Virginia O'Brien

MGMs Deadpan Diva

The Authorized Biography

Virginia O'Brien: MGMs Deadpan Diva
© 2018. Robert Strom All rights reserved.

All illustrations are copyright of their respective owners, and are also reproduced here in the spirit of publicity. Whilst we have made every effort to acknowledge specific credits whenever possible, we apologize for any omissions, and will undertake every effort to make any appropriate changes in future editions of this book if necessary.

No part of this book may be reproduced in any form or by any means, electronic, mechanical, digital, photocopying or recording, except for the inclusion in a review, without permission in writing from the publisher.

Published in the USA by:
BearManor Media
P O Box 71426
Albany, Georgia 31708
www.bearmanormedia.com

Printed in the United States of America

ISBN   978-1-62933-219-2 (paperback)

Book & cover design and layout by Darlene Swanson • www.van-garde.com

Virginia O'Brien

MGMs Deadpan Diva

The Authorized Biography

By Robert Strom

Virginia O'Brien, MGM's Beautiful Deadpan Diva.

Contents

	Foreword by James Gavin	vii
	Preface by Robert Strom.	xi
Chapter One	The Daughter of Captain O'Brien	1
Chapter Two	Meeting the People	17
Chapter Three	The Beginning of the MGM Years	29
Chapter Four	Sothern Breezes	51
Chapter Five	Enter Superman	87
Chapter Six	Virginia Was a Lady	99
Chapter Seven	Hello Baby	119
Chapter Eight	Deadpan Solo	173
Chapter Nine	Saluting MGM.	209
	Virginia O'Brien Portraits	261
	Acknowledgements	265
	Bibliography	269
	Index	273
	Filmography, Discography, Radio and Television Appearances	277
	Bibliography	289

Foreword

Virginia O'Brien's deadpan singing was born organically, the result of a bad case of stage fright. Later Keely Smith would adopt that comic style. Cher is said to have done the same. Virginia was first, doing it wittily and famously. It happened in some of the most acclaimed MGM musicals of the 1940s: *Ziegfeld Follies, The Harvey Girls, Till the Clouds Roll By, Thousands Cheer,* and *Du Barry Was a Lady.* Whether crooning of a birthday that had gone wrong ("Did I Get Stinkin' at the Club Savoy"), a manhunt on the old frontier ("The Wild, Wild West"), the non-glamour of showbiz ("Life upon the Wicked Stage"), or her obsession with a man who's determined to bump her off ("Say That We're Sweethearts Again"), O'Brien held a poker face, except when her eyes rolled wryly heavenward or from side to side. In films where love conquered all and women lived for romance, she was the skeptic—a sleek, big-city brunette who played courting and heartbreak for laughs.

Popular as she was, she never became a top-rank star. O'Brien had a lead role in just one film, the Red Skelton comedy *Merton of the Movies* (1947). Otherwise, like Lena Horne, she was mainly an MGM utility player, dropped into nightclub scenes or production numbers as a dash of spice. The public knew little about her. To this day, even hardcore movie buffs are in the dark about the off-camera O'Brien, who died in 2001.

Now, thanks to Robert Strom's richly researched, engaging biography, O'Brien is finally getting the full spotlight. Where she came from, how her persona evolved, what it was like to be a stock performer at the legendary Dream Factory of movie musicals—all this is vividly detailed in Robert's book. Having released others about Peggy Lee and Gypsy Rose Lee, Robert knows a thing or two about unusual performing women. Happily, he shows that there was much more to O'Brien than her novelty image, and that her career was far from over after MGM. O'Brien appeared memorably in TV and cabaret—she toured in a package show with Sally Rand, Cass Daley, Beatrice Kay, and Allan Jones, and she even became mayor of a small town. Hers is an overlooked Hollywood story that deserved telling. Robert has told it wonderfully.

James Gavin,

(James Gavin's books include *Stormy Weather: The Life of Lena Horne* and *Is That All There Is?: The Strange Life of Peggy Lee.*)

Lena Horne and Virginia O'Brien in *Till the Clouds Roll By.*

Preface

"I was so terrified on opening night, the director had to push me on the stage. When the spotlight hit, I froze. My knees actually knocked together like castanets. My arms were paralyzed at my sides. My eyes were wide with fright. I could move my mouth and shoulders, but everything else was rigid. But I kept singing! As I sang the audience began laughing. When it was over, I ran to the wings and cried."

These are the words of Virginia O'Brien, recalling her opening night at the Los Angeles Assistance League Playhouse. Seventeen-year-old Virginia, a Los Angeles native, was appearing in *Meet the People*. The show, a music comedy revue, was Virginia's theatrical debut. Following her graduation from North Hollywood High School, Virginia's voice teacher encouraged her to audition for the revue. Not only was she cast, she also had a solo in the show. Neither could have known that this would launch Virginia's career in every medium of the performing arts.

She honed her new-found "deadpan" performance style after the director told the devastated newcomer that she hadn't spoiled the show as she had assumed. She had quite the opposite effect; she stopped the show. Although she probably didn't know it at the time, two weeks after opening night the name who would sign her to a seven-year contract with the studio that had, "More stars than in the heavens," was in the audience. Louis B. Mayer, laughing with the rest of the audience, saw her potential. MGM soon added another star to its heavenly rooster: Virginia O'Brien.

This book follows Virginia's journey as a singer-comedienne who eventually appeared in twenty movies, sixteen of them at Metro-Goldwyn-Mayer. Her work there led to radio appearances, personal appearances with big bands and war bond rallies. At MGM, she met and worked with the biggest movie stars of the 1940's. Some, like Eleanor Powell and Lucille Ball, would become close friends. Eight-time co-star, Red Skelton, introduced her to her first husband.

It's a happy journey, devoid of many of the pitfalls of fame. Virginia O'Brien has been described by those who knew her as a "great lady," a kind person who "always called everyone by their first name." Some fans opposed the title of this biography. With voices raised in protest they said, "Virginia O'Brien was no Diva!" For a short time, I considered changing the title.

After consideration, I decide to keep the term "Diva," which does not always refer to a demanding, difficult to work with artist. The diva in the title was a talented, beautiful woman who was neither difficult, nor demanding. She was a professional who cared about her art, and whose way with a song always left 'em smiling and wanting more. This is the true essence of a diva. This is Virginia O'Brien.

Robert Strom

June 2017

Chapter One

The Daughter of Captain O'Brien

Woodrow Wilson began his second term in 1919. *The Magic of Oz*, the thirteenth book in L. Frank Baum's popular Oz series, was published one month after his June 7th death. Movies were still silent. Some of 1919's biggest screen stars were Charlie Chaplin, Mary Pickford, Mabel Normand, Douglas Fairbanks, and Roscoe "Fatty" Arbuckle. New songs included Marion Harris' recording of "After You've Gone," and Ben Selvin's instrumentals, "Dardanella" and "I'm Forever Blowing Bubbles," the later was number one for four weeks.

E.R. Burroughs added *Jungle Tails of Tarzan* to his volumes about the King of the Jungle. In Hollywood, director D.W. Griffith had a huge success with *Broken Blossoms* starring Richard Barthelmess and Lillian Gish. At Paramount, Griffith's contemporary, Cecil B. DeMille, triumphed with *Male and Female* and its star, Gloria Swanson. The wealthiest men in the nation were John D. Rockefeller and Andrew Carnegie, until Carnegie died on August 11, 1919. Several people who would find their fame and fortune in show business were born in

1919: Nat King Cole, Betty Garrett, Liberace, Anita O'Day, and a Los Angeles-born Irish-American girl named Virginia O'Brien.

Virginia O'Brien came from solid Irish stock. Her grandfather, James O'Brien, was born in Ireland in 1840. As was her grandmother, Johanna O'Brien (nee Dwyer), in 1837. After marrying and immigrating to the United States, they had their first child in 1875. J.J. O'Brien was born in Iowa. Four years later, Joseph was born in Indiana. Annie, born in 1878, was the first of their children born in Nebraska. Virginia's father, Thomas Francis O'Brien, was born in Nebraska on September 18, 1881. Margaret was born there in 1883.

By 1900, James and Johanna had settled in San Francisco with their five children. The O'Brien residence in San Francisco was at 6 Mariposa Terrace. The fate of their home in the 1906 earthquake and fire is unknown. Mariposa Terrace, which was between Harrison and Folsom, is no longer there.

Virginia's mother, Edna, was born on February 3, 1887 in Missouri. The 1900 US Census shows thirteen-year-old Edna living at 1628 Cherry Street in Kansas City. Her father, J. William Cox, was a barber. Cox had married Luttie M. Davis on May 16, 1886. In addition to Edna, they had Rubey, who was born Mary Rubey Cox on September 23, 1888.

Thomas Francis O'Brien and Edna Lee Cox were married in Santa Barbara on January 30, 1918. The marriage was witnessed by Edna's sister, Rubey McDonald, and the man she would later marry, Lloyd Bacon. Family lore says that Civil War General Robert E. Lee was a relative on her mother's side. This explains Virginia's first and middle name, Lee for the general, and Virginia for his home state. General Lee was not the only public figure in the family. Those that she grew up with included her own father, his brother, and her Aunt Rubey's husband. Rubey was sometimes spelled in the traditional manner, Ruby.

The marriage license of Thomas Francis O'Brien and Edna Lee Cox. Witnessed by Virginia's aunt, Rubey and film director Lloyd Bacon. Rubey and Lloyd would soon marry.

On October 7, 1918 thirty-seven-year-old Thomas O'Brien prepared to put on a different uniform. He registered for World War I. At that time, the O'Briens lived at 1933 Childs Avenue in Los Angeles. While he was assigned the rank of 1st mate, he was not deployed. On November 18, forty-two days after Thomas signed his registration card, World War I came to an end.

In the year Virginia was born, her father's name and image were in the *Los Angeles Times* frequently. The young officer was making a name for himself, and rising quickly through the ranks of the Los Angeles Police Department.

Thomas O'Brien was the Captain of Detectives in the Los Angeles

Police Department. Later, he would serve as a Los Angeles District Attorney. Captain O'Brien was known for his honesty, and was definitely seen as a hero.

The *San Bernardino County Sun* reported his waiting for "zero hour" in the California town of Dulzura with justice agents and members of the LAPD to capture several escaped convicts. Captain O'Brien and his team also seized an armored truck, 400 Springfield rifles, and 155,000 rounds of ammunition.

Less than a month after the birth of his daughter, the May 9, 1919 issue of the *Los Angeles Times* printed an article that revealed the standards and commitment of Thomas O'Brien. The headline said it all: "New Head for Purity Squad." Former head of the squad, Sargent Hackett, appointed O'Brien. The concluding paragraph read: "Detective O'Brien has already served four times in the same position, and according to Chief Butler, is considered the best versed man in the police department in handling the work of suppressing vice and liquor violations."

On July 2, 1919, the headline of a brief article in the *Los Angeles Times* read: "Seems John Doe Likes Whiskey." Sargent Thomas O'Brien filed the complaint that Doe, who is described as a "well-known court habitué," had stolen sixty-six cases of whiskey valued at $2,400. O'Brien recovered thirty-four of the cases.

Detective Sargent O'Brien was mentioned in a prominent case in the November 30, 1919 issue of the *Los Angeles Times*. This time the headline was in all caps: "DRUG FIENDS MAKE CRIME WAVE." This case involved the arrest of "hop heads," "snow snorters," and "needle men." Arrests were made based on the authority of two detective sergeants who were narcotics experts; Thomas O'Brien and Lloyd Yarrow.

The 1920 California Census was conducted shortly after Virginia Lee O'Brien was born on April 18th of 1919. Like her fellow MGM contract players Ann Miller, Jane Powell, and Debbie Reynolds, Virginia was an Aries. It is a birth sign known for the tenacity needed to survive the ups and downs of show business. Being a fire sign also gave these ladies the spark that set them apart from other performers. Each had that individual flare that "lit up" their scenes and songs.

In a 1992 interview, Virginia said that she and her siblings were all born at home because her mother "had a thing about hospitals." At the time of Virginia's birth, the family lived at 2638 Benedict Street. In the months after she was born, her father's heroics continued to be documented in the *Los Angeles Times*.

Prior to the birth of Edna and Thomas O'Brien's last child, his work for the Los Angeles Police Department continued to make news. Some of his more memorable heroics are summarized here in four articles published between 1920 and 1924. The *Los Angeles Times* reported on February 11, 1920 the arrest of one Charles Scott. Scott and four others robbed the Home Savings Bank on Vermont Avenue. Officers Thomas O'Brien, Jesse Winn, and Joseph Taylor trailed Scott to his hotel room where he was counting $1,205, his share of the $7,095 stolen.

Detective O'Brien's reward of $750 was featured in the June 19, 1920 edition of the *Santa Ana Register*. The reward, lowered from $1,000, was for the work O'Brien had done that led to the arrest of Eddie Daley for "violating the narcotics act." O'Brien had worked for a year collecting evidence against Daley.

"On Trail of Daring Courtroom Looter" ran a headline in the *Los Angeles Time* on August 18, 1920. Beneath was a photo of Detective Sargents Thomas O'Brien, Herman, and James Cline inspecting a courtroom safe. This time the amount stolen was $24,000.

Thomas O'Brien was a detective lieutenant by 1922. Along with Edward Dalton, a special investigator for the American Banking Association, O'Brien set a trap for pickpocketer E.F. Carney.

When O'Brien and Dalton boarded a street car, Carney followed, as expected. He was arrested when he picked Dalton's wallet. This incident was reported in the *Los Angeles Times* dated December 20, 1922.

In 1923, four-year-old Virginia became a big sister. Mary O'Brien was born on June 30th of that year. Mary would also go on to work in films. Her career was very short. She made five films between 1944 and 1945. In four of those films she played uncredited parts. The only film in which her character had a name was 1944's *Moonlight and Cactus*. She played the small role of Amanda.

Mary's feelings about her involvement in the preforming arts were made clear to this author by Mary's niece, Virginia's first-born, Terri. In a conversation, Terri O'Brien shared the funny story of her aunt shouting one day as she backed her car out of the driveway, "I'm not doing this anymore!" The "this" referred to show business. Mary got her wish, and found happiness elsewhere.

**Captain Thomas O'Brien in 1927.
Courtesy of Terri O'Brien.**

The Daughter of Captian O'Brien

In October of 1929, when Virginia was ten, her father was given the job of protecting Los Angeles District Attorney Buron Fitts. Fitts was corrupt, and eventually would be removed from office due in part to Thomas O'Brien's efforts to clean up the LAPD. However, in 1929 it was his job to keep Fitts from being killed. One of the detectives under Captain Thomas had overheard a group of gangsters say, "We are going to burn down Fitts and McDonald the first time we see them." McDonald was a bootlegger who claimed to have paid Los Angeles police officers half a million dollars over a span of five years to protect him.

"Honest Tom" was Captain O'Brien's nickname. He must have been "Patient Tom" as well. He would have to be to put up with his wife's sense of humor. Edna's antics were much like those of Virginia's friend, Lucille Ball. One of her favorites was to put her hair in pigtails, blacken her two front teeth, get in the car, and speed through the city. She did this until she was pulled over. When the officer approached to give her a ticket, she announced, "I'm Thomas O'Brien's wife!"

Other family members held jobs of distinction in Los Angeles. Thomas O'Brien's brother, Patrick Peter O'Brien, was Los Angeles' postmaster. When she spent a day with Uncle Patrick, Virginia later told her daughter that she was sure the P.P. on his Los Angeles residence stood for Patrick O'Brien. She found this childhood memory funny. Edna's sister, Rubey, was married to the film director Lloyd Bacon. It was Uncle Lloyd who gave young Virginia her first glimpse at the art of making motion pictures. She was especially thrilled when she watched her uncle filming a number with her hero and role model, Ruby Keeler.

In an interview with writer and film historian Dan Van Neste,

Virginia told him of her experiences visiting Uncle Lloyd at work:

> "I never bothered to observe what was going on beyond watching Busby Berkeley work. Later, at MGM, I realized how complicated and dangerous making musicals was."

Lloyd Bacon, Virginia's uncle by marriage, was a prominent director in Hollywood. Bacon was at the helm of 130 films, including *42nd Street*, *Footlight Parade*, and *The Fuller Brush Girl*.

This sounds odd now, but at that time filming could be dangerous. Directors from Busby Berkeley to Vincente Minnelli, who would direct Virginia, often employed cranes to get the "aerial" shots they were known for. Over the years, musical comedy stars performed with injuries from scalding steam, poorly executed special effects, and the pleasant, but costly, delays due to pregnancy. Some of these were in Virginia O'Brien's future.

Prior to her watching Uncle Lloyd and Busby Berkeley working, Virginia had another memorable encounter with a famous director of the silent era. She is reported to have made her film debut in one of Mack Sennett's comedies. Unfortunately, her walk-on part was uncredited, and the title of the film remains unknown.

Even so, the youngster was not especially impressed by her visits to Hollywood's sound stages. She had a serious side, and the desire to follow in her father's footsteps. Her interests lay in business and clerical studies.

Her early schooling was at Micheltorena Elementary, where she and her fellow students sang the school song: "Oh Micheltorena charming is thy name. How we love to sing it spread abroad its fame. Linked with California thus thy name appears. Oh Micheltorena music to our ears." As a teenager, she attended Eagle Rock and North Hollywood High Schools.

When Virginia was seven, Uncle Lloyd had a bit of drama, and he wasn't on a film set. His boat experienced engine trouble and lost its anchor. The *Rubey B* was named for Virginia's Aunt Rubey. Luckily, the boat drifted ashore at Huntington Beach, and no one was hurt. The article on this incident was in the *Santa Ana Register* on August 30, 1928. With a postmaster, a police captain and a famous film director in the family, the O'Briens were frequently in the newspaper.

By the time she was twelve, Uncle Lloyd and Aunt Rubey had a new boat. Christened *Lightnin'*, it was named after the hit Broadway play written by and starring Lloyd's father, Frank Bacon. The Bacons were staying at the Hotel Del Coronado for three weeks, reported the *Los Angeles Times* on June 28, 1931. Anchored off shore, the *Ligntnin'* was there for a party. Virginia was on-board with friends and relatives Fran Shortell, Steve Watson, Harry Barris, and Frances Bacon.

Lloyd Bacon's boat, *Lightnin'*, was featured in *Marine Magazine* in 2014. In part, the accompanying article read: *It was built in 1929 for movie director Frank Bacon; in its Hollywood career, it hosted Bing Crosby and other names you know. Bacon's enthusiasm extended to entering a race from Los Angeles to San Francisco and almost winning. Disqualified on a technicality, in disgust, he sold the boat to Don Owen.* Rechristened the *Pat Pending*, the boat is still harbored on San Francisco Bay. It is still in the Owen family.

On June 1st of 1933, fourteen-year-old Virginia got her first taste of publicity. On that date, *The Eagle Rock Advertiser* ran the headline, "Presents Pupils in Recital Sat." The piano students of Juanita Grizzell Taylor were presenting a recital at the Thomas F. O'Brien home, 5418 Dahlia Drive, to which the public is invited. The article lists Virginia's younger sister Mary as having a piano solo.

It's unclear as to whether Virginia sang, played a solo, or both. Her songs were "Love's Caprice" and "Romance." On "Love's Caprice," student Max Heindl plays the piano solo, which indicates that Virginia probably sang the tune.

Tommy Daly, Mary Aitken, and Virginia are the students listed on the performance of "Romance." Since Tommy Daly performed a saxophone solo earlier in the program, it is possible that Mary Aitken played the piano and Virginia sang this song as well.

Another memorable adventure she related to author Dan Van Neste was the trip she took with her family when she was fifteen. In 1934, the O'Brien family boarded a ship in New York City. From there they sailed on to Havana, Guatemala, and Panama. This was an expensive trip during the Great Depression.

By the time the O'Briens reached Hawaii on their return voyage it was 1935, and Virginia turned sixteen. The family was joined by Aunt Rubey in Honolulu. Rubey, identified as Mrs. Lloyd Bacon in a *Los Angeles Times* blurb, hosted an aloha party at the Alexander Young Hotel's roof garden. Rubey's nieces, "Misses Frances Shortell and Virginia O'Brien," were mentioned.

The family had already been in Honolulu for five weeks, having arrived on July 26, 1935 aboard the *President Hoover*. This was all reported after the fact. The short article was seen in the August 5th edition of the *Los Angeles Times*. Barely six months after visiting her family in Hawaii, Uncle Lloyd divorced Aunt Rubey. It was the end of a fifteen-year romance.

On December 19, 1935, again in the *Los Angeles Times*, the headline read: "Mrs. Lloyd Bacon Wins Divorce From Director." Virginia and Fran Shortell were photographed standing on either side of their aunt. Both were witnesses in the divorce, as was Virginia's mother, Edna. Lloyd, who initiated the divorce, then later dropped it, was not in court. However, he was represented by three lawyers: Ronald Button, Julien Hazard, and Joseph Reina. Rubey won the decree and was awarded $125,000. No mention is made of the couple's home at 8235 Lincoln Terrace.

Virginia, Rubey Bacon, and Fran Shortell appear in court during Rubey's divorce from director Lloyd Bacon. Photo courtesy of Terri O'Brien.

In the beginning of 1936, Thomas O'Brien had commissioned plans to have a new home built for his family in the San Fernando Valley. The style of the home was known as Monterey. The house was designed by Leo Bachman. Builder William Mellenthin, who built sixty-eight homes in the valley, constructed the three-bedroom, two-bathroom home. A photo of Virginia's new residence was seen in local newspapers on February 2nd of 1936.

The O'Brien residence was built for
Deputy District Attorney Thomas F. O'Brien in 1935.

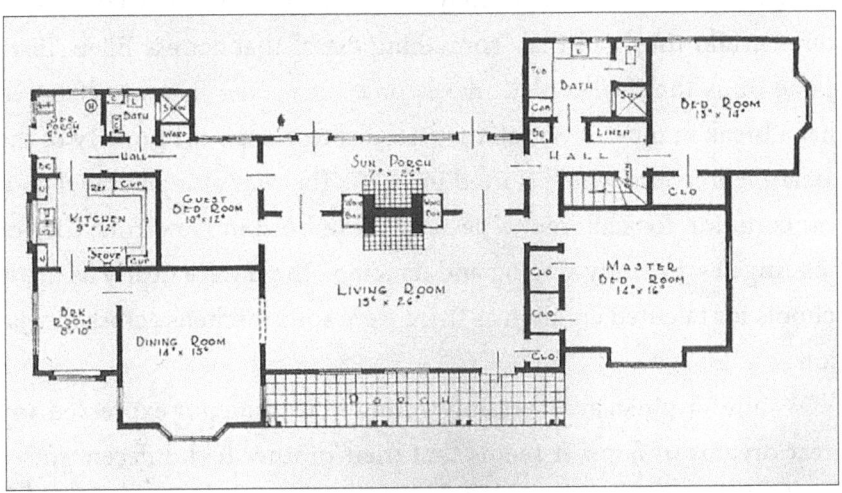

The floorplan of the O'Brien home at 12036 Laurel Terrace, North Hollywood.
Note the double fireplace that separates the living room from the sun room.
Photos courtesy of Terri O'Brien.

"Honest Tom" continued his dedicated efforts to make Los Angeles safer. On August 4, 1937, the *Los Angeles Times* ran a United Press article titled "Hunt Thugs Who Broke Film Strike." As directed by the district attorney's office, Deputy District Attorney O'Brien began to hunt for twenty gangsters from Chicago.

He told the press that the gangsters had been "imported" by the brother of a high-ranking city official. Their purpose was to pose as guards at the striking studios. Once they were in place, they began to intimidate the "… striking studio craftsmen" into returning to work. His success resulted in a return to a safe work environment at Virginia's future workplace.

Virginia and her sisters grew up during the years when thousands flocked to the town called Hollywood. These newly arrived citizens were certain they had that "something extra" that actress Ellen Terry spoke of as the quality that makes one a star. The majority believed that a break in movies was all they needed to escape the poverty of the Great Depression, which started in 1929. This was also an era when it was common for children, especially those born in New York City or Los Angeles, to study singing and dancing. There were nearly as many schools for talented children as there were soup kitchens across the nation.

While Virginia, and certainly young Mary, had not expressed any great dreams of fame, it seems that their mother had different ideas. A gifted musician who played several instruments and sang, Edna O'Brien had stars in her eyes. Motivated by her sister, Rubey, who may have promised showbiz opportunities courtesy of Uncle Lloyd, Edna is remembered as a stage mother. Perhaps not as relentlessly driven as Gypsy Rose Lee and June Havoc's Mama Rose, but a stage mother nonetheless.

Virginia, and one can safely assume Mary, began to study voice and dance. To be a dancer, like future friend Eleanor Powell or the popular Ruby Keeler, and not a singer, was her only show business dream during her adolescence. Still, her early training in the performing arts was, for the beautiful teenager, more for fun than anything else. But children grow, and Virginia was already at her full height of 5 feet 7½ inches. As she grew, she discovered a new-found gracefulness, and with it, new dreams.

Virginian O'Brien North Hollywood High School 1937.

2

Chapter Two

Meeting the People

Vernon Dent and Eunice Munsy were married on August 27th of 1938. Silent screen comedian Harry Langdon and his wife Mabel, the only guests, acted as best man and matron of honor. Vernon Dent was a character actor who eventually worked in 433 films. In 1979, Eunice Dent reminisced with author and film historian Edward Watz about her wedding day. She recalled having lunch wife Harry and Mabel Langdon at the El Facile restaurant in Santa Barbara.

The foursome then drove to Bob Murphy's nightclub on La Cienega Blvd., where they had dinner. While it wasn't "nightclub time at all," Eunice told Watz, they were entertained by Murphy's star, Virginia O'Brien:

> She sort of gave us a solo concert performance. We were very impressed with her—she was good. Of course, we had an awful lot of fun that night.

Seven short years after entertaining Vernon Dent and his new wife, Virginia met the actor again. He was cast as the engineer of Atchison, Topeka and the Santa Fe in *The Harvey Girls*. Then in 1947, Dent appeared as a silent film comedian in *Merton of the Movies* with Red Skelton and Virginia.

Virginia earned $25 a week singing at the House of Murphy.

While singing at Bob Murphy's in 1938, Virginia continued to pursue her first show business dream. She still hoped to be a tap dancer. As a child, she had been in awe of Ruby Keeler. Now another female tap dancer inspired her to continue her classes. Decades later she spoke of this time with film historian Dan Van Neste, saying, "I was a good tap dancer. After all, I had the best teachers."

One of the teachers Terri O'Brien remembers her mother speaking of was Louis DaPron. Born in Indiana six years before Virginia, DaPron was a gifted dancer and dance teacher since childhood. His career in movies began when two choreographers at Paramount Pictures, LeRoy Prinz and Nick Castle, hired him as an assistant dance director. His big break came in 1941 when DaPron became Rudy Keeler's choreographer for her last musical, *Sweetheart of the Campus* (Columbia Pictures).

DaPron's most memorable collaboration was with tap dancer extraordinaire, Donald O'Connor. Under contract now at Universal Studios, Louis DaPron was the choreographer for a young dance team called the "Jivin' Jacks and Jills." The stand-out talent in the group was Donald O'Connor, who blended both comedy and dancing.

With teachers like Louis DaPron, and others in his league, Virginia obviously gained skill and confidence. Sometime prior to her theatrical debut in 1939, she found the bravery to make her first screen test. Sadly, she told Dan Van Neste, "... *during my screen test, I wore a yellow dress that made me look taller than the Empire State Building!*"

Her failed screen test was the first sign that Virginia should change her course. Those "just for fun" singing lessons became more serious. The gifted teenager progressed further with her singing than she had with her dancing. In a 1988 interview for the *San Francisco Chronicle*, Virginia discussed the new goal her failed screen test inspired: "All right," she said, "I was willing to expand my dreams. Become a combination Ruby Keeler-Ethel Merman."

Aside from her admiration for Merman, there was another connection. Both singers had studied with singing coach Al Siegel (1906 - 1966). Merman, keeping her "no training" legend alive, would deny having worked with Siegel. This white lie was dispelled by Erskine Johnson in his "Hollywood News" column. Appearing in nationwide newspapers, Johnson's news on August 18, 1943 stated he has taught a singer a trick or two. There were Sophie Tucker and Ethel Merman and Virginia O'Brien... Dorothy Lamour and Martha Raye....

Ethel Merman had an impressive career on Broadway, having starred in five musicals, for a total of 1,320 performances. During this same time, she also appeared in eight movies, and eleven short movies she made in the early 1930's. She did all of this before Virginia decided she would dance like Ruby Keeler and sing like Ethel Merman.

It isn't surprising that Merman influenced Virginia. The famously untrained singer was the idol and ideal of a legion of young singers from the time she first stepped on the stage of the Alvin Theatre with Ginger Rogers in *Girl Crazy*. Her first Broadway musical, *Girl Crazy*, ran for 272 performances (Opened: October 14,1930; Closed: June 6, 1931).

The name Ethel Merman, and her powerhouse style, would come to haunt Virginia O'Brien. As she stood in the wings awaiting her debut in the Los Angeles production of *Meet the People*, singing her solo in Merman's style was her intention. As described in the introduction for this book, that was not the outcome. The outcome was better. This is because it was truer, the essence of a new style—the Virginia O'Brien style.

Stage fright is common even among the most famous performers. In her case, stage fright hit at the right time, and the right place. Had it not, word would not have spread about the girl who stopped the show at the Los Angeles Assistance League Playhouse. It is unlikely that Louis B. Mayer would have gone to see another Merman imitator. Fate, and fright, gave birth to Virginia O'Brien.

The original program for the production of *Meet the People* at the Hollywood Playhouse begins with the credit, "Entire Production Staged by Danny Dare." Henry Myers was the revues lyricist, while Jay Gorney wrote the music.

A caveat below these credits stated: "Any similarity between the order of the program and what you see on the stage is purely accidental." Typical of a musical revue, it gave the producer and director the option of pulling sketches and songs that flopped.

The show opened with all twenty-six cast members in a sketch titled, "The Legend of Sleeping Beauty." The roles, in addition to the obligatory Prince Charming, included: six Ladies in Waiting, two newspaper boys, a gangster, a Fuehrer, a radical, a policeman, and The Spirit of California. The state's spirit was played by actor Jack Albertson, later known for his roles in *Willy Wonka & the Chocolate Factory* (Grandpa Joe), *The Poseidon Adventure* (Manny Rosen), and as Ed Brown on the sitcom *Chico and the Man*.

Three members of the Joad family, from John Steinbeck's *The Grapes of Wrath*, also appeared. Tom Joad was played by one Tex Brodus, Pa Joad was portrayed by actor Elliot Sullivan, and Ma Joad by Virginia O'Brien. Brothers Ben and Sol Barzman wrote the sketch, with music by George Bassman. Following the first sketch, various cast members performed in *Meet the People*: *The Unwritten Law, Mr. Capra Goes to Town, I am an Artist, Design for Earning a Living*, and *The Stars Remain*.

The Stars Remain had three parts: She (Janice Chambers), He (Robert Davis), and Another She (Virginia O'Brien). Next up was *The Battle of the Century*, and *Hurdy Gurdy Verdi*. The ninth sketch found Virginia as Zanuck's Secretary in *Zanuck in Darkest Washington*. She didn't return until the fifteenth sketch, *A Statement of Policy*, appearing again with the entire cast.

Virginia opened Act II as Offenbachette in *Let's Steal a Tune from Offenbach*. Sketches seventeen through twenty-one were: *The Dictator at Home, Fancy Footwork, A Fellow and A Girl, The Same Old South* (Mr. Mason and Mr. Dixon were the two characters), and *Light Meat or Dark*. Many Guatemalans were required for *In Chichicostanango*, and Virginia was one of them. She sat out the twenty-third sketch, *It's All Right, Joe*. She then reappeared to sing the title song in the next-to-last sketch, *Elmer's Wedding Day*. The entire company was on stage for the finale, *All This and Hollywood Too*.

The *Los Angeles Times* would cover Virginia's career from beginning to end. Sources indicate that her first mention in the venerable newspaper came on January 16, 1940. Considering her youth and beauty, it's appropriate a stunning photograph was all that was needed. The simple caption read, "Scores Revue Hit—Virginia O'Brien is credited with being a consistent show-stopper in *Meet the People* at the Assistance League Playhouse."

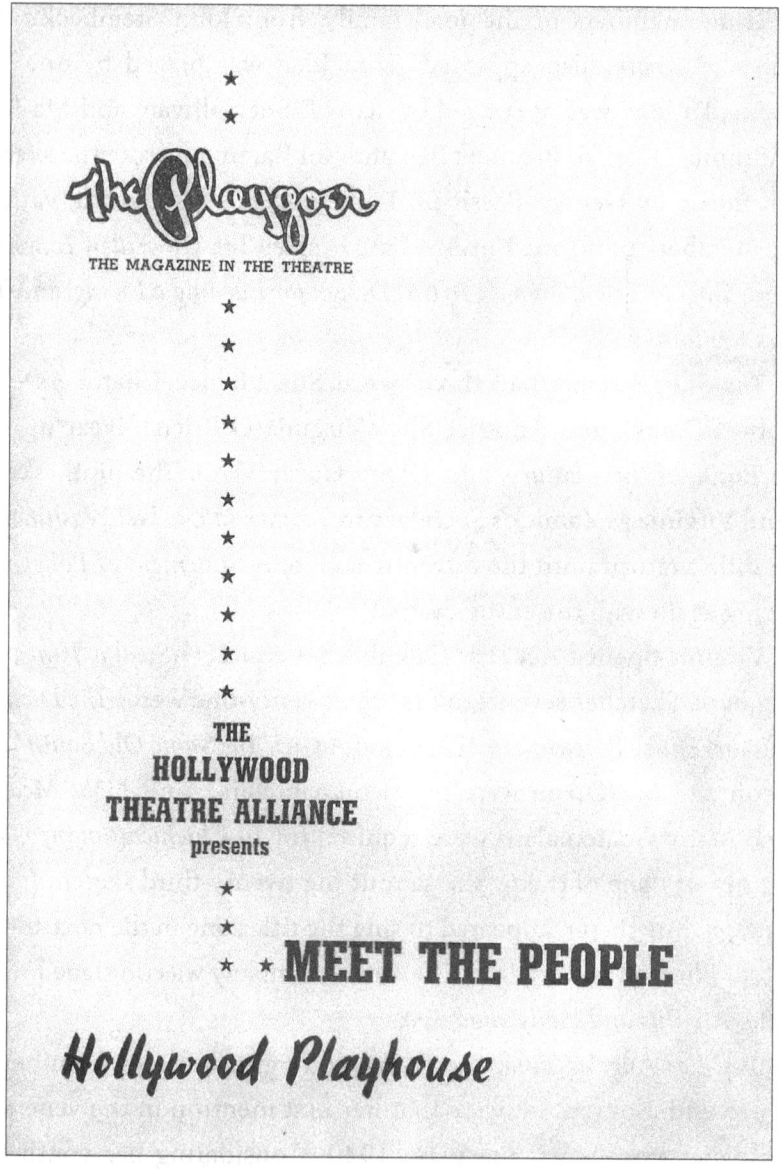

The original issue of *The Playgoer* program for the Los Angeles production of *Meet the People*.

The show had a second opening. This event was covered by the formidable Hedda Hopper. Her February 10, 1940 column mentioned an addition to the show: "Nineteen-year-old Nanette Fabares taps the width of the stage in nothing flat...sings, does pantomime, and looks like Hepburn...." As for Virginia, Hopper summed it up by simply stating, "Virginia O'Brien still holds top honors." Nannette Fabares would become Virginia's co-worker at MGM, after changing the spelling of her last name to Fabray.

Soon after, on March 7th, an article in the *Los Angeles Times* bore the headline, "Find Awarded Stage, Screen Roles." The details read:

> Virginia O'Brien (yes, she's from the *Meet the People* cast, too) has been snapped up by the Roaring Lion at Culver City (meaning M.G.M.) for an important part in *Strike Up the Band*, which has Judy Garland and Mickey Rooney as a team. She is the daughter of Deputy District Attorney Thomas F. O'Brien. The film find is to receive a further baptism in the theater before she does the picture. She will appear in the New York musical show *Keep Off the Grass*.

The comment that Virginia came from the cast "too" was in reference to the number of "movie-colony raids" made on *Meet the People*. The cast changed often, as new discoveries left for screen tests and contracts with various studios. Another cast member, soon to be mentioned along with Virginia, was William Orr.

Meet the People was the subject of a photo-essay published in the February 26, 1940 issue of *LIFE* magazine. Titled "Pretty Girls, Witty Songs Make *Meet the People* Hollywood Hit," the three-page spread appeared in the theater section. "This winter," the article began, "to its own astonishment, Hollywood has produced a theatrical smash hit."

On opening night only 125 people attended the show in a "playhouse seating 400." After the first reviews were published, *Meet the People* was sold out for three weeks in advance.

Photo by Richard Tucker© Billy Rose Theatre Division,
The New York Public Library for the Performing Arts.

The photographs from the show in *LIFE* included Fay McKenzie as "The Sleeping Beauty" in the sketch that satirized "Hollywood's intellectual inactivity," Bill Orr impersonating both Eleanor and Franklin Roosevelt and Bernice Parks who sang the torch song "Sugar Hill" and danced a torrid rhumba as a Guatemalan. Beneath a lovely photo of Virginia, the caption read: "Virginia O'Brien is a swing-singer with a new technique. She croons softly, hardly moves a muscle, but keeps busy with her eyes. Warner Bros. signed her up." Obviously the reference to Warner Brothers was incorrect.

"Virginia O'Brien, a songstress with a distinctive style, has been signed to M-G-M." The March 18, 1940 review of *Meet the People* mentioned the show's success in "getting some of its people into the movies. Another cast member was William Orr, an expert impersonator with a keen sense of humor, has been signed to a Warner contract.

Considering all the roles she played, her dialogue, and lyrics, it's no wonder that Virginia battled stage fright. The praise of Louis B. Mayer must have eased her worries for the remainder of the run. Contract signed, Mayer wanted to present his latest discovery to moviegoers as soon as possible. Fate stepped in again when Virginia was asked to open in Lee Schubert's new Broadway show, *Keep Off the Grass*.

The Schubert show would be familiar territory for Virginia. Like *Meet the People*, it was a musical comedy revue. A slightly disgruntled L.B. Mayer gave Virginia his blessing to head to New York City and begin rehearsals for the show, which was scheduled to open in the spring of 1940. He may have been hesitant, but it proved to be a wise choice.

Before her departure from Los Angeles, *Meet the People* and several members of its cast won what amounted to a standing ovation in print. Tom Treanor of the *Los Angeles Times* dedicated his "Hollywood's Showcase" section in the *Los Angeles Times Sunday Magazine* (May 26, 1940) to *Meet the People*. The two-page article featured the photographs of Virginia, Jane Clayton, Lois Ranson, and Bill Orr. The four were among the "kids" who set a rags to riches record.

Treanor reveals that in spite of their talent, it wasn't until *Meet the People* opened that O'Brien, Clayton, Ranson, and Orr were considered worthy of screen tests. Prior to the revue, all four had received "thumbs down" from movie producers.

Meet the People, at the Assistance League Playhouse, where those tagged as "hamateurs" played, changed that with its sold-out performances. The keys to its success as a show, and for cast members, Treanor surmised, stemmed from three things. First, it positively refused to give them star billing. There was no star, and everyone appeared in about 12 numbers apiece besides the two or three feature spots. Second, cast members never took an encore, no matter how hard cash customers clapped. Third, no cast member was paid more than another. When the box office was especially good, everyone received the same bonus.

Treanor, like everyone who reviewed the show, singled Virginia out. "She is a card in the way she sings," he wrote. "Hotcha stuff with a deadpan. She'd bowl 'em over in pictures, sure." Others mentioned for standout turns went on to successful careers, Jack Albertson and Jack Gifford among them. With Tom Treanor's praise ringing in her ears, Virginia departed for New York, and the Broadway stage.

The cast of *Keep Off the Grass* included two big stars of theatre and film, the great Jimmy Durante and Ray Bolger. Virginia would work with both stars again at MGM. In *The Harvey Girls* she was Bolger's love interest. She appeared with Durante in *Two Girls and a Sailor*, in which he performed his theme song, "Inka Dinka Doo." Virginia would also appear with *Keep Off the Grass* star Jane Froman some years later.

As the newcomer, the twenty-year-old O'Brien was still learning. With hard work and talent, she more than held her own. Brooks Atkinson, the theatre critic for the *New York Times*, was a powerful man. His opinion could close a show, and make or break a star.

His review of *Keep Off the Grass* included the following praise for a certain tall, beautiful singer "… a dead-pan singer who convulses the audience by removing the ecstasy from high pressure music." The favorable reviews for Virginia's performance continued with a mention from a man even more powerful than Brooks Atkinson.

In the 1930's and 40's, columnist Walter Winchell ruled Broadway. Winchell could make or break a *show*. To have a favorable mention in his column was a stamp of approval that entertainers cherished. He covered the opening of *Keep Off the Grass* in his Broadway column on May 26, 1940 with these words:

Virginia stopped the show when she appeared in
Keep Off the Grass on Broadway in 1940.

"The event of last week was the opening of *Keep Off the Grass*, a revue.... It was freighted with big names, Jimmy Durante, Ray Bolger, Ilka Chase, and Jane Forman.... The *Times* and *News* critics enjoyed it, the *Mirror*'s man being only excited by Virginia O'Brien's indifference."

A review by a member of the Canadian Press took note of Virginia's sending up her co-star, singer, Jane Froman. Leon Edel of Canada wrote, "The dry-voiced Virginia O'Brien, who with her face as stiff as a poker, parodies every one of Miss Forman's songs in sardonic monotones."

Virginia's numbers brought about a change in *Keep Off the Grass*. Fifty-nine years later, Virginia told Dan Van Neste what happened when her song started to outshine Durante:

"Jimmy had a monkey act (in the show), and I was on just before he was. But after Walter Winchell wrote that a newcomer (meaning me) 'left Schnozolla in the shade,' they changed the sequence of the show, because he wouldn't follow me."

Stealing a bit of the spotlight from the seasoned, and beloved, "Schnozolla" was no easy feat. Goodnight, Miss O'Brien … wherever you are.

Chapter Three

The Beginning of the MGM Years

Over the years, Hollywood studios from "poverty row" operations to the big-league companies like Warner Brothers, Paramount, and MGM invented the formula used to create movie stars of their contract players. The path to potential stardom usually followed the same progression: small "walk on" roles usually uncredited and without any dialogue, credited "walk on" or "bit" parts with a line of dialogue (the young ingénue with classic lines like, "Tennis, anyone?"), credited supporting roles that appear throughout a film, a co-starring role with second billing and, finally, if you were driven and lucky, stardom with top billing and the role that "carried" the picture.

At every step of this proscribed route, publicity was crucial to a contract player's success. By the time Virginia O'Brien made her debut in 1940's *Hullabaloo*, the publicity department at Metro-Goldwyn-Mayer was a well-oiled machine. Working hand in hand with the studios photographers, they made certain that photos of the new contractees were seen as often as possible in newspapers and magazines.

The careers of Louella Parsons and Hedda Hopper were born out of the need for constant publicity. A "mention" in either Parsons' or Hopper's column was worth its weight in gold. Wise stars cultivated friendships with one, or both gossip mavens.

Another popular columnist was Harrison Carroll. On April 5, 1940, his "Behind the Scenes in Hollywood" column linked Virginia's name with another newcomer. "Bob Stack and Virginia O'Brien," Carroll reported, "of *Meet the People* are a twosome there...." He had spotted them dancing at the popular Los Angeles nightspot, La Conga. It sounds cliché, but, in truth, Virginia and Robert Stack were good friends. The friendship lasted another sixty years.

"Singer Signs Film and Stage Tickets" was the headline of a notice in the April 23, 1940 issue of the *MGM Studio News*. That piece read as follows:

> "Virginia O'Brien, whose distinctive style of singing won her local stage prominence overnight, has been placed under long-term contract at M-G-M, and will start there following an engagement in New York in *Keep Off the Grass*."

Prior to the opening of *Hullabaloo*, Edward Schallert of the *Los Angeles Times* announced that Virginia's first film break would come in the new "Nick Carter" film. Detective Nick Carter was portrayed on the screen by MGM's own Walter Pidgeon. This new, as yet untitled film, would be Pidgeon's third as the sleuth.

"Virginia, of course, was the striking young lady who sang The Stars Remain in *Meet the People*, the long-lived stage revue," Schallert informed readers, "and who later went east to appear in the short-lived *Keep Off the Grass*." Schallert closed his August 13, 1940 column with, "It's going to be very interesting, indeed, to see how her type will register in pictures."

What was more interesting was the fact that the "Nick Carter" mystery would not be Virginia's screen debut. This worked in her favor. In the film that MGM quickly fitted her into, two songs got the O'Brien treatment. The Walter Pidgeon film offered her no chance to do what Louis B. Mayer had hired her to do, which was to sing.

Another debut came before her film bow. Paul K. Damai wrote the column "Radio Short Circuits," in which he reviewed Virginia's first record on August 18, 1940. This was the 78rpm Columbia recording of two songs from *Keep Off the Grass*. He found that she "... begins each side normally enough...." It was during the second chorus of "Clear Out of This World" and "Two in a Taxi," that she revealed her comedic talent, and, as Damai observed, "... suddenly goes crazy and bids fair to claiming the title of the world's most eccentric songbird."

MGM's publicity team had already been working on increasing the public's awareness of Virginia O'Brien. Her work in *Meet the People* and *Keep Off the Grass* were lauded. She was, in both cases, the "deadpan" singer-comedienne who "stopped the show." Her discovery by Louis B. Mayer, along with photographs of the naturally beautiful girl, piqued the public's interest. When would she make her big screen debut?

Movie audiences got to see, and hear, Virginia for the first time when *Hullabaloo* opened in the U.S. on October 25, 1940. Cast in the small role of Virginia Ferris, she was lucky that her talent was singing. If this role, like her next two, gave her only a few lines of dialogue, it did give her the opportunity to sing in the style that made her unique, and instantly identifiable. Initially, Virginia was only to sing one song in *Hullabaloo*, but she performed the first so well that they added another solo for her at the end of the film.

The first song movie audiences watched her deliver, like no other singer before or since, was "Carry Me Back to Old Virginny." The second was "Jeanie with the Light Brown Hair." Both were traditional favorites, long known to Americans.

Actually, two singers perform solos of each. First, a young African-American tenor named Charles Holland sings each in a traditional manner, lending to each a style that was close to operatic. In a juxtaposition that includes gender, ethnicity, and style more than the other two, Virginia follows him. Her interpretations are wildly different. She swings both, and infuses them with her comedic flair. Here was a singer who was fresh, original, and funny all at the same time.

MGM's power spread far and wide via the many columns written from Hollywood and published around the world. One such column was "Harold Heffernan, from Hollywood." Readers of the Newcastle Sun in New South Wales (Australia) could read about Virginia O'Brien on November 2, 1940.

Heffernan's article was titled "Hollywood Is No Longer Training Potential Stars." Two paragraphs were devoted to the young singers, who most Australians were reading about for the first time. "Virginia O'Brien, a pretty, singing youngster," Heffernan's piece began, "attracted the attention of Metro-Goldwyn-Mayer when she appeared in a Hollywood home talent show about six months ago."

She wasn't immediately ready for a screen appearance. Heffernan gives credit to the head of MGM's scouting department, Billy Grade, for sending Virginia to Broadway. Grade announced that after her Broadway show closed, Virginia would then be ready for a startling role. Metro studio executives attended *Keep Off the Grass* regularly. Virginia developed at such a rapid rate, that the studio had her return to film a song for *Hullabaloo*. One song, as previously mentioned, suddenly become two.

This was accomplished during the break between the Broadway closing and the road tour of *Keep Off the Grass*. Heffernan claims that few knew that Virginia was under contract to MGM while she was accumulating so much admiration and name value on Broadway. While this seems to contradict the fact that her signing with the studio was announced widely, Heffernan's point is well made. Metro decided that she was so good it could not afford to let her escape despite her lack of training.

Virginia on tour with *Keep Off the Grass*.

Giving her autograph to fans during the tour of *Keep Off the Grass*.

When *Keep Off the Grass* played Detroit in November of 1940, it was reported that, "Detroit has never seen anyone like Virginia O'Brien, who was brought back for six curtain calls." Here was ample proof that her show-stopping number in *Meet the People* was not just a fluke. Virginia had impressed New York theatre-goers, and, more importantly, the theatre critics. With a Broadway success under her belt, Virginia was ready to return to her home town and her new home studio.

The young Miss O'Brien was doing double duty in Detroit. In addition to appearing in *Keep Off the Grass*, she and other young stars were also among Louella O. Parsons' Hollywood Stars. This troupe was appearing at the Warner Theatre in between movies. Along with Virginia, hostess Parsons' *Hollywood Stars of 1941* were Binnie Barnes, Robert Cummings, Brenda Joyce, Sabu, June Preisser, William Orr, and Mike Frankovich.

Miss Parsons' announced in her column dated November 25, 1940, that while Virginia was still on the road with *Keep Off the Grass*, her next film assignment awaited her in Hollywood. "Virginia O'Brien, who went over like a million with Detroit audiences," Parsons' gushed, "will play Eleanor Powell's sister in *Lady Be Good* for M-G-M."

Even though her contract with Metro-Goldwyn-Mayer assured her of seven years of film work, Louella still wondered why, "… some Broadway producer hasn't signed this girl … critics orchided her all over the place, she's so different." It is a valid point. True, *Keep Off the Grass*, had a short run, but Virginia was so successful in it. Yet, she never returned to Broadway.

Now reviews from her first movie began to appear. "Virginia O'Brien, whose dead-panning of a southland song satire just misses being a definite high spot," reported the *Pittsburgh Post-Gazette* on November 30, 1940. Her "satirical singing" was called "a treat." That same paper featured a photograph of Larry Nunn and Leni Lynn on December 5th. Nunn and Lynn played Frank Morgan's children in *Hullabaloo*, which was opening at the Warner Theatre on December 6, 1940. Patrons could see Virginia on-screen first, and stay to see her in-person following the movie.

Morgan was a superb leading and character actor, best known

for playing Professor Marvel, the Wizard, and a few smaller parts in *The Wizard of Oz*. His character in *Hullabaloo*, Frank Merriweather, is something of a braggart and con artist. A character not unlike many he would play brilliantly, including Professor Marvel. Merriweather is an actor with the ability to do thousands of voices.

At one point in the film, MGM plugs its upcoming movie, *Boom Town*, by having Merriweather perform a scene from the movie. That scene allows him to "imitate" the stars of *Boom Town*: Clark Gable, Spencer Tracy, Claudette Colbert, and Hedy Lamarr.

The cast of *Hullabaloo* (left to right) Charles Holland, Donald Meek, Virginia, Larry Nunn, Leni Lynn, Frank Morgan, Virginia Grey, and Dan Dailey.

Morgan is ably assisted in *Hullabaloo* by another *Wizard of Oz* alumni, Billie Burke. She plays the role of Penny Merriweather, one of Merriweather's three ex-wives. Virginia Grey is his daughter, Laura Merriweather. Both Morgan and Grey are trying to break into radio at the same station. In the beginning, they do not know that they are father and daughter. Frank Merriweather, and his daughter are unemployed, and neither has any luck at the station, but Virginia O'Brien and Charles Holland do. As Virginia Ferris, and the Bell Hop, they both audition successfully.

When Frank Merriweather is finally given a chance to perform on-the-air, he does all of the voices in a hilarious take-off of the legendary Orson Welles' radio play, *The War of the Worlds*. Merriweather's broadcast has the same effect on its listeners as Welles' radio play, in that it sets off a nationwide panic. Merriweather loses his sponsor and is fired. Of course, everything comes together at the end, with O'Brien and Holland singing on Frank Merriweather's new radio show.

The review from the *Harrisburg Tribune* summed up Virginia's screen debut thus: "Virginia O'Brien sings a torch song version of a Stephen Foster melody with a few preliminary wiggles and shakes." *Showman's Trade Review* found Holland and O'Brien to be "stand-outs."

Shortly after the opening of Virginia's second film, *Sky Murder*, at the Fox Theatre in Los Angeles, Virginia took to the stage of that same theatre, among others. Between screenings of Shirley Temple's *Young People*, Virginia was joined by actress Binnie Barnes and the young star known only as Sabu. This was a scaled-down version of Louella Parson's *Hollywood Stars of 1941* that was seen in Detroit and Pittsburgh.

There is no record of what Virginia sang during these performances, but based on how MGM's publicity department operates, it is likely that she sang "Carry Me Back to Old Virginny" and "Jeanie with the Light Brown Hair" from *Hullabaloo*. If time permitted, her show-stoppers from *Meet the People* and *Keep Off the Grass* were probably on the program as well.

Virginia's second film must have been a disappointment to her growing number of film fans. She didn't sing a note in the 1940 release, *Sky Murder*. Starring Walter Pidgeon, *Sky Murder*, was the third and final installment in a series of mystery-comedy films, which included *Nick Carter, Master Detective* (1939), *Phantom Raiders* (1940) and *Sky Murder* (1940).

The character, a favorite among the readers of the popular "Dime Novel" magazines, was introduced in the *New York Weekly* (Vol. 41 No. 46) on September 18, 1886. In addition to the trio of movies starring Walter Pidgeon, the detective also had a radio series bearing the same title as the first movie, *Nick Carter, Master Detective*.

Sky Murder opened on September 27, 1940. Lucille LaVonne, Virginia's uncredited role, is a member of a troupe of six chorus girls who appear to entertain a Washington Senator. Lucille speaks one line. Virginia's memory of her work in the quickly made *Sky Murder* was, *"I did a lot of screaming in that one."* Soon the screaming would end, and laughter took its place.

A lobby card for *Sky Murder*. Virginia is on the right, looking over Walter Pidgeon's shoulder.

Lounging while Walter Pidgeon solves the crime in *Sky Murder.*

Chapter Three, Part Two: Lullaby Groucho

At the beginning of 1941, Hollywood sent several of its newest talents north to entertain in the state capitol, Sacramento, where they performed at a banquet hosted by California Governor Culbert L. Olson for the state's 54th Legislature. Traveling with Virginia were Mary Heally, Charles Holland, and the Stoud Twins. Actor Charles Irwin would be the master of ceremonies. *The Oakland Tribune* covered the story on January 23, 1941. Charles Holland, who appeared with Virginia in *The Big Store* and *Hullabaloo,* was referred to as "Charles Holland, colored tenor...."

Louella Parsons' column of February 3, 1941 reported on the response to Virginia's appearance in *Hullabaloo.* Miss O'Brien "was given a rousing reception" after the film was screened at Camden. Parsons noted that critics, unlike the public, did not care for *Hullabaloo.*

Nevertheless, MGM had already made $600,000 on a film that cost $300,000 to make.

Before production on her third movie began, Virginia scored a double victory. Her performance at a legendary Hollywood restaurant, and its mention in Louella Parsons' column on March 20, 1941. Parsons raved about Virginia again:

> "The ovation they gave Virginia O'Brien at the Screen Actor's ball when she sang 'Sleep My Baby,' 'My Old Kentucky Home' and 'Jeanie with the Light Brown Hair' in her own peculiar style was terrific. The applause fairly shook the Coconut Grove, bearing out my contention that this girl, who was with me on my personal appearance tour last year, is in a class by herself. Virginia looked so pretty. She was in a party with Dan Dailey Jr., Bill Orr, and his mother, and I was glad that some of the Metro executives were there to see the reception given her."

Parsons also announced Virginia's next screen assignment: "I was told today that Virginia goes into one of the top spots in the Marx Brothers Comedy with Tony Martin and Virginia Grey." For now, that movie was titled *Step This Way*, and promoted as the most lavish musical for this trio since *A Night at the Opera*. The title would change, the "lavish" was missing and Virginia's "top spot" was one song. But, as usual, one song was all she needed to leave a lasting impression. There was, however, another personal appearance for the singer before filming started.

Following her success at the Coconut Grove, Virginia found the time to make a personal appearance in Rhinelander, Wisconsin. On April 15, 1941, three days before her 22nd birthday, she appeared there as an "Added Attraction." Heading the bill was a group called Three Bits of Rhythm. Also featured was Donna Andrich, who was billed as a "Sophisticated Dancer Direct from New York."

The show was at the Riverside Nite Club, which proclaimed itself "Rhinelander's Brightest Spot," and boasted a "seating capacity of 10,000—approximately 100 at a time." Only in Wisconsin! One can imagine Virginia's great relief upon her return from the hinterlands to Hollywood.

In her third outing for MGM, Virginia was cast in a movie that saw her working with leading men bearing the monikers Groucho, Chico, and Harpo. By 1941, the off-screen antics of the legendary team of brothers had cooled some.

Gone were the days of two or more of them, each with a suitcase, entering an elevator to perform an outlandish practical joke only they could pull off. As the elevator started its ascent, the brothers stripped and put their clothes into the suitcases. When they arrived at their floor, they exited the elevator in the nude. Police were called when the Marx Brothers pulled this pre film-career stunt.

Even so, they were still up to mischief on the set of *The Big Store*. Virginia shared her happy memories of that time with journalist Dan Van Neste:

> "That was too much fun! They (the Marx's) were always doing something funny, disappearing, etc. You could never get them all on the set at the same time ... And so clever! A lot of the film was ad-libbed. They had doubles for the roller skating scenes, but did most of the skating themselves. Groucho turned out to be such a good friend. I later appeared on his radio show."

As Kitty, a sales clerk, Virginia was on the staff of the "big" store known as Phelps Department Store in the movie. As the film opens, we learn that Hiram Phelps, who owns half the store, has died. Martha Phelps (Margaret Dumont) owns the other half. Hiram's share of the store is willed to his son, Tommy (Tony Martin), a singer who would rather build a music conservatory than run a department store.

Worried about her nephew's future, as well as her own, Martha hires one Wolf J. Flywheel (Groucho) to keep an eye on the store's shifty manager, Grover (Douglas Dumbrille). Frivolity and murder attempts ensue, with Flywheel aided and abetted by Ravelli (Chico) and the ever-silent Wacky (Harpo).

The tradition of Groucho, Chico, and Harpo having solo, musical numbers continued in *The Big Store*. Chico shares his piano with Harpo, and together they play "Mama Yo Quiero." Harpo outdoes himself, playing with a mirror image of himself on "Mozart's Sonata in C Major." This is followed by his singular interpretation of "Beethoven's Minuet," which he performs on the harp, cello, and violin (most film historians agree that the violin was actually played by the film's musical director, jazz violinist Georgie Stall).

Groucho has the big production number "Sing While You Sell." Like the Pied Piper of Hamlin, Groucho dances and slinks through each department, gathering more of the staff along the way. En masse, they follow him to Kitty (Virginia O'Brien), who is in the infant's department.

Singing "Rock-A-Bye Baby" in *The Big Store* (1941).

The melody of "Sing While You Sell" segues into "Rock-a-Bye Baby." Virginia, hand on the cradle, she slowly rocks, no expression on her expressive face, begins singing the song in the traditional fashion. The tempo shifts, the rocking cradle speeds up to a rate so fast that, had there been a baby inside he would have flown out! Throughout, Virginia's face remains frozen in nonchalance. Just as soon as it began, Virginia's solo ends all too quickly, with the singer shooting an off the hip phrase, "Shoot the talcum to me, Malcolm!"

A scene from *The Big Store*. Left to right: Marion Martin, Harpo, Groucho, Virginia, and Chico.

The production number ends with the stars and the chorus standing on a platform that slowly begins to move forward, sliding several feet across the expanse of the store. Standing next to Groucho, Virginia is thrown off balance slightly as the platform starts its journey. Groucho takes her hand, in what looks like an unrehearsed moment of gallantry, and steadies her. Hand in hand, they ride it out together.

At the end of the ride, Groucho, Virginia, and some of the chorus are deposited into a waiting elevator. If you watch very closely you will see Groucho turn to Virginia and say something as the doors close, and the number ends.

The Big Store opened on June 1, 1941. Many felt that it was not up to the standards of previous Marx Brothers classics like *Duck Soup* and *A Night at the Opera*. After its release, the brothers announced their retirement from movies. They reunited just once, for 1946's *A Night in Casablanca*, but *The Big Store* was their last film at MGM.

"I believe it important to record with you the splendid contribution of the motion picture industry through the motion picture production committee ... and camp recreation of which Edward Arnold is chairman." Thus began a letter to Norman Chandler of the *Los Angeles Times*.

The letter was from J.J. Christian from Camp Roberts. This was a thank you to the movie stars who entertained at the camp in June 1941. Christian went on to rave about "One of the greatest shows in Army history, including such talent as Laurel and Hardy, Red Skelton, Chico Marx, Donna Reed, Joan Leslie, Virginia O'Brien, and Margaret Whiting."

Backing up the singers who performed at Camp Roberts was the Universal Studio orchestra with Jerry Adler. 20,000 soldiers saw the two-and-a-half hour show in an amphitheater. The letter concluded with, "I cannot amply express my own gratitude and that of my fellow officers and of the men in Camp Roberts. The motion picture industry deserves the plaudits of all Americans for this kind of rallying to the cause of keeping the morale of our Army boys at a high level."

On June 14 and 15, nation newspapers including the *Los Angeles Times* all reported on the huge group of Hollywood stars who entertained troops at three military camps. The show was titled *Hollywood Stars on Maneuver*, and entertained 20,000 soldiers at California's

Camp Roberts. Future performances at Camp Hunter Leggitt and Fort Ord were expected to draw between 70,000 and 80,000.

The list of performers taking to the stage at Camp Roberts and Fort Ord read like the 1941 edition of Who's Who in Hollywood: Jack Benny, Ray Bolger, Burns and Allen, Claudette Colbert, Marlene Dietrich, Carol Landis, Dick Powell and Joan Blondell, Martha Raye, the Ritz Brothers, and Virginia O'Brien. The two-hour show was free.

Hollywood on Maneuver performed at several military camps during June 1941. Virginia is fourth from the right, between Dick Powell and Marlene Dietrich. Photo courtesy of Kevin John Charbeneau.

Another blurb appeared in the "Tattletale" column in the June 15, 1941 issue of the *Los Angeles Timesi*, which began, "There was great excitement among soldiers at Camp Roberts." A bus rolled into Camp Roberts carrying movie stars who were performing that evening. On board with Virginia were Laurel and Hardy, Joan Leslie, Jane Withers, Buddy Peppers, Ella Logan, and Red Skelton.

**Virginia singing for the troops at Fort Ord,
where she stopped the show (1941).
Photo courtesy of Kevin John Charbeneau.**

The soldiers didn't know about these shows until the day before the performance when sound trucks arrived to set up. The 60th Signal company from Fort Lewis in Washington State quickly built the stage. The entire tour was under the auspices of the Hollywood Motion Picture Defense Committee. A lengthy article with six photographs was published in the October issue of *Screenland* magazine.

In her book about the work she and her sisters did during World War II, Maxene Andrews of the Andrews Sisters remembered Virginia's USO and Hollywood Canteen performances. Andrews wrote that Virginia was among the early heroes of those who performed in USO productions. Maxene also revealed that it was Lucille Ball who helped Virginia overcome two of her fears. The first was the common fear of flying. Unfortunately, this came after Bob Hope's invitation to join him on the first of his many overseas tours.

When Virginia was asked to greet and entertain wounded GIs at a Bay Area veteran's hospital, she asked to be excused. Lucy helped her with her fear of hospitals by making her feelings clear. Ball simply said, "Virginia, you *have* to do it." Virginia knew her friend was right. Letting down the bedridden soldiers anxious to see her was not acceptable. With Lucy by her side, Virginia entered the hospital and performed. After that she spent six weeks visiting only military hospitals on her first solo tour.

Early on there seemed to be some confusion about the genre applied to Virginia's singing. She was obviously not a classical artist. Technically, she wasn't a band singer, or, in 1940's jargon, a "canary." Even so, it was not unusual to see blurbs with a title like, "Singer Cast In 'Masie' Movie." This item, which appeared in papers on June 29, 1941, read:

> "Virginia O'Brien, dead-pan singer who first attracted attention with her appearance in the Hollywood production of *Meet the People*, is adding another to her list of screen appearances with the announcement that she has been signed by Metro-Goldwyn-Mayer for a role in *Ringside Maisie*, starring Ann Sothern. Miss O'Brien will present a new musical number, "Boogie Woogie Maisie." The picture is directed by
>
> Edwin L. Martin, and produced by J. Walter Ruben."

Unfortunately, one thing here was premature. When *Ringside Maisie* reached the screen, Virginia did not sing "Boogie Woogie Maisie." Such are the ways of Hollywood directors and producers. It is even possible that the song was never written. Nevertheless, MGM's publicity machine continued to find ways to get Virginia's name in print. One method of doing that was to take advantage of her beauty. Beauty tips from columnists, and supposedly from Virginia herself, were seen in newspapers and magazines.

"Health, Beauty and Poise — How to Improve Your Personality" was a column by Veronica Dengel. Virginia's beauty was on display when her photograph graced the column on July 23, 1941. This was because Miss Dengel was writing about "The Oval Face Again." She claims that parting one's hair in the middle, as Virginia did, was becoming to the oval face. Other remarks included:

> "Virginia O'Brien (MGM feature player soon to be seen in *Ringside Maisie*) is wearing the perfect type of evening dress for summer use ... I also want to call your attention to Virginia's face — the perfect oval."

Over the years, Virginia's beauty was mentioned often. In his book, *The MGM Stock Company,* author James Robert Parrish explains Virginia's appeal perfectly. "She was that rare item: a comedienne who was also a looker." This combination of humor and glamour was something she shared with Lucille Ball, who managed to perform slapstick without losing her femininity.

The response to Virginia on the screen was the same as seeing her on the stage. Live or on celluloid, she stopped the show. *Variety* reported on the audience response to Virginia in *The Big Store*. On August 18th, at the illustrious Gopher Theatre in Minneapolis, viewers applauded after Virginia sang "Rock-a-Bye Baby" at every showing:

> "Applause is an extremely infrequent occurrence at the Gopher, or any other local house. It occasionally breaks out at the start of a cartoon comedy, but very seldom otherwise, and thus, the manifestations provoked by Miss O'Brien are regarded in local trade circles as all the more remarkable."

Was Virginia O'Brien the daughter of Fanny Brice? Hollywood has always loved a good rumor. This was one that was going around during the summer of 1941. Jimmy Fidler, the Los Angeles reporter known for his "In Hollywood" column, called this a "… silly, hard-to-squelch rumor…." It wasn't true. The O'Brien's had the birth certificate to end any speculation.

For several decades, stars and studios courted two powerful columnists. One was Louella Parsons, the other was Hedda Hopper. Virginia was mentioned frequently by "Lolly" and Hedda, who was famous for her trademark hats. Hopper mentioned Virginia twice in four days in 1941.

First on August 3, 1941:

> "Little Virginia O'Brien sang for $25 a week at the House of Murphy, and glad to get it. Joined up with *Meet the People* and was a tremendous local success with producers. So she went into a Broadway show on the strength of the hit she made here…."

Hedda's August 7, 1941 column contained the following:

> "My old friend Bob Murphy, of *The House of Murphy*, is a nervous wreck over his new singer Dotty Simms. She's a "nacherl" from Jacksonville, Fla., with a repertoire as sensational as her chassis, but after the way he lost Virginia O'Brien to the movies, Bob's become leery of talent."

Virginia accompanied Edward Arnold, Binnie Barnes, Connie Boswell, Eddie Cantor, Linda Darnell, and Ann Rutherford to San Francisco on Friday August 8, 1941. The stars were traveling to appear at the dedication of the first United Service Organization recreational center. The center was built on land donated by the city. San Francisco labor union members volunteered their time to build it. The supplies were donated by the citizens of San Francisco. The event was seen in nationwide newspapers.

Chapter Four

Sothern Breezes

Virginia's next movie at MGM, 1941's *Ringside Maise*, was an installment in a popular series of films. Ann Sothern's "Maisie" movies were more popular, and more numerous, than Walter Pidgeon's short-lived career as Nick Carter. Beginning in 1939 with *Maisie*, and ending in 1947 with *Maisie Undercover*, Ann Sothern played Brooklyn's brash but loveable Maisie Ravier ten times on film.

Maisie Ravier was the stage name of the fictional burlesque star born Mary Anastasia O'Connor. The part was given to Sothern when MGM's original choice, Jean Harlow, died suddenly at age 26 on June 7, 1937.

In *Ringside Maisie*, the fifth of the ten Maisies, Virginia O'Brien played "Herself" for the first time. She would go on to play herself four more times over the course of her film career. In the 1940s, it was common for a studio's contract players to appear as "Himself" or "Herself" in another star's movie. Bob Hope and Bing Crosby did this often in each other's movies, as did the team of Alan Ladd and Veronica Lake when they appeared in the film version of the popular radio show, *Duffy's Tavern*.

Virginia had one great song in *Ringside Maisie*. "A Bird in a Gilded Cage" bears a similarity to "Carry Me Back to Old Virginny" and

"Jeanie with the Light Brown Hair," in that it was written, and became a popular hit, before Virginia was born.

In 1900, songwriters Arthur J. Lamb and Harry Von Tilzer collaborated on the ballad. The lyrics came first, written by Lamb in 1899. Tilzer casually worked out the melody as a group of his friends listened. He knew "A Bird in a Gilded Cage" would be successful when he noticed that the ladies in the group were crying. According to sources, over two million copies of the sheet music were sold in 1900.

Of course, Virginia O'Brien put her personal stamp on the song. It was a performance she would repeat many years later on comic Ed Wynn's television show to great effect. As with "Rock-a-Bye Baby" in *The Big Store,* Virginia begins "A Bird in a Gilded Cage" with the traditional feeling and tempo. Then *the* trademark Virginia O'Brien look comes across her face, her shoulders moved up and down faster, and a new bird is born. That gilded cage is swinging now.

Lady Be Good opened on September 1, 1941, exactly one month after the opening of *Ringside Maisie*. This was the second film in which Virginia worked with Ann Sothern. It was the first time Virginia appeared with funny man Red Skelton, and it certainly wouldn't be the last. MGM's great tap-dancing star of the 1930's and 1940's, Eleanor Powell, joined the fun, and she and Virginia would go on to become great friends.

Original MGM Caption: BOUFFANT IN BLUE SOUFFLE ... Is Virginia O'Brien, who poses in an Adrian-designed gown for her role in Metro-Goldwyn-Mayer's musical *Lady Be Good*, which stars Eleanor Powell, Ann Sothern, and Robert Young. Miss O'Brien will be remembered for her "deadpan" singing in *Hullabaloo*. Norman McLeod directs *Lady Be Good*, with Arthur Freed producing.

Virginia's solo moment in *Lady Be Good* came with her singular version of "Your Words and My Music." As the husband and wife songwriting team of Dixie Donegan and Eddie Crane, Ann Sothern and Robert Montgomery perform the song first. "Your Words and My

Music" tells the story of the best part of Dixie and Eddie's love story; their marriage is happiest when she is writing words to blend with his music.

Nightclub Compere (Phil Silvers) introduces Lull (Virginia O'Brien) who sings "Your Words and My Music". *Lady Be Good* (1941).

"Your Words and My Music," which is sung next by actor John Carroll, was actually written by MGM's in-house songwriters Nacio Herb Brown and Arthur Freed. Brown had been composing music, while Freed, also one of MGM's most successful producers, supplied the lyrics. The song they are best known for, "Singin' in the Rain," was first published in 1929.

Virginia brings her singular style to "Your Words and My Music." The performance is deadpan. The tempo is brighter. In the middle of the song, Virginia stops singing and quickly asks, "I wonder where I parked my car?" This was guaranteed to get a laugh, and she added it to her comic repertoire.

As Red Skelton's girlfriend, Lull in *Lady Be Good*. "She's only happy when she eats," says Skelton, as Joe Willet.

Shortly after the opening of *Lady Be Good*, Harold Heffernan's September 5th "On the Film Front" column ended with, "Virginia O'Brien... singer of eccentric songs, has installed the most astonishing auto horn.... When Virginia presses the button to warn traffic, the first few bars on her hit song, 'Two in a Taxi' come pouring out."

"Two in a Taxi" was one of four songs that Virginia recorded on the Columbia label. The others were "This is Spring," "Clear Out of This World," and "I'm an Old Jitterbug." All four were from her short-lived Broadway show, *Keep Off the Grass*.

As no other cast members recorded songs from the musical, Virginia's recording comprised, in a sense, the only Broadway soundtrack of *Keep Off the Grass*. It should be noted that "Clear Out of This World," is not the Harold Arlen—Johnny Mercer song with the similar title of "Out of This World."

The October 1941 issue of the popular movie magazine *Screenland* featured a lengthy article titled "Hollywood Makes Me Laugh." Accompanied by numerous photos, the article focused on the shows that Hollywood stars put on at military bases like Fort Ord and Camp Hunter Liggett. Virginia was among a large group of stars that included Jack Benny, Claudette Colbert, Joan Blondell, Dick Powell, Marlene Dietrich, George Burns, and Grace Allen.

Virginia's performance was a hit. "The boys applauded vigorously after every act, but it was really Virginia O'Brien who stopped the show." The article was attributed to a woman with the single name, Liza. Virginia, Liza, and four of the younger lieutenants had dinner together after the show. This, based on the impact of Virginia's performance, must have been the highlight of the lieutenant's day. Liza reported:

> "Most of the boys didn't know who Virginia O'Brien was, and when she came out she got just the amount of applause

any would get until—and it was only about a 30th of a second until she broke into that dead pan swing and really knocked the boys for a loop. They just wouldn't let her go, and made her do number after number, with each song topping the previous one."

Liza, who may have been enlisted herself, concluded her comments about her first encounter with Virginia by stating, "… I wish my year were up and I could go back to Hollywood to see more of Miss O'Brien because there's one really swell girl!"

The news of Virginia's touring various military bases continued with an article in the December 9, 1941 issue of the *Oakland Tribune*. Camp Shows, Inc. had a variety unit called The Sunshine Revue. At the time, the unit was going "to Camp Roberts at Monterey to open a 4000-seat theater tonight." Twelve chorus girls, dancers, comedians, and singers were slated for another two-and-a-half-hour show. After the performance in Monterey, the unit was traveling to Sacramento. The film stars on this tour were Edward Arnold, Joe E. Brown, Brenda Marshall, Ruth Hussey, and Laraine Day. Virginia performed in the show and joined the other stars in dedicating a USO hut in Salinas the same day.

Virginia and Ann Sothern went directly from working on *Lady Be Good* into rehearsal for *Panama Hattie*. On Broadway, the show starred Virginia's singing idol, Ethel Merman. MGM bought the rights for the film adaptation, and cast Ann Sothern in the title role. The part of Flo Foster went to Virginia. Flo's romantic interest was played by Red Skelton. This was their second film together; by Hollywood standards they were on their way to becoming a film team. They didn't know it at the time, but their fourth silver screen coupling would follow *Panama Hattie*.

A wardrobe test for *Panama Hattie* (1942).

The New York Times film critic was fine with one of Virginia's songs, but the other one made him uneasy:

> "To be sure, some of the music is fetching. Virginia O'Brien sings 'Fresh As a Daisy' humorously, though her other number, 'At the Savoy,' is in decidedly questionable taste."

In *Panama Hattie* Virginia sings "Fresh as a Daisy" to
Ben Blue, Rags Ragland, and Red Skelton.

That "questionable taste" was key in the decision to assign "Did I Get Stinkin' at the Savoy" to Virginia. Originally, as she revealed years later in an interview with Dan Van Neste, the song was to be performed by Ann Sothern. After screening the footage of Sothern's performance, it was decided that her interpretation of the song was too salacious.

Van Neste writes, "The delightful 'Fresh as a Daisy' was delivered at lightning speed. Another of her numbers, "At the Savoy," really raised eyebrows...." Virginia remembered the controversy, and the outcome. "There was a big tadoo about that number. Ann Sothern filmed it first. Walter Donaldson wrote the song for her to sing and staged it for her. But the Hays office objected to the way she did it (on a table as if she were drunk). MGM wanted to use the number, and they thought I could get away with it."

Where Virginia sang it sober, recalling how "stinkin'" she was last night; Ann sang it as if she was still intoxicated. Virginia's up-tempo, frozen-faced rendition removed the sexual innuendo of Sothern's languid approach. Today the thought of a woman having one too many is not nearly as shocking as it was in 1942. Even with Virginia's comic slant, the song's topic was objectionable to those who felt that drinking to the point of inebriation was "un-ladylike."

The quintessential British butler (Alan Mowbray) is startled when Flo (Virginia O'Brien) makes her intentions clear while singing her up-tempo, predatory version of "Let's Be Buddies." Original *Panama Hattie* lobby card, 1942.

A rare photograph of the cast of *Panama Hattie* at the film's finale. Photo courtesy of Kevin John Charbeneau.

Chapter Four, Part Two: Sing for Your Soldier

On February 2 and 3 of 1942, the *Los Angeles Times* covered the opening of the U.S.O. clubhouse. Located at the intersection of Cahuenga and Hollywood Boulevard, the gathering place for soldiers and movie stars was a 6,000-square-foot building. Edward G. Robinson was the guest of honor on the first night.

One thousand soldiers attended the klieg-light ceremony where they met stars like Robinson, Ann Sheridan, Nancy Kelly, Barbara Britton, Jinx Falkenburg, and Virginia O'Brien. Like the famous Hollywood Canteen, the U.S.O. clubhouse was a place servicemen went to eat, relax, and be entertained by the stars who volunteered nightly until the war came to an end. For young men leaving from the Port of Los Angeles, dancing with Ann Sheridan, Bette Davis, or Ginger Rogers was an unforgettable thrill.

The *Los Angeles Times* covered the Hollywood scene in their section titled "Hither and Yon With Stars," on February 19, 1942, mentioning another O'Brien. "Mary O'Brien, 18-year-old sister of Virginia O'Brien, was a hit when she entertained at a Southern California anti-aircraft camp, and elsewhere."

In March 1942, Virginia joined a group of celebrities and movie stars who would be performing for the crews of freighters and tankers from all parts of the world. The whole venture would be launched, according to the *Los Angeles Times*, dated March 6, at Convoy Cabaret.

Convoy Cabaret was held at the Yugoslav Hall in San Pedro, California. A group called Bundles for Bluejackets was hosting the gala event. In attendance, there would be at least two "Hollywood celebrities" seated at each table. They were there to entertain "seamen from all ships of the United Nations" currently docked in Los Angeles Harbor.

These men, who were "fighting the Axis," were Russian, Dutch, British, Scandinavian, and American. The long list of stars included Kay Francis, Dolores Del Rio, Carole Landis, Fay Wray, Charles Laughton, and Joan Bennett. Actor Gregory Ratoff acted as host. The *Los Angeles Times* piece concluded by informing its readers that this was a Hollywood tribute to the courage of the men who go out unarmed in the deadly submarine lanes.

"The Home Front," a *Los Angeles Times* feature from March 9th, reported on the party, and the challenges it presented. "No police department in the world could cope with 1,000 seamen … a dozen assorted nationalities, fighting over 100 of the world's most beautiful women within the confines of a single building."

And yet, the event was a success. Journalist Treanor reported that the four-hour party went without a single fight inside the hall. He felt that the scattered fights outside, "didn't count." Careful planning triumphed. The men were served by Kay Francis, Carole Landis, Mrs. Darryl Zanuck, and a bevy of "B girls."

Charles Laughton offered the only serious presentation. The actor, who was called back for an encore, recited Lincoln's Gettysburg Address. Laughton had a tough act to follow, the inspired princes of tap dance, the Nicholas Brothers. In addition to Virginia, other lifting their voices in song were Carol Bruce and Irene Manning. Thanks to the Victory Committee, Ray Noble's orchestra played. The evening ended in what must have been the longest conga line ever seen in Hollywood.

Sidney Carroll's column about the comings and goings of Hollywood was carried by numerous newspapers. In the March 22, 1942 *Oakland Tribune*, Carroll wrote, "Alyn Sees Town." This was one of the first times readers saw Virginia's name alongside that of "fiancé" Kirk Alyn. She was giving the Broadway dancer a tour of Hollywood even though, as Carroll reported, "he should know it by now, having been out here a couple of times on movie bids that didn't pan out."

The time Virginia and other stars spent entertaining the troops was rewarding to them as performers and patriots. More importantly, was the effect these shows had on all of our armed forces. "Actors' Role in Building Morale Told Ad Club" was on the front page of the *Los Angeles Times* on March 25, 1942.

The Advertising Club held a luncheon at the Biltmore Hotel on March 24, where it was reported that the Army considers the work as important as weapons. Kenneth Thompson, secretary of the Screen Actors Guild, stated, "We send individual stars and small groups of stars on tours through the camps all over the country...giving free performances in theatres, mess halls, hospitals and parade grounds." Five of those stars were at the luncheon: Charles Laughton, Rosalind Russell, Martha O'Driscoll, Michele Morgan, and Virginia.

The only one who performed that day was Virginia, who sang some of the songs she sings for soldier entertainment, light, modern pieces. Rosalind Russell was given special mention for having performed at seven camps in Texas, where she did four shows a day.

The following day, the luncheon was mentioned in "Hither and Yon with the Stars," the aforementioned *Los Angeles Times* column by Edward Schallert. "Rosalind Russell's speech was thoughtfully and impressively given, and had a touch of humor besides," Schallert reported. He also noted that, "Virginia O'Brien clicked with her songs."

Virginia's second film of 1942, *Ship Ahoy*, reunited her with the star she admired most at MGM, Eleanor Powell. Also on board was Red Skelton, but this time he was not Virginia's love interest. The role went to Bert Lahr. *Ship Ahoy* was screened for the press on April 4, 1942 in New York City.

Backstage Lothario "Skip" Owens (Bert Lahr) tries to impress the woman of his dreams, Fran Evans (Virginia O'Brien). Encountering him later on the ship she calls him the "Lepracorn."

Virginia's generosity went beyond the time she spent entertaining the military. One generous act, reported on April 12, 1942 in the *Los Angeles Times*, also showed that Virginia didn't have the overblown ego of some celebrities: "Virginia O'Brien is twice a week giving lessons to Virginia Perry of North Hollywood High, who wants to imitate her deadpan style."

During the war years, Hollywood produced a wide variety of patriotic films. Known as "flag wavers," these movies were made to boost national pride. Many of these movies, such as James Cagney's *Yankee Doodle Dandy*, were musicals with production numbers that prominently featured the "Stars and Stripes."

A portrait in the wild print dress Virginia wore when she sang "Poor You" to Bert Lahr in *Ship Ahoy*.

There were more serious efforts too. Not just dramatic films, but documentaries about battles aboard and the manufacturing of supplies here at home. A new series of "episodic" documentaries was announced by Virginia's studio. Covered by Edwin Schallert in the April 29, 1942 edition of the *Los Angeles Times*, the films were to be a series titled *Now We Are 21*.

"These films would be a right-up-to-the-minute building of the new Army," Schallert reported. Like the new soldiers, the directors were from the younger group at M.G.M. Among them were Jules Dassin, Fred Zinneman, and Edward Cahn. The stars selected were also younger talents like Gene Kelly, Patricia Dane, and Virginia.

It was also reported by Louella Parson's that writer Edgar Allan Woolf, one of Hollywood's' best and most prolific writers, was assigned to the series. Woolf died in 1943. After his death, there were no further reports of the project. The filmographies of others involved have no record of it.

The next time Virginia's name and image appeared in the *Los Angeles Times* it was in a lighter, romantic feature. One of the three photos shows her helping a young soldier to his feet. This was Corporal George Kislingbury, and the article that told the tale was "Corporal's May Day Dream Has Just the Right Ending" (May 1, 1942).

As the story goes, Corporal Kislingbury took a tumble as he delivered a basket of May flowers at Virginia's doorstep. With a mysterious picture tucked inside his shirt, he made the journey from the Biltmore Hotel's U.S.O. sitting room to a home in the fertile San Fernando Valley.

There is the implied "Once Upon a Time," and the presence of MGM's publicity department is present, as the story unfolded. The "hopeful but unabashed" Corporal walked "straight to the home of slender brunette, Virginia O'Brien ... for it was the picture of this fair actress he carried in his blouse."

The idea of this first of May ritual was for the young man to leave the flowers on the doorstep of his beloved, knock, and then flee before she appeared. The punishment if caught, would be a kiss. Corporal Kislingbury "... stumbled—accidently, of course—just as the fair Virginia swung the door [open]...." The blushing man in uniform was helped to his feet. Having nabbed him, Virginia had the right to kiss him, and so she did.

"Ah, the merry month of May," said Corporal Kislingbury with a sigh.

Harrison Carroll had the syndicated column "Behind the Scenes in Hollywood." On May 16, 1942, Carroll mentioned another singing O'Brien. "Hollywood Party Line: Virginia O'Brien's kid sister, Mary, gave a singing audition for Buddy De Sylvia and may be in movies soon. She graduates from high school this summer." Buddy De Sylvia was one of the founders of Capitol Records. Mary did make a few movies, but the results of the vocal audition are unknown.

A British battleship, or man-of-war, dropped anchor in a port near Hollywood. The secrecy was probably to keep the ship's exact location unknown. The ship's name was not reveled either. What is known is that on May 21, 1942, nationwide newspapers carried a blurb headlined, "Movie Stars Give Show on British Battleship." This was the first time the Hollywood Victory Committee had presented a show on a ship.

Virginia was there for that inaugural shipboard performance. Basil Rathbone was the host. Others there to entertain were Gracie Fields, Reginald Gardiner, and Roy Rogers. Virginia and Roy were old friends. Rogers had dated Mary O'Brien before Dale Evans appeared on the scene. The two used to play duets on the piano and sing at the O'Brien family home. The crew must have been thrilled to see Fields and Gardiner, who were both born in the UK. Rathbone was British as well, but he was born in South Africa.

"I Fell in Love with the Leader of the Band" was Virginia's solo in *Ship Ahoy*. Only a handful saw the song on the screen, though the *St. Louis Star and Times* mentioned it in a review printed on June 3,

1942. How many saw the number before it was cut from *Ship Ahoy* is unknown. The enthusiastic swing tune finds Virginia backed by the Dorsey orchestra and falling for various musicians as they each take a solo. Also unknown is the reason for removing the song. It would not be seen until it reappeared in 1945.

Far left: Roy Rogers and Virginia O'Brien are among the first entertainers to perform on a ship during WWII. Also pictured are Captain Jack Bolton and Gracie Fields (center, wearing a long strand of pearls). At the far right, Basil Rathbone has his hand on the shoulder of his wife, Ouida.

"... *Ship Ahoy*," wrote Marion Boone, "... is a lame excuse for the use of the spy theme." Writing for the *St. Louis Star and Times,* Boone titled her June 6, 1942 review of *Ship Ahoy* "Spies Are Not Popular, Especially in Musicals." She explained her belief by pointing to Alfred

Hitchcock's mysteries and thrillers as films in which spies "... fit appropriately into the scheme."

While she did not appreciate Eleanor Powell tapping out a coded message to trap enemy agents, she did acknowledge the skill with which Eleanor, working with drummer Buddy Rich, executed the "flashy dance" with "brilliant style."

An original lobby card for MGM's *Ship Ahoy*. Left to right Virginia, Bert Lahr, and Eleanor Powell.

In her closing paragraph, the journalist singled out Miss Powell's supporting cast:

> "The audience, especially the younger element, goes for Red Skelton in a big way, and additional clowning of some merit is done by Bert Lahr and Virginia O'Brien, the sob-faced singing comedienne."

Virginia, Eleanor Powell, and Red Skelton in *Ship Ahoy*.

Dressed for a shipboard costume party, Bert Lahr puts the moves on Virginia in *Ship Ahoy*.

The finale of *Ship Ahoy*, "It's the Last Call for Love." Far left second row is Frank Sinatra. First row left to right: Red Skelton, Eleanor Powell, Tommy Dorsey, Virginia and Bert Lahr.

As we have learned from Virginia's fingernail treatment, beauty hints espoused by famous film actresses have been going on since the advent of films, since the creation of our earliest "movie stars." Virginia's beauty secret for clear eyes was the sixth in the series Beauty Hints published, with an accompanying photo of the smiling Miss O'Brien, in the *Kilmore Free Press* on June 25, 1942 (Victoria, Australia).

> "Clear eyes are important for beauty, says Metro-Goldwyn-Mayer starlet, Virginia O'Brien. She has a simple treatment for the tired look that results from eye strain, glaring lights, or late nights. Fill a small round bottle with ice water, close it, dry the outside, and use it as a compress for the eyes alternately."

Hollywood, being Hollywood, used these beauty hints from the starlets of 1942. Virginia's accomplishments were also referenced. The "popular radio artist" had appeared in "several"

MGM films, six to date. Also promoted was the upcoming *Ship Ahoy*, with "… Eleanor Powell, Red Skelton, and Tommy Dorsey's Band.

Original MGM Caption: THERE'S AN ORIENTAL INFLUENCE … to Virginia O'Brien's dusty pink dinner gown with its sequin-trimmed tunic and accordion-pleated skirt. The attractive player will be seen with Eleanor Powell in the Metro-Goldwyn-Mayer film "Ship Ahoy" with Red Skelton and Bert Lahr. Gown designed by Kalloch. Photo: Author's collection.

Virginia's friend, Groucho Marx, was a man of letters. His letters have been published in books such as his own *The Groucho Letters: Letters from and to Groucho Marx*. This book is comprised of the letters that Groucho donated to the Library of Congress in the mid 1960's.

In 1992, Groucho's daughter published *Love, Groucho: Letters from Groucho Marx to His Daughter Miriam*.

For those who feel that based on her appearance in *The Big Store* with the Marx Brothers, and her stint as the singer on Groucho's *Blue Ribbon Town* radio show, indicated that Groucho may have liked the deadpan singer a bit more than he let on, his letter April 18, 1942 to Miriam offers some insight:

Ambassador Hotel - Los Angeles

Dear Miriam,

I'm sitting here with Virginia O'Brien. Wish you were here to see us dancing cheek to cheek.

Love,

Silent Cal Englund

Miriam's annotation reads: Virginia O'Brien was a singer I had a crush on. "Silent Cal" (after Silent Calvin Coolidge), was my father's private name for George Englund, because he claimed that George never talked either.

"Curtain Calls: From Singing Wins Her—Virginia O'Brien Scores When Stage Fright Evolved New Type of Comedy." Wood Soanes wrote this article for the *Oakland Tribune* on June 24, 1942. It is interesting to read, as it shows how stories change over the years. Periods of time become longer or shorter, people are credited with things they may or may not have done. It seems the only consistent thing is Virginia's comments:

> "There is increasing evidence of the popularity of a young (girl) who does torch songs with reverse English—Virgin-

ia O'Brien, who recently had not only a song, but a good comedy role in *Ship Ahoy*.

Miss O'Brien has been touted by press agents ever since she hit the jackpot in *Meet the People*, that intimate review prompted and produced a group of disgruntled youngsters who believed they had talent, but couldn't interest film magnates. Some of them did, including Miss O'Brien.

The other day she broke down, and confessed to an inquiring AP reporter, seeking data on the development of her singing method, that it was purely accidental, just as most of the big comedy hits were accidental. Charlotte Greenwood discovered the humor of her famous camel walk when she slipped and fell during a dance, wrenched her back, and couldn't get off all fours to make her exit. Other stars have had similar trials that paid big dividends.

Well, Miss O'Brien simply got stage fright … and a smart director. She is the daughter of a deputy district attorney in Los Angeles, Thomas F. O'Brien, and she studied law, but liked singing better than she liked Blackstone.

When she heard that *Meet the People* was in rehearsal, she decided to take a whack at it. 'So I auditioned for a part,' she recalled. 'I didn't expect to get it. In fact, I didn't greatly care, and I was really surprised when they told me I'd do.

'I had tried to emote. I just couldn't. It was awful, and I started to wish I'd never seen the inside of a theater. Something happened to my nerves, and the muscles of my face virtually froze.'

After working with her for hours, stage director Danny Dare, so the story goes, walked off into the wings making hoarse animal noises and tearing at his hair. It was almost time for the premier, and he had no likely substitute singer for a couple of more important ditties.

Suddenly, an idea struck him. There was plenty of emotional singers, and he had the only frozen-faced one of record. Rehearsals started all over again on a new angle, and the rest is more or less history. MGM signed her before the show left Hollywood with the understanding that she could finish the run. She did a couple of years later in New York, paused to appear in a flop, *Keep Off the Grass*, and then returned to the studio and her home town. Since then she has been in *Sky Murder, Hullabaloo, Ringside Maisie, Lady Be Good*, and several others, not only singing, but acting with a frozen pan."

Headline, the *Los Angeles Times,* June 29th 1942: "War Heroes Hailed by Thousands." *Times* journalist Tom Cameron covered the long day honoring the fifteen Americans and Britons who "... overcame fear and caution to serve brilliantly their native lands...." It was almost as if this day was, in a way, the inspiration for the MGM musical, *Thousands Cheer*. That film began filming six months after this salute to veterans with, among other things, a parade with thousands cheering along its route.

Hollywood's glamour girls draw names to see which soldier they will escort at the Cocoanut Grove. Courtesy of Terri O'Brien.

Like the film, there was an exciting evening of entertainment awaiting these soldiers. The article had a photograph of eight "Hollywood glamour girls" drawing the names of the heroes they would escort to a dinner dance at the legendary Cocoanut Grove. Along with Virginia were Dorothy Lamour, Ruth Hussey, Ann Sothern, Jean Rogers, Patricia Morrison, Lynne Carver, and Claudette Colbert. Others, not seen in the photo, included Betty Grable, Susan Hayward, Carole Landis, and Alexis Smith. The master of ceremonies was the comedian known as Banjo Eyes, Eddie Cantor.

Columnist Edward Schallert continued to praise Virginia in the *Los Angeles Times*. On July 20, 1942, he wrote, "Virginia O'Brien scored so well at the preview of *Panama Hattiei*, she's expected to speed ahead at MGM., and there is talk of possible big doings for her in *Du Barry Was a Lady*, which will be produced by Arthur Freed. She plays the friend of Ann Sothern in "Hattie" and sings very effectively."

An August 2, 1942 review of *Ship Ahoy* in the *San Bernardino County Sun*, with no byline read, "Tops too, are the ten new songs numbers, with Virginia O'Brien in her best role to date, literally stopping the show with her interpretation of 'At the Savoy.'

As an up-and-coming MGM star, Virginia was publicized around the world. This photo appeared in the *Mirror* of Perth Australia on July 25, 1942. Caption: Tennis is a sideline for Virginia O'Brien, pretty "deadpan" singer who warbled her way into an MGM. picture contract. Now she's busy with Ann Sothern in "Ringside Maisie".

On August 18, 1942, Virginia O'Brien was called upon to make an appearance on the radio show *Command Performance*. The host was one of Hollywood's most popular actors, Cary Grant. Virginia was first up with the song "Go to Sleep My Baby." This was followed by a comedy skit with Cary Grant and Joan Davis. Then listeners heard the sound of a San Francisco fog horn, as requested by a member of the armed forces.

The song Cow, Cow Boogie was a big hit at the time, performed by Freddie Slack and his orchestra, backed singer Ella Mae Morse on the tune. Host Grant then introduce the pianist Jose Iturbi, who played his rendition of Fire and Ice. Cary Grant and Bert Lahr closed the show with a comedy routine about Lahr owing money to the IRS.

The IRS must have been pleased with Virginia during the period of time. In an interview with author Dan Van Neste, she stated that she was getting five-thousand dollars a week when she made a personal appearance.

Not all of her live performances generated money, as over the years she would take part in many benefits. Such was the case when she was one of the featured stars in the *Red Cross Victory Revue*. This "Soldier Benefit Revue" was also billed as the *Valley Victory Varieties*.

The event benefited not only the Red Cross, but local hospitals as well. It was unique in that it was presented simultaneously at the Fox and Capitol theaters on Tuesday August 25th of 1942. Joining Virginia was comedian Rags Ragland, who appeared with her in the film version of *Panama Hattie*, as well as on Broadway with Ethel Merman.

Other members of the all-star show were Joan Blondell, Carmen Miranda, Ethel Waters, Phil Silvers, and Hoagey Carmichael. *The San Bernardino County Sun* promoting the show in their August 21, 1942 edition called Virginia the girl with the "dead pan," the oomph shoulders and one of the best swing singers in Hollywood.

By the 1940's, the brilliant silent film comedian Buster Keaton, who had a face as immobile as Virginia's, was a gag-writer at MGM. For now, his glory days were over, but Keaton would rebound in the Judy Garland musical *In the Good Old Summertime*. For now, he was earning a living, and teaching a young Lucille Ball the art of physical comedy.

Betty Boone wrote a regular column for *Screenland* magazine titled "Inside the Stars Homes." In the November 1942 issue of *Screenland*, readers were invited to Virginia's home. Three photos showed Virginia preparing for Thanksgiving dinner.

The traditions the O'Brien family indulged in prior to the outbreak of WWII were "stopping for the duration." This included the desserts that Virginia and younger sister Mary would prepare together. In their place, a fruit "Knox Sparkling Gelatine" would be served.

While Virginia was busy being "funny for money," her mother, Edna, and their O'Brien's cook followed Virginia's suggestion for the holiday dinner. Those suggestions included fruit cocktail with wine sauce, string beans, sour cream biscuits, Hawaiian sweet potatoes, and turkey with oyster dressing.

The epitome of MGM glamour. Virginia circa 1942.

Seven recipes from the O'Brien household were included. "If Old Man Rationing or the priorities or something else make pineapple scarce," Virginia said she would prepare an "... ornamental vegetable platter." The cooked cauliflower center was covered in Hollandaise sauce.

Betty Boone offered her impression of Virginia, and her family. "MGM's favorite little comedienne looks like a typical American college girl," Boone wrote. She added that Virginia laughed easily and, "she's much prettier than she allows herself to be on the screen." The reporter found a home filled with laughter.

Switching to Virginia's film career, during her visit, Virginia received four calls telling how the audience reacted to her at the preview screenings of *Panama Hattie*. She was, in the words of the Metro executives who called, a "smash." Boone mentioned her upcoming movie. "If she's half as amusing in *Du Barry Was a Lady*, you're going to ache from laughing...."

Virginia's appearances at Army camps were made during her spare time. The O'Brien's would also be hosting "... Army, Navy, Air Corps, and Marine servicemen" during the holidays. It was mentioned that deputy district attorney O'Brien, who collected Navy books, had recently joined the merchant marines. This would be his third war.

The O'Brien sisters had gin rummy and charades into "relay races." For their new version of gin rummy, the party guests were divided into two teams. Betty Boone described the proceedings, "... tables are set up in both living room and playroom, and numbered. You are supposed to play your game as fast as you can: the winners of the first table get into the winners of the first table that finishes, and the idea is to get through the required number of games ahead of all the rest. You change partners each time and your tally is credited with "first" finishes, wins, and scores."

For the guests arriving after the traditional turkey dinner, Virginia planned to serve a buffet supper of turkey sandwiches and coffee. If coffee was rationed, soda and fruit punch would be served. Another of the O'Brien girls' relay race party games, "Quotations," would be played.

As she had with relay gin rummy, Betty Boone described how to play this version of charades. "Two teams are formed. An umpire makes out a list of slogans, quotations, picture titles, or whatever is decided on, and stands with them in the hall. His partner plays exciting, swift-tempo music. The teams take over two rooms and the captains of each one dash to the umpire for the first title.

Thanksgiving dinner with the O'Brien's.
Screenland magazine, November 1942.

"Each gets the same title, and the idea is for each team to choose someone to act out the title, then have the rest guess. The minute a team guesses, its captain dashes out for the second title, the team finishing first wins."

In the November 11, 1942 "Theater Topics" entertainment column, it was noted that "Sphynx-faced Buster Keaton... appeared on a movie set where dead-pan Virginia O'Brien was holding forth."

Keaton watched Virginia go through her paces before commenting, "Virginia has the pulsating appeal of a tray of ice cubes." O'Brien matched with, "He looks like a fugitive from Mt. Rushmore." (*The Lincoln Star*, Lincoln, Nebraska)

Several years later, dressed in his trademark silent-screen outfit, Buster visited Virginia on the set of *Du Barry Was a Lady*. He sat on her lap, and neither moved a muscle as the camera caught the moment. The two remained friendly, and crossed paths in the future when both guested on Ed Wynn's television show. During the filming of *Merton of the Movies*, starring Red Skelton and Virginia, it was suggested that Buster join the cast as her father. While Skelton loved the idea, it didn't work out.

One more beauty hint was offered in the December 1, 1942 edition of Queensland's *Evening Advocate*. Beneath a photograph of Virginia in dark glasses, the caption read, "With the hot weather coming, there's always the danger that overexposure to the sun and wind will make the skin dry and brittle. MGM actress Virginia O'Brien demonstrates you can enjoy the sun without spoiling your complexion. Use, she says, turban or kerchief to protect your hair, a good layer of cold cream for the skin, and don't forget the dark glasses."

American newspapers were not to be outdone. The *Lansing News Journal* brought its readers all the latest, vital news from the set of Virginia's next film, *Ship Ahoy*. First in the December 2, 1942 edition, Virginia's fingernails were discussed for the first time in print. Titled

"Virginia O'Brien Airs Trick for Fingernails" claimed that Virginia had the longest fingernails in Hollywood. How did she grow and maintain her half-nice nails? "Oil does the trick," the star revealed.

A fashion photo from a 1942 Spanish publication. Original Caption: El atractivo vestido que luce Virginia O'Brien, actriz de la Metro-Goldwyn-Mayer, es de créspon crema con adornos negros y tiene la ventaja de dar la impresión de esbeltez.

This fascinating story came from the set of the movie then called *I'll Take Mania*. That title was changed to *Ship Ahoy* before the film was released. The details of her nightly nail-care routine included wrapping each fingertip in cotton that had soaked in warm olive oil. When the cotton had cooled, Virginia put on the white cotton gloves she wore as she slept. The article ended with this promise: "The young starlet guarantees this nail care as a sure cure for split, broken, or injured fingernails." Women everywhere must have been eternally grateful.

Virginia's fingernails were nothing compared to the item the *Lansing State Journal* published on December 24, 1942. Eleanor Powell and Virginia discovered how to "Shine in Blackout." By mixing a fine-grain luminous powder into their makeup, the ladies achieved "a glow easily discernable in the dark."

As 1942 was coming to a close, things were definitely looking good for the young, rising star. Soon they would shift into high gear. A handsome, young actor who could literally sweet her off her feet was about to fly into her life.

Modeling the latest fashions was part of the job for any raising starlet at MGM.

The handsome actor Kirk Alyn was Virginia's first husband, and the screen's first Superman.

Chapter Five

Enter Superman

Virginia seemed to shy away from the spotlight and the gossip columns where her romantic life was concerned. She was seen on the town with actor Robert Sterling, and another man she dated for a time was the Broadway star John Raitt. Yet she didn't seem to have a suitor who looked like husband material. This is why gossip columnists, including the well-connected Louella Parsons, were genuinely surprised when they learned that Virginia had suddenly married actor Kirk Alyn in October of 1942. Some didn't think the couple would marry so soon due to the May 2, 1942 announcement that Virginia and Kirk had postponed their wedding "for the duration." The marriage took place in Yuma, Arizona. If the young couple had hoped to keep their wedding day out of the Hollywood newspapers, they had certainly chosen the right location.

Born on October 8, 1910, Kirk Alyn was nine years Virginia's senior. His given name was John Feggo, Jr. The son of parents who had immigrated from Hungry, John spent his childhood in the town of Wharton, New Jersey. Visitors to Wharton can find a plaque that commemorates his life in the city's municipal building.

During the 1930s, he lived in New York City, where he found work in the choruses of three Broadway musicals: *Girl Crazy* (with

Virginia's singing hero, Ethel Merman), the patriotic *Of Thee I Sing*, and *Hellzapoppin'*.

The first six years of their marriage could not have been easy on the young couple. Unable to find regular work in films, Kirk gave up acting for a time and worked at the Douglas airplane plant. There would also be separations due to the war. At least the newlyweds had a brief honeymoon before returning to Los Angeles, where Kirk began looking for work, and Virginia was back at MGM filming her eighth film.

Kirk Alyn and Virginia circa 1942.

On Saturday, December 12, 1942, KGLO-CBS broadcast *Soldiers with Wings*. The program was broadcast from the West Coast training center in Santa Ana, California. This was where aviation cadets received their training. Major Eddie Dundstedter's Army band provided the music. The announcer that evening, Sergeant Ben Gage, was married to one of Virginia's co-workers at MGM, the Million-Dollar

Mermaid, Esther Williams. Along with Virginia, the great husband and wife comedy team of George Burns and Gracie Allen would interview the cadets.

Five days after the *Soldiers with Wings* program, a large photograph of Red Skelton and Virginia appeared in newspapers across the country, including the December 17, 1942 edition of *Wilkes-Barre Record* (Pennsylvania). The caption read, "Red Skelton lends an ear to deadpan Virginia O'Brien as she sings a song in MGM's *Panama Hattie*... Ann Sothern plays the title role."

Even the citizens of Canonsburg, Pennsylvania were curious about Hollywood. On November 18, 1942, that town's paper, *The Daily Notes*, reported news from the set of *Du Barry Was a Lady*. "Everything happens to Du Barry," the tiny blurb began. Everything included the birthday of director Roy Del Ruth, the birth of Gene Kelly's daughter, Kerry, and Virginia's marriage.

The December 31, 1942 issue of *Variety* included a review of *Du Barry Was a Lady*. It was decidedly less than glowing:

> "With the weak plot and weaker dialog, Skelton has a tough time living up to his rep as a funnyman. Ball does a bit better, while Kelly, whose forte is terping, suffers from the histrionic and singing demands of his role and lack of opportunity to make with the feet. Virginia O'Brien is disappointing too, except for the one tune she's given, 'Salome Was the Grandma of Them All,' in which she literally sparkles."

1943 began with a sobering event. In Superior Judge Benjamin Scheiman's courtroom, Virginia's father suffered a heart attack. The *Los Angeles Times* reported the news on January 6, 1943. Thomas O'Brien "... was talking to a court attaché when he slumped to the floor. Dr. Marcus Crahan, Jail Physician, administered first aid." He was taken to Cedars of Lebanon Hospital, where he was reported in fair condition.

The closing paragraph of the article read, "O'Brien, father of Virginia O'Brien, actress and singer, is a veteran of the Spanish-American War. A master mariner, he lately has been spending his leisure time instructing Coast Guard candidates." While she was certainly concerned about her father, and may have hoped for time off to be with him, the pace of Virginia's career continued to increase.

One of Virginia's fans wrote to *Photoplay* magazine from the Naval Air Station in Norfolk, Virginia. The letter won the prize for Best Parenthetical Picture.

> *At first I thought she was just funny and so I laughed, but I soon sat up and took notice. I thought she was beautiful—but dumb.*
>
> *Now I think she is one of the best comediennes Hollywood has introduced in a long time. The more I see her the more convinced I become that here is a girl who has the best of them all beat.*
>
> *She's beautiful (from the right angle). She can sing (if she wants to). She can act (if she tries to). She can keep an audience in an uproar (always). Young and old like her (and always will). Everybody talks about her (though sometimes they don't quite remember her name).*
>
> *Who is she? Well, she's that most glamorous sour-puss crooner, none other than Virginia O'Brien. Give us more pictures with Virginia—she's good for what ails us. She's a laugh tonic if there ever was one.*
>
> *R.T. Winstead, Seaman 2nd Class*

Photoplay published the letter in the January 1943 issue. For his efforts, Seaman Winstead won the prize of one dollar. In 1943 that was enough to see one of Virginia's movies, twice.

The January 16, 1943 radio broadcast of *Command Performance* was hosted by Jeanette MacDonald. She introduced each performer, including Dale Evans and The Mills Brothers. The performers, and the songs they presented were, Dale Evans: *Why Don't You Fall in Love with Me?*; Virginia O'Brien: *Rock-a-Bye Baby*.

Virginia's song was appropriately preceded by a soldier's request to hear the sound of a baby cry, as he missed his own. Violinist Eddy South and his orchestra played. The Mills Brothers sang a beautiful rendition of *(On the) Banks of the Wabash*. Eddy DeBaron and his orchestra played the popular hit, *Brazil*. Virginia returns to sing *Carry Me Back to Old Virginia (Virginny)*. Eddy South and his orchestra played their encore of the *St. Louis Blues*. The show closed with Jeanette MacDonald honoring a request to hear *Ava Maria*.

"Prescription for Warmth" was the title for a review of *Panama Hattie* in the January 19, 1943 issue of the *Abilene Reporter*. Readers were advised to go see the MGM musical rather than "… sitting around shivering from the low temperature…." Of the three sailors, Ben Blue was the favorite: "… it's no effort for him to be funny."

Of Virginia, the uncredited reviewer wrote:

> "Then there is Virginia O'Brien, dead-pan comedian who brought the house down singing her tale of getting stinko at The Club Savoy."

Fans hungry for more of Miss O'Brien were treated to a photograph of her with Robert Stack. The photo was in the February issue of *Silver Screen* magazine. Stack is best remembered for playing Elliot Ness in television's *The Untouchables*. Playing the FBI agent who took down Al Capone won him the Best Actor in a Dramatic Series Emmy in 1960. He and Virginia remained friends for another fifty-eight years.

On March 27, 1943, newspapers such as the *Mason City Globe-Gazette* featured a photo of Groucho Marx and a beautiful younger singer. The caption read, "RADIO'S RAFFISH ROMEO - That devastating man about town, Groucho Marx, tries his charm on Virginia O'Brien, who'll join him on *Blue Ribbon Town*, which opens on KGLO-CBS Saturday from 9:15 to 9:45 p.m."

Groucho Marx, Virginia O'Brien Will Star in *Blue Ribbon Town* is the bold headline above a small article, which reads, in part:

> "The rib-tickling antics of this raffish Romeo are supplemented by the glamour in the person of Barbara Stanwyck, vocal vigor in the persons of Virginia O'Brien and baritone Donald Dickson, and music under the supervision of Robert Armbruster.
>
> "Groucho Marx seems to have finally found a happy niche in radio," stated *Variety* in a review of the premiere broadcast of *Blue Ribbon Town*. The positive review felt the program benefited from a "smart linking of entertainment to a merchandising idea." The material was praised, as was guest star Barbara Stanwyck. "Miss Stanwyck dovetailed perfectly into Marx's comedy methods ... sparking his wisecracks, tossing him lines in a sketch."
>
> Virginia, while praised for offering "satisfactory filler" between comic sketches, was not given full points for her "jived-up" "She's a Bird in a Gilded Cage." The *Variety* critic felt this was due to Virginia's expressions going unseen on radio. She did receive kudos for muffing her lines, which gave the host "the opening for his funniest ad lib."

Other radio shows were created specifically to support overseas troops during World War II. Virginia was a favorite on these. Her appearances were usually prompted by members of the military, who wrote letters asking to hear Virginia sing.

These commitments, as well as interviews and photo shoots for magazines, kept her busy while the studio prepared her newest movie. This, her eighth at Metro, would be the beginning of a friendship with Lucille Ball. It was their first film together.

Thousands Cheer was the first of two movies she would make with Gene Kelly, and the first of four with Judy Garland. Opposite Kelly was singer Kathryn Grayson. For Virginia and Kathryn, who made three movies together, it was the beginning of a lifelong friendship. Castmates with whom she had worked before included Red Skelton, Ann Sothern, and Eleanor Powell. *Thousands Cheer* also marked the screen debut of conductor Jose Iturbi.

What *Thousands Cheer* lacked in plot it compensated for in the wide variety of musical numbers performed by an all-star cast. Female lead Kathryn Grayson has the most songs. Grayson sings "Daybreak," "I Dug a Ditch," "Three Letters in the Mailbox, "Let There Be Music," "United Nations on the March," and "Sempre libera" from Verdi's opera, *La Traviata*.

One of the most memorable moments in *Thousands Cheer* came when, backed by Benny Carter and his band, the lovely Lena Horne sings a song that became one of her trademarks, "Honeysuckle Rose." Jose Iturbi is shown conducting for Grayson, and playing piano for Judy Garland who scored big with the swinging "The Joint Is Really Jumpin' in Carnegie Hall."

Virginia reprises "Rock-A-Bye Baby" three years after having sung it in *The Big Store*. One musical highlight in *Thousands Cheer* comes when Bing Crosby's brother, Bob Crosby, and his orchestra play sweetly while two of MGM's young starlets, Gloria DeHaven and June

Allyson, sing "In a Little Spanish Town" in close harmony. Before the song veers toward cloying, it is pleasantly interrupted by Virginia. Per her custom of the raising and dropping of her shoulders, she propels the tune from sweet to swing.

"In a Little Spanish Town" deadpans Virginia in *Thousands Cheer*. Left to right: Bob Crosby, Gloria DeHaven, Virginia, and June Allyson.

The number begins with DeHaven and Allyson in front of Crosby's group, while Virginia, unseen at first, stands on a riser among the musicians. The camera pans up to her as she sounds her first, very distinct note. Then, as if by magic, she is transported through the orchestra until she's placed on stage between DeHaven and Allyson. Crosby and the two women watch with contagious joy as MGM's only deadpan vocalist takes over. In later years, "In a Little Spanish Town" became one of the staples of Virginia's nightclub act.

Just prior to the release of *Thousands Cheer*, Edward Schallert's

August 24, 1943 column in the *Los Angeles Times* mentioned Virginia's little sister. Mary O'Brien had been signed for the upcoming Walter Wanger production *When Ladies Fly*. Schallert wrote of Mary:

> "It seems that Mary is a singer, but strictly on the 'straight' side, and that she also looks likely for romantic leads. She has been offered several contracts but has been waiting for the right part, and she likes the one proffered her in the film at Universal. She is, incidentally, a graduate of North Hollywood High School."

Thousands Cheer opened in New York City on September 13, 1943, and in Los Angeles on December 30, and was a hit. The film garnered Academy Award nominations for Best Color Art Direction, Best Color Cinematography, and Best Score—Musical. Praise was lavished on the film by *The New York Times*, which reported, "It's a veritable grab-bag of delights. Musically there is something for all tastes, from Jose Iturbi to boogie-woogie." Early in the filming of *Thousands Cheer*, it was announced that Virginia would be reunited with Groucho Marx. The comedian asked her to be on his new radio show.

An advertisement for
Groucho's radio program.

Groucho's *Blue Ribbon Town* was sponsored by the Pabst brewery, the producers of Pabst Blue Ribbon beer. In 1876, the beer had begun winning contests, receiving numerous blue ribbons for first place. Six years later the company added a blue ribbon to the neck of their beer bottles. In late 1942, they hired Groucho Marx to host their radio show. Groucho hired Virginia at the beginning of 1943. *Blue Ribbon Town* was broadcast on CBS from March 1943 to August 1944.

Groucho and Virginia promoting his
radio show *Blue Ribbon Town*.

Pool was never the same after Virginia and Groucho played.

Chapter Six

Virginia Was a Lady

Hollywood Canteen Chatter was the official newsletter of the establishment where service men could relax and be entertained by movie star volunteers. The chatter in the March 10, 1943 issue paid homage to stars of Irish descent in an article titled "Wearin' O' The Green," which read:

> "All of us have a little Irish in our background somewhere, and we're proud of it. This week brought St. Patrick's Day, so we thought it would be nice to salute some of the Irish stars who have, and are doing, much to keep American morale tip-top, George M. Cohen, daddy of them all, will be greatly missed. Jimmy Cagney, his successor via "Yankee Doodle Dandy," makes us proud to be marching with Uncle Sam. At the canteen we've seen and been entertained by Pat O'Brien. now performing somewhere-off-shore are Irene Dunne, Virginia O'Brien, Spencer Tracy, George Murphy, and Jimmy Dorsey...."

Columnist Gladys Rowley put a note from her son in the March 27, 1943 issue of the *Nevada State Journal*. He was telling her of his adventures in Hollywood. At the Hollywood Canteen, he danced with

Deanna Durbin and Veronica Lake. He enjoyed Virginia's company, and the "swell jokes" of film comedian Hugh Herbert.

By 1943, more stars were joining the war effort. Virginia was one of hundreds who went on tour to sell war bonds and performed at military camps in USO shows. In February of 1943, a new canteen was opened at Fort MacArthur. Allen Dundee, of the *Long Beach Independent*, reported this news on March 28th. To celebrate the opening, radio station KHJ was broadcasting a special. Eddie "Banjo Eyes" Cantor was the emcee, and Freddy Martin and orchestra would accompany Ginny Simms, the King's Men, Bill "Bojangles" Robinson, and Virginia.

"Groucho Marx seems to have finally found a happy niche in radio," *Variety* stated in a review of the premiere broadcast of Blue Ribbon Town. The positive review felt the program benefited from a smart linking of entertainment to a merchandising idea. The material was praised, as was guest star Barbara Stanwyck, "Miss Stanwyck dovetailed perfectly into Marx's comedy methods ... sparking his wisecracks, tossing him lines in a sketch...."

MGM's own blonde beauty, Lana Turner, graced the cover of the March 1943 edition of *Photoplay*. "If you had your choice of being someone else, whom would you like to be?" was the question presented to readers on page fifty-four. The question was answered by five of Hollywood's beautiful stars.

"I Wish I Were—" was a two-page feature with photos of Virginia, Anne Shirley, Ruth Hussey, Ann Sheridan, and Kathryn Grayson. Beside each was a photo of who they wanted to be, and the reasons for their choice. Ruth Hussey, who wanted to be Emily Post, explained, "I'd like to have her sense of fitness, her inner assurance for my own."

Eleanor Roosevelt, one of the most admired women of the time, was who Ann Sheridan chose. "I envy her ability to meet all kinds of people—every possible kind of person—in a warm and friendly manner," was one reason behind Ann's choice. Kathryn Grayson envied and wished to be Walt Disney. She felt he must have a deep sense of achievement.

Groucho and Virginia enjoyed success on his 1943 radio show.

Virginia wished she were Clare Boothe Luce. She gave the following reasons for her selection:

> "I've always been afraid of strangers. I'm still shy. But Clare Boothe Luce simply expands when she meets strangers. She sparkles. People stimulate her and inspire her, and I'm

sure she does better than her best when she has an audience.

She's a true cosmopolitan too. She's been everywhere, met everyone and even seen everything. I've scarcely been outside of my home state, California. She's known for a long time all about things that I'm just beginning to discover."

The statuesque brunette also revealed that she wanted to be a "fragile blonde," like her cosmopolitan Congresswoman hero.

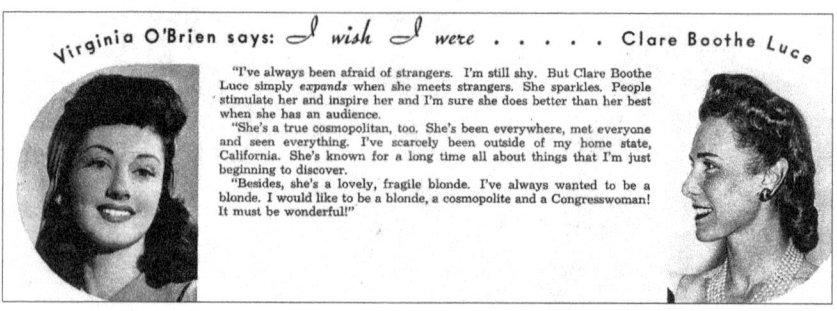

"I Wish I Were—" from *Photoplay,* **March 1943.**

Australia's *Radio Call* magazine ran an ad for *Ship Ahoy,* which was playing at the country's Metro Theatres. On the same page of the April 4, 1943 issue, was a small article titled "Dead-Pan Star's New Picture." Virginia was the only member of the cast to receive individual attention. Eleanor Powell, Red Skelton, and Bert Lahr did not have similar articles. In part, the *Radio Call* article read:

"Virginia O'Brien, who has developed her own original style of dead-pan torch singing... adds to the zest and comedy on Metro-Goldwyn-Mayer's new musical, *Ship Ahoy,* starring Eleanor Powell and Red Skelton. Virginia was born in Hollywood on April 18th, and that in itself is highly original.

A magazine ad for *Ship Ahoy*.

The article went on to recap Virginia's performance in *Meet the People* as a revue produced by youngsters. The claim was made that her stage debut was on her birthday. This is not correct. The stage revue *Meet the People* opened in December of 1940.

Mary Bailey was the beauty editor at *Motion Picture* magazine. Her column was titled "Thru the Ages" in the May 1943 edition of the movie magazine. It featured eight photographs of Virginia to illustrate beauty in two different time periods.

Four photos showed her in the Marie Antoinette-style wig she wore in *Du Barry Was a Lady*. The other four show her as she appeared in the 1940's. "The fundamental steps to beauty haven't changed through the ages," Bailey wrote of Virginia's beauty routine, whether it be in 1943 or the days of *Du Barry*. "There's no difference in *what* she's doing—it's the way she's doing it," Bailey contended.

Virginia was on the air again on May 15th of 1943. The "Commanding Officer of Command Performance," was said to have her photograph riding in the flying fortresses and brightening the walls of GI shacks all over the world, was Joan Blondell. Talent commanded to perform included Dick Powell, Judy Canova, Martha Tilton, Eddie "Rochester" Anderson, and the Sportsman Quartet. Miss O'Brien sang "Did I Get Stinkin' at the Club Savoy," from *Panama Hattie*, to riotous effect.

Popular columnist Erskine Johnson had long been a Virginia O'Brien fan. She was mentioned often in his nationwide column over the years, so it is no surprise that on June 29, 1943, the entire column was about her. Erskine was launching a crusade he hoped would affect some change for the better in her film career.

The column announced Erskine's launching of GVOIRROITHA on Miss O'Brien's behalf. Johnson wrote:

> "Now that Virginia O'Brien has completed the Hollywood cycle—from *Meet the People* to *Meet the People*—it's

high time for movie audiences to meet the... "Get Virginia O'Brien Into Romantic Roles Or Into The Hero's Arms."

He suggested that the members of the group wear "Meet Virginia O'Brien" buttons. Erskine took issue with the fact that the handsome leading men seemed to avoid her, due to her being typed as a comedienne. Furthermore, with the expectation of Bert Lahr pecking her on the arm once, she had never been kissed on-screen.

Shifting gears, Erskine wrote about the reel versus the real:

> "Off the screen, Virginia O'Brien is the antithesis of her celluloid self, a very beautiful young lady, indeed. People, in fact, have been known to do a double take upon meeting her... and say 'Not THE Virginia O'Brien?'"

This reaction, Erskine continued, was due to what people remembered best, that poker-faced style of singing. As not to irritate her employers, the columnist pointed out that Virginia was not complaining. Also, when she received her paycheck, she was seen smiling the warmest smiles in Hollywood....

Next the newspaperman listed his reasons for launching his campaign. Among them were her obvious glamour, and its effect during the filming of *Du Barry Was a Lady*. The studio ordered one of her scenes to be filmed again. When she asked the reason, she was told, "You looked too beautiful. You're supposed to be a comedienne."

The second reason behind the "GVOIRROITHA" made more sense. This was her ability to act. It was not as obvious as her glamour, due to the limits of her roles thus far, but Erskine knew something that audiences didn't:

> "Several months ago, before Myrna Loy decided to return to the screen, studio bosses looked at some of Virginia's film scenes and decided she would be a splendid Nora... in

the Thin Man series. She was given a script to read and told to prepare for the role.

Whether their intentions were serious, is doubtful. It seems like a ploy to nudge Loy in front of the cameras. Of course, she returned to the role that was rightfully hers alone. Erskine played the publicity game, and said simply, "Virginia lost the role." He then went on to write about the part she played, and the familiar name of her current film.

> "...Virginia is working on the film version of *Meet the People*, the Hollywood revue in which she made her professional debut... she was frightened into her career. The dead-pan was a natural... was a sensation, and won a film contract before the show closed."

While the role of "Woodpecker" Peg was typical of her other screen appearances, with four numbers, two of them dead pan, Erskine stated there was little chance to act, and no romance. The last is only semi-accurate. She was ardently pursued by Bert Lahr. Still, Erskine concluded, "But now, we hope things are going to be different." Essentially, they weren't.

Virginia had a "secret," and it was announced by E.B. Radciffe on the Fourth of July. Radcliffe was a fan of Virginia's singing. His July 4, 1943 column bore the headline "Virginia O'Brien's Secret." Virginia herself confessed the secret. As the subtitle states, "Made Known By Frozen-Faced Comedy Star, Who Was Frightened Into A Phenomenal Film Career".

Mr. Radcliffe felt that using old-fashioned firecrackers or dynamite might change Virginia's sphinx-like expression. Not just a small amount of explosives, he wrote, but a bigtime Fourth of July event or something equally startling to change Virginia's on-screen carryings-on....

Du Barry Was a Lady was a successful Broadway musical starring Ethel Merman. MGM's Cowardly Lion, Bert Lahr, was Merman's co-star. The words and music were written by Cole Porter. When Metro acquired the film rights, Merman and Lahr were out, as was the bulk of Cole Porter's score.

Red Skelton was cast in Bert Lahr's dual role as Louis Blore and His Most Royal Majesty, The King of France. Ethel Merman was replaced by Lucille Ball as both May Daly and Mme. La Comtesse Du Burry (her singing was dubbed by Martha Mears).

New characters were added for Gene Kelly and Virginia. They too would play two parts. Kelly was Alec Howe and Black Arrow. Virginia was cigarette girl Ginny and Mme. du Barry's lady in waiting. As Ginny, she was hopelessly in love with Skelton's Louis Blore.

Virginia sings her one number as Ginny. Taking a break from her duties as a cigarette girl, she performs a mock striptease while singing the praises of "Salome." This is the same song that the offices of the Production Code had removed two years earlier from *Panama Hattie*. Among the lyrics cut from the song to remove the "sex suggestiveness" were "That makes 'em answer nature's call…," which were replaced with "That takes the wallflowers off the wall."

Completely removed were these lyrics about Cinderella, to wit "That naïve way they say she got that prince. The clock struck twelve, she lost her shoe, but do they tell you in what boudoir they found all the prince's fingerprints." The same fate befell "A fig for Gypsy Rose Lee's teaseroo. Except for zippers what's she got that's new? Beneath her modern streamline strip, there's nothing but that same old hypnotizing version of the hoochy koo."

When *Du Barry Was a Lady* opened at the Empire Theatre in London's Lelcester Square, the August 1 edition of the *Sunday Pictorial* had this brief note in the "New Films" column: "Expensive technicolor version of the Cole Porter musical. This proved to be the biggest disappointment of the week. It's garish, crude and gaudy, but it has two redeeming features, the dead-pan darling Virginia O'Brien, also Tommy Dorsey and his band."

Lucy and Virginia in *Du Barry Was a Lady*.

The cast of MGM's *Du Barry Was a Lady* recording the films finale. Left to right: Virginia O'Brien, Gene Kelly, Lucille Ball, Tommy Dorsey, and Red Skelton.

Virginia poses in her gown by MGM custom designer Irene for the "Salome" number in *Du Barry Was a Lady*.

The cast of *Du Barry Was a Lady* sings Cole Porter's "Friendship."

On August 14, 1943, *Command Performance* invited Rosalind Russell to be the Mistress of Ceremonies. During that broadcast, audiences were treated to a wide variety of musical entertainment. Russell introduced Jimmy Wakely and the Rough Riders, who performed "Cowboy in the Clouds." MGM star Xavier Cugat was there with his choir and orchestra to add some Latin flavor to the proceedings. Carlos Ramirez sang "Armour, Armour." The beloved comedienne Judy Canova provided the laughs. The laughs continued when Virginia sang of her ill-fated romance with a masochistic boyfriend, with "Say We'll Be Sweethearts Again."

"Dead Pan Virginia O'Brien Thaws Out and Even Smiles." Could this headline be true? The article about this historical event carried no byline when it was published in the *Brooklyn Daily Eagle* on August 15, 1943. The first paragraph read:

> "Virginia O'Brien is Hollywood's first glacier-face to melt. Buster Keaton and Ned Sparks, classic examples of the iceberg expression, stalked through film after film without cracking a smile. Virginia bade fair to follow in their frosty tracks, but failed to reckon with heat—in the form of torrid tunes and a 'stripless' strip tease."

Here was another reference to the impact of the "Salome" number in *Du Barry Was a Lady*. Told again, in her own words, was the story of her stage-fright induced style. She also spoke of being "hypnotized" by the microphone that first time she recorded a song for a film appearance. Her "ice cube" technique sprang from a real case of nerves.

It wasn't until *Ship Ahoy* that she managed "a smile and a wink." The deadpan remained intact while the actress herself began to show signs of "coming to life." This change was credited to Red Skelton's playing cupid. Skelton aimed for Virginia's heart and struck with a "dart" named Kirk Alyn. Alyn, a houseguest of the "brick-haired comic" who became a frequent visitor to the set of *Du Barry Was a Lady*.

The article claimed the couple "eloped during the filming." Thus, matrimony combined with the success of her new film brought about the "defrosting" of the comedienne. The result was songs that allowed her to arch her eyebrows and even smile. Famed director Roy Del Ruth saw her as the "frozen version of a red-hot mama." Another comparison to Buster Keaton soon followed.

> "To look at pretty Virginia O'Brien, as the singing (deadpan) comedienne of MGM's Technicolor musical comedy *Du Barry Was a Lady*, now at the Capitol Theater, you'd never think she burns with the fevers and fires of a crusader," began an article appearing in the *Brooklyn Eagle* on August 27, 1943. Virginia's crusade was against the word "mugger." The word had supposedly turned her into a "zealot."

Virginia felt that the word should not be associated with criminals.

Her plans to remove "mugger" from use by the police was, the article claimed, spelled out in a letter she had written to the owner of New York's Capitol Theater, Harry A. Gourfain. Virginia, slated to appear in the theatre's next *Stars in Person* show, had promised to see "Police Commissioner Valentine and J. Edgar Hoover, and all the crime reporters I can reach." Virginia felt that the word belonged to "stage folk." To make her case, she listed the comedians referred to as "muggers," Ned Sparks, Fred Allen, and Buster Keaton among them. She claimed that she and Fanny Brice, as women, were the only "muggettes" in show business.

Turning to the dictionary for support, Virginia stated, "I can't understand how it happened no dictionary supports that usage. On the contrary, all authorities establish the claim of the comedians." According to the dictionary she consulted, the definition of a "mugger" was "one who makes audiences laugh by grimacing and other unexpectedly amusing motions." One smells the MGM publicists at work here. If that is the case, they succeeded in promoting *Du Barry Was a Lady* and Virginia's upcoming appearance at the Capitol Theater. The closing quote attributed to Miss O'Brien is, "I hope Police Commissioner Valentine and the reporters will have the time to receive my formal complaint, and heed my request that police and reporters desist from misusing the word 'mugger.'"

Hedda Hopper's "Looking at Hollywood" column from the September 28, 1943 issue of the *Los Angeles Times*, reported on the O'Brien sisters. According to Hopper, Mary had completed her work on *When Ladies Fly* and would be traveling to New York to meet Virginia. From New York the two would go to Texas to visit their half-brother Jack. Sargent O'Brien had been wounded overseas and was "ensconced in a hospital" in Texas.

Double deadpan: Buster Keaton visits
Virginia on the set of *Du Barry Was a Lady*.

"Virginia O'Brien—A Musical Buster Keaton in Skirts," was the title of an article that appeared in the October 3, 1943 issue of the *Oakland Tribune Magazine Pictorial*. There were four photos accompanying the piece: one of Keaton with the caption "Sad-Eyed Buster Keaton founded the frozen-faced school." Below that there was a photo of Virginia with the caption, "Here is Virginia with Bandman Tommy Dorsey singing, "Friendship" in *Du Barry Was a Lady*." The last photo in this vertical row claimed, "Another master of the blank look is Arthur Treacher, whose many rolls as a butler have frozen his face."

The best, and biggest photo, accompanying this article was of Virginia. It's a casual, at-home photographer showing the young singer at her loveliest, and she's smiling! The appropriate caption reads "This is just to prove that Virginia O'Brien actually can smile." The short article beneath her photo reported the following:

> "It's about time you were becoming better acquainted with Virginia O'Brien (remember her Salome ditty from "Du Barry Was a Lady"?). Virginia is the girl who took up where Buster Keaton left off. The only time she smiles is on payday. And then she laughs out loud. She's also the songbird you saw in *Ship Ahoy* and *Panama Hattie* delivering her lines so dead-panedly. It happened this way:
>
> Virginia had toyed with the idea of being a dancer or a lawyer. But she ended up taking singing lessons. Friends said with her voice and her smile she could go a long way in a movie. So she auditioned for *Meet the People*. The sound effect was good, but not   a smile could she muster.
>
> Maybe the director was tired of toothpaste advertising, maybe he didn't find life so tempting that day... maybe.... Anyway, the deadpan diva caught his fancy and he kept her at the mike trying one song after another... "Without a smile, please." Call it a director hunch or a directors' dyspepsia, but Virginia's style of singing caught on like wildfire.
>
> And now she's no longer scared stiff and would like to turn on a smile... Hollywood cries "No, no a thousand times no." Maybe OPA unfreezes things, but never Hollywood, not when there's gold to be dead-panned. At home and at parties, Virginia can smile and smile and smile, but when the cameras start to roll its blackout for Virginia.

A portrait in the gown and jewelry she wore in *Du Barry Was a Lady*.

She really doesn't mind (you wouldn't either if you got her check) and she gets a kick startling her friends with a dazzling smile one minute and a graveyard glare the next. Her ability doesn't come so easily as you might think, and she practices every day before her mirror so she CAN'T do what most pretty girls want to do... SMILE.

Other than keeping MGM's publicity people employed, this type of "fluff" piece revealed nothing about Virginia's personal life. But it served its purpose, keeping her in the public's eye, and this time, with the bonus of a beautiful photograph.

For the second time in 1943, Mary Bailey, the beauty editor for *Motion Picture* magazine, chose Virginia's image to grace her featured article. Bailey's advice in the November issue was to "Keep Lovely … Keep Working." The four photographs of Virginia show her practicing Mary Brian's beauty "Do…" tips, some of which were also seen in Australian newspapers.

> "Take to lovely Virginia O'Brien's suggestion and keep your hair braided or up-swept so stray wisps will fit under a protective cap. After work, says Virginia (whom you'll see in MGM's *Meet the People*), brush your mane out."

"Brush your mane out," sounds like beauty tip for MGM's mascot, Leo the Lion. The photos show Miss O'Brien caring for her hair, nails, and eyes. Bailey's "For the Ladies" feature plugs not only *Meet the People*, she also recommends the use of Yardley's Zinnia Face Powder, Maybelline and Hinds' hand lotion. Product placement, and celebrity endorsement 1943-style. It is not known which, if any, of these beauty practices Virginia actually employed. Brief articles such as these were created to give an up-and-coming star a public persona.

Virginia returned to the airwaves for the 27th November, 1943 broadcast of *Command Performance.* This time the host was actor Herbert Marshall. Announcer Harry von Zell introduce guests, including singer Anita Ellis, Virginia, Edgar Bergen, Charlie McCarthy, and Frances Langford.

Modeling the latest fashion in 1943.

The Hollywood Reporter was on the scene for this Christmas Eve celebration:

> "At seven o'clock, on Christmas Eve, 1943, Eddie Cantor, dressed as Santa Claus, arrived at the Hollywood Canteen and started to dispense gift duffel bags to the first group of ten thousand G.I.s who attended between that evening and Christmas Day. The entertainment was extra special.

"Extra special" is a bit of an understatement. Various orchestras played until midnight. The soldiers were entertained by Red Skelton, Amos 'n' Andy, and Edgar Bergen. The singers included Bing Crosby and Virginia.

On December 31, 1943, newlywed Virginia attended the wedding of David May II and actress Ann Rutherford. David May II was the heir to the May Company, a successful chain of department stores. The wedding took place at the Beverly Hills estate of Tom and Anita May. MGM's Ann Rutherford played Carreen, Scarlett O'Hara's sister in *Gone with the Wind*. Other guests included Laraine Day, Maureen O'Hara, Jackie Cooper, Robert Stack, and Deanna Durbin (who was known to friends as Edna May). With that announcement, 1943 came to a close.

Virginia made numerous radio appearances in the 1940's.
Courtesy of Terri O'Brien.

Chapter Seven

Hello Baby

1944 was a very busy year for Virginia. She appeared on at least one radio show per month, complete appearances three movies, a fourth, *The Harvey Girls*, began filming, and she also continued to perform at various benefits and local military bases.

The February 1944 issue *of Movieland* magazine reported on Virginia's patriotism and generous nature. Throughout the war it was not uncommon to see soldiers hitch-hiking and, unlike today, all got rides easily. That is exactly what Virginia did as she headed toward Army camp to entertain the troops. The *Movieland* article is titled "Uniformed Hitch-Hiking in Hollywood." Here is the sweet story of Virginia and her soldier:

A switch on that "if-I-could-only-meet-Claudette Colbert-Rita Hayworth-Lucille Ball-Linda Darnell-" dream of all lads in uniform, is told by dead-pan Virginia O'Brien. Virginia picked up a hitch-hiking soldier on her way to play a show at a nearby Army camp. The soldier belonged at that particular camp. He was tremendously grateful and excited—but he confessed that he couldn't go to the show. He was late and would undoubtedly be given k.p. duty.

Sure enough, he was. But Virginia, who has a soft place in her heart for service men, didn't forget the boy. After she was through with the show, she went searching for him. She found him in the kitchen, as predicted, at k.p., with five other sad youths. None of them had seen the show.

Original MGM Caption: Not so deadpan a diva is raven-tressed Virginia O'Brien, whose familiar ice-cube expression has been melting with each succeeding picture. Having launched her career as a glacier-faced songstress, Virginia gave fans their first view of her smile in *Du Barry Was a Lady*. Since then it has been flashed in such star-packed musicals as *Meet the People* and *Two Girls and a Sailor*. An Army camp favorite, Virginia has made hundreds of appearances before servicemen since Pearl Harbor. She is currently vocalizing for her initial album of recorded music. Selections were all chosen by servicemen's votes. Photo: Author's collection.

Virginia told them to cheer up. Without an accompanist, she launched into one of her dead-pan songs. The boys loved it. She gave them an encore. They applauded her until the top kick arrived to see what all the row was about. He came to bawl the men out, but stayed to cheer Virginia.

When she was ready to leave, the boy she picked up turned to the other boys and shouted, "All right now, three cheers for Ethel Merman!"

Virginia and Henry Fonda prepare for a show at a tour of military camps. When he enlisted in the Navy, Fonda said, "I don't want to be in a fake war in a studio." Alan Eichler Collection.

This enthusiastic, yet misguided cheer must have made the singer smile. She was, after all, a fan of Broadway's brassy belter. Sharing her Army camp story with the readers of *Movieland* showed that she had a great sense of humor.

Yank magazine devoted a full page to it's pin-up girl in the February 18, 1944 issue. Wearing the form-fitting dress designed for her appearance in *Du Barry Was a Lady*, Virginia, one hand on her hip, looks more sophisticated than she has since her film debut. She is the Valentine pin-up, standing in front of a huge heart made entirely of roses. A note on the page opposite her photograph reads: *Valentine's Day Greeting to the GIs in the Southwest Pacific from Virginia O'Brien, who came forth with this picture of hearts and flowers—and what's more—O'Brien. YANK wishes she could deliver the greetings personally, but Virginia's busy taking bows for her role in MGM's Du Barry Was a Lady.*

How the GI's felt about her was obvious from all of the letters they sent, requesting a song on *Command Performance*. Those letters brought her back to the radio show ten days after the publication of *Yank*. The entertainer affectionately known as "Banjo Eyes," Eddie Cantor, was the host. That evening's talented cast brought Ginny Simms, the King's Men, and tap legend Bill Robinson to listeners. Freddy Martin and his orchestra, a group Virginia would work with again, provided the music.

Being of Irish descent made March 17 an important day in the O'Brien family. On St. Patrick's Day of 1944, several of Hollywood's Irish-American stars were honored, as they were yearly, by the Catholic Film and Radio Guild. Virginia was among the group that attended a war bond rally, where the honorees received statues of St. Patrick and St. Bridgid.

The statues were a gift of the Eire Four Provinces Club, and the event was hosted by the Ancient Order of Hibernians. Among the other recipients were Pat O'Brien, Una O'Connor, Ruth Hussey, Martha O'Driscoll, Maureen O'Hara, James Cagney, Thomas Mitchell, Maureen O'Sullivan, Bing Crosby, and J. Carroll Naish.

Virginia's name would appear twice in Ohio's *Akron Beacon Journal* in 1944. The first time was in the February 2, 1944 edition. Marlene Mains, the talented twelve year old who imitates Virginia so brilliantly in the Our Gang Comedy *Calling All Kids*, was "… a former Akronite…." She also had a small role in *Heaven Can Wait*.

For a short time, at the beginning of 1944, there was news that Virginia would be cast in a dramatic role in MGM's *Dear Barbara*. Susan Peters was announced as the star. The supporting cast was to have included Jimmy Durante and the studio's younger O'Brien, Margaret. Virginia's *Hullabaloo* co-star, Frank Morgan, was slated to portray a character similar to "… his telegrapher in *The Human Comedy*." The proposed new role for Virginia was also mentioned in the *Showman's Trade Review*, dated January 22, 1944. That magazine reported that Virginia would "change her screen personality in her newest picture."

Marlene Mains imitates Virginia in the Our Gang Comedy *Calling All Kids.* Author's collection.

Two Girls and a Sailor struck gold with the pairing of June Allyson and Van Johnson. Between 1944 and 1951, Allyson and Johnson were *America's Sweethearts.* The couple made five movies together. Their joint effort in 1944 was *Two Girls and a Sailor.* The second girl in the title was Gloria DeHaven. Virginia was along for the ride, but just barely.

"Take It Easy" was Virginia's musical moment in this, her 10th movie at MGM. It's a pleasant song that cast her as a type she had played before, a young lady who wants romance but has difficulty in finding it. In this case, it's because she's "too tired, too tired...." Hence, her reason for taking it easy. The added attraction here is that the song, and Virginia's costume, are a spoof on the wildly popular "Brazilian Bombshell," Carmen Miranda.

The song was no match for "In a Little Spanish Town," and certainly less memorable as "Salome." While popular, *Two Girls and a Sailor* was criticized for being too long for a standard musical comedy, which were roughly 75 to 90 minutes in length.

Virginia's mold as Metro's "specialty singer" had been cast. Her performances were always a highlight that audiences looked forward to and remembered long after the closing credits. Yet, sometimes the formula worked against her. This was the case in *Two Girls and a Sailor*. "Take It Easy" gave her around two minutes of screen time. Even so, reviews were positive. The *St. Louis Post-Dispatch* took notice. "Miss O'Brien does Take It Easy, a song the beautiful deadpan comedienne fried over a slow fire…." (June 9, 1944).

Terri O'Brien loves her mother's singing of "Take It Easy." She, and the author, agree that it is probably Virginia's most underrated performance. Terri properly points out that the segue from Xavier Cugat's band, and the animated Lina Romay, to the shot of Virginia laying on her side is truly funny. Virginia's lazy Carmen Miranda send up is a delight. From tossing the maracas over her shoulder to her batting eyelashes and yawning, it is a number that displays all of her comic talent.

While her screen time may have been limited in *Two Girls and a Sailor*, it did not go unnoticed. In his diary, Sergeant Merle Alan Fisher of Company B, 1st Amphibious Tractor Battalion, 1st Marine Division, made this entry on June 21, 1944. "In the evening saw *Two Girls and a Sailor* with Virginia O'Brien. What a woman." A few weeks later in the July 7th edition of the *Cincinnati Enquirer*, it was noted that Virginia took her "… leisurely [time] to needle the devil out of the Miranda dynamics. The success of *Two Girls and a Sailor* must have pleased Mr. Mayer.

Louis B. Mayer had become a successful mogul through an interesting combination of hard work, conventional family values, an eye for talent, and his acquired "know how." His eye for Virginia's natural talent and unique style gained her a coveted seven-year contract. She fit into Mayer's vision of MGM as one big, happy all-American family.

It was this know-how that gave him the foresight to purchase the rights to the show in which he discovered her, *Meet the People*. Here was ready-made material that he could produce quickly, and featured her in a role that required little preparation on her part.

So, *Meet the People* went before the cameras in the later part of 1944. Virginia was the only cast member who had also appeared in the theatrical production of the show. Other cast members from MGM's family she had worked with before included June Allyson and Lucille Ball. Dick Powell, who later would marry June, was Lucille's leading man.

The story revolved around shipyard worker Powell, who was also an aspiring playwright. Virginia played a Rosie the Riveter type, a welder known as Woodpecker Peg. The weak plot was trussed up with music. Popular 1940's singer Vaughan Monroe contributed "In Times Like These."

June Allyson, known as "the blonde with the brunette voice," sang "I Like to Recognize the Tune." The song is backed by Vaughan's orchestra. He and Virginia vocalize with June Allyson. The song includes a bit of dancing, a rarity for stoic Virginia. The King Sisters join in for added sparkle.

Virginia, Bert Lahr, Lucille Ball, and Dick Powell in *Meet the People*.

Virginia's solo went on to become something of a theme song, and her most requested number. Author Dan Van Neste writes:

> It was sphinx-like, Virginia's inimitable rendition of "Say We're Sweethearts Again," which stole the show. Audiences roared as the forlorn Peg laments the romance had ended till you tried to poison my food." It was classic O'Brien.

Meet the People: June Allyson and company collapse at the end of "I Want to Recognize the Tune."

Another show-stopper for Virginia. "Say That We're Sweethearts Again" from *Meet the People*.

The best reviews appeared in the diaries of the women and men in the armed forces. In his journal, Roy Hugh, who went from the rank of private first class to brigadier general, wrote:

April 16th, 1944 Lockbourne Field, Ohio "Went to one of the most entertaining shows I have ever seen, *Meet the People*, with Dick Powell, Lucille Ball, Virginia O'Brien, Vaughan Monroe, and Spike Jones Orchestra. The show was very, very good.

In April and May of 1944, Virginia returned to radio with appearances on *Command Performance*. The first of these was on April 22, with Gene Tierney hosting. Virginia's leading man from *Hullabaloo*, Frank Morgan, stopped by. Martha Tilton sang "Besame Mucho." Country music fans were treated to "Easy Rocking Chair" by Roy Acuff and his Smoky Mountain Boys.

The May 27 broadcast of *Command Performance* was a true musical treat. "Dixie diva," Dinah Shore, was the Mistress of Ceremonies. The popular thrush opened the show with "It Had to Be You." Baritone Dick Haymes was another guest.

In July, Haymes would invite Virginia to be the guest when he hosted a program called *Everything for the Boys*. The highlight was certainly Louis Jordan, who performed "Is You Is or Is You Ain't My Baby." When this show was rebroadcast on June 10, 1944, a photo of Dinah, Virginia and Louis appeared in newspapers such as the *Pittsburgh Courier*.

While filming *Meet the People*, Lucille Ball and Virginia both had their husbands nearby. Staff Sergeant Desi Arnaz drove from Camp Arlington every time he got a pass. Kirk Alyn, who worked as a "... swing shift inspector at one of the large California war plants..." was a "technical adviser" on the film (Author's Note: Kirk Alyn worked as an airplane mechanic at the beginning of WWII).

Virginia, Dinah Shore, and Louis Jordan having fun on the WWII radio show *Command Performance*.

Modern Screen reported this in its June 1944 issue. Another cast member, Bert Lahr, became a father on the only day when three-hundred extras were on the set. This situation "... ran up a fancy cigar bill."

Monday June 5 was the day that the new WHP radio program, *Inside Hollywood*, made its premiere broadcast. Two days earlier, the *Harrisburg Telegraph* carried an article that summarized the proceedings. "Each program will deal with the trials and tribulations encountered by those who are recognized as true stars and genuine box office attractions...." Virginia was the first guest to tell listeners of "... the hard work plus the unusual experiences she met in the long climb to her present position." Upcoming guests included Basil Rathbone, Mickey Rooney, and Donna Reed.

Another radio appearance was broadcast on July 22, 1944 from

LaGarde General Hospital in New Orleans. Virginia was the guest of the Armed Service Forces show *Visiting Hour*. The *Circleville Herald*, dated July 14, makes no mention of the songs she performed. In addition to her visit, wounded soldiers at the facility appeared in a segment called "Ask the Doctor."

Virginia's name was seen by the citizens of Akron, Ohio again on July 18. Four days after the broadcast of *Visiting Hour*, she was the guest of singer Dick Haymes. The Radio Time Table in the *Akron Beacon Journal* said the Haymes-O'Brien teaming would be "… a rollicking session." The radio program, also heard in Australia, was *Everything for the Boys*. Those "boys" were the fighting forces of the USA.

"… not once in my entire career," states the Metro-Goldwyn-Mayer actress. This was Virginia's comment in a blurb from various newspapers dated September 10, 1944. She was talking about how she could go unrecognized in public. In *The Cincinnati Enquirer*, that very brief piece began, "Whenever Virginia O'Brien, lovely 'dead pan' singer wants to travel incognito, she merely remembers to smile. Smiling, or not, she couldn't be missed at her next WWII benefit performance."

Perris Hill Park Bowl, an amphitheater in San Bernardino was the site of a huge *Army Airfield Benefit Show* on Friday, September 29, 1944. Numerous articles appeared in Los Angeles area newspapers. This fundraiser, at which the stars appeared gratis, had one of the most impressive roosters of any Army benefit in California.

A special attraction was a number of "noted composers" who were going to sing their own songs that evening. This list included L. Wolfe Gilbert ("Waiting for the Robert E. Lee" and "Ramona"), Jack Norwood ("Shine on Harvest Moon") and Albert von Tilzer ("Take Me Out to the Ball Game"). One September 9th article featured a lovely photo of the smiling Miss O'Brien and actor Reginald Gardiner. They were singled out:

"Reggie Gardiner, comedy star of Twentieth Century, will have a featured role in the coming doings as will that 'deadpan' star of the M.G.M. studio who has wowed so many members of our armed forces during her trips to various theaters of operation."

Others on the bill were Joe E. Brown ("... he of the yawning mouth who is a soldiers' favorite), Jack Carson, George Murphy, Jane Wyman, and Arthur Treacher. Just prior to the event, excitement grew when one of the most popular entertainers of the World War II years was added to the bill, Martha Raye.

Even as Virginia was performing at Perris Hill Park, another benefit was in the works. This was an annual fundraiser known as The Sheriff's Show. Held at Shrine Auditorium from October 5th to October 11th, in 1944 it was produced by the comedy team Abbott and Costello.

On the nights Virginia's appeared, October 6th and 7th, some 6,600 saw each show. Pinky Tomlin, who wrote the popular song "The Object of My Affection," was the master of ceremonies. Also appearing those two nights were Jack Carson, Arthur Treacher, and Dale Evans. On subsequent two-night appearances, audiences were entertained by William Bendix, Georgia Gibbs, Jack Benny, and Martha Tilton.

The 1944 Christmas broadcast of radio's *Command Performance* was an event to remember. The two-and-a-half-hour show had a guest list which included nineteen stars, the Ken Darby Chorus, and Major Meredith Wilson and the Armed Forces Radio band. *Photoplay* magazine published a photograph of the shows "Carol-singing Sextette."

This 1944 photo was captioned: "Resort to Beauty ... Holiday time too often means over-exposure to sun and wind, causing after-weeks of dry peeling skin and brittle hair. Virginia O'Brien, Metro-Goldwyn-Mayer actress, demonstrates what to do to protect the skin and still enjoy the sun." Similar beauty tips had been given in Australian papers in 1942. In truth, Terri O'Brien told the author that Virginia was a sun worshipper who sometimes went overboard with her tanning.

Wendy Wilde was the name that Mr. and Mrs. Cornel Wilde hung on their daughter. Gossip columns that December 24th announced that the Wildes were inviting other new celebrity parents to a party for Wendy. Virginia had hopes that Kirk Alyn would be home from the merchant marines to a special note. Left by Santa Claus, it disclosed that he and Virginia would be eligible for the Wilde's party in 1945.

Judy Garland, Ginny Simms, Dinah Shore, Virginia O'Brien, Frances Langford and Dorothy Lamour have recorded disc after disc of Christmas carols which are to be sent to the lads overseas – and all parts of the world. What a sextette! The gals have recorded some of them in harmony – and others as solos – but either way, you know that they will sound like angel voices to our boys at the fighting fronts. Courtesy Terri O'Brien.

The blurb titled "Virginia Goes to Drama" wasn't the first time, nor would it be the last, that readers were misled. According to the *Eugene Guard* (Eugene, Oregon), published on Christmas Eve 1944, Virginia's next appearance marked "… her first departure from strictly deadpan roles…." In *The Harvey Girls*, she was reported to have a role with "… light dramatic characterization…."

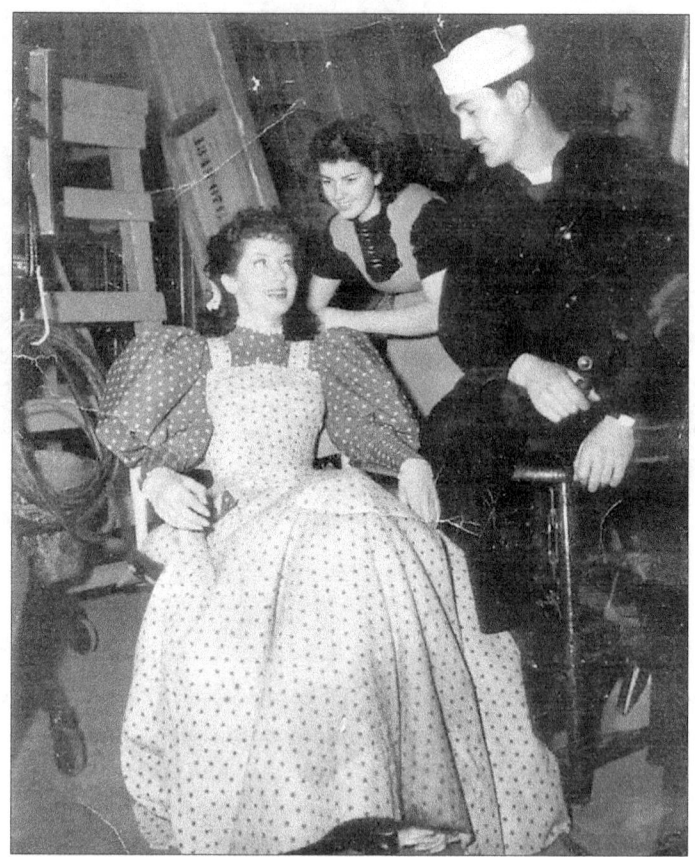

Merchant Marine Kirk Alyn visits his wife on the set of
The Harvey Girls. Virginia's MGM hairdresser, Helen Young,
stands behind Virginia. Photo Courtesy of Terri O'Brien.

Christmas Day 1944 brought the happy news that Kirk Alyn would soon be seen in the new Hopalong Cassidy film. Along with Roy Rogers, William Boyd (aka Hopalong Cassidy) was one of the most recognized film cowboys of all time. Alyn would play the saloonkeeper who was acting, reluctantly, as town sheriff. "Hoppy's" bid for re-election as sheriff was in jeopardy due to the action of the "Forty Thieves" of the title. This marked the beginning of a longtime friendship between William "Hoppy" Boyd and Kirk "Superman" Alyn.

The December 1944 cover of the Spanish movie magazine, *Primer Plano*.

Erskine Johnson's "In Hollywood" column should have been titled "*Only* in Hollywood" on January 24th, 1945. Hollywood is the only town where a newspaperman could have written about fingernails.

> "Virginia O'Brien has pared her fingernails—an inch and a quarter from quick to tip (Red Skeleton once accused her of sleeping on a perch)—for a role of a lady blacksmith in *The Harvey Girls*."

Virginia's involvement in *Ziegfeld Follies* was announced in the *Los Angeles Times* on January 31, 1945. This would be one of MGM's musicals that featured a cast of nearly all of its singing and dancing stars.

The February issue of *Silver Screen* magazine had eleven photographs of Virginia. They were seen in a two-page photospread titled "Thawing Out Frozen Face." They showed Virginia at home with the members of her family. She was shown playing the piano, working in the garden, and singing with her sister, Mary. The captions revealed the following: her father painted as a hobby, for relaxation Virginia sewed and "scribbled," and was a weekly entertainer at the Hollywood Canteen. Photos from the movie magazine are seen below with their original captions.

Virginia does a deadpan aria as her sister Mary accompanies on the piano and her mother joins in with her harmonica.

Virginia likes the exercise of chopping wood.

Virginia lives with her family on a North Hollywood ranch. In her spare time, she takes active interest in it and…

… loves playing with her niece, Diane.

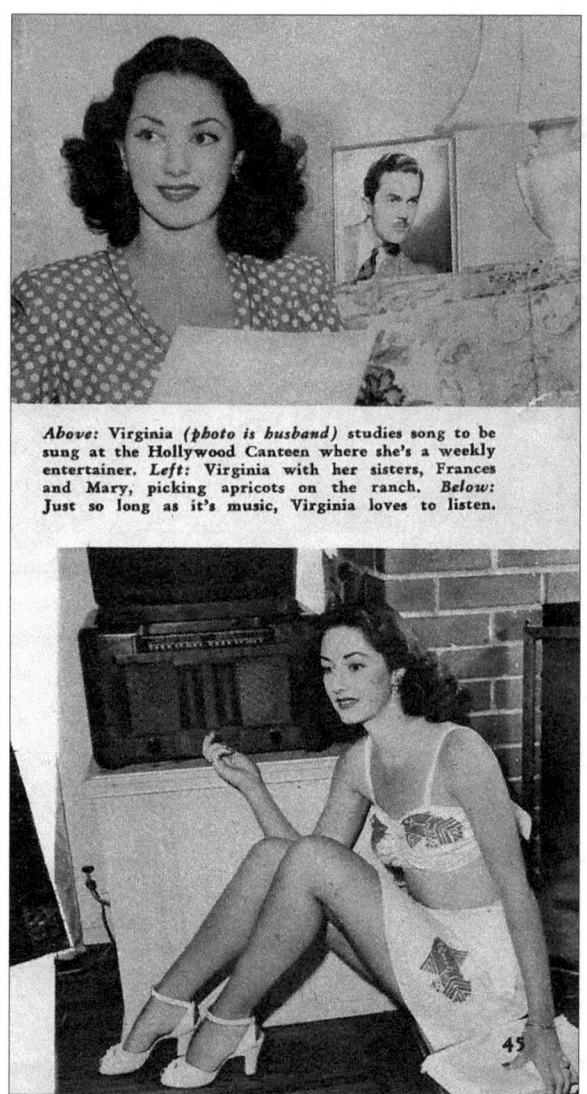

Above: Virginia *(photo is husband)* studies song to be sung at the Hollywood Canteen where she's a weekly entertainer. *Left:* Virginia with her sisters, Frances and Mary, picking apricots on the ranch. *Below:* Just so long as it's music, Virginia loves to listen.

Virginia studies her lyrics. Note the photo of Kirk Alyn behind her. The starlet keeps up on the latest hit tunes on the radio.

Virginia and her sisters, Fran and Mary, picking apricots at the farm.

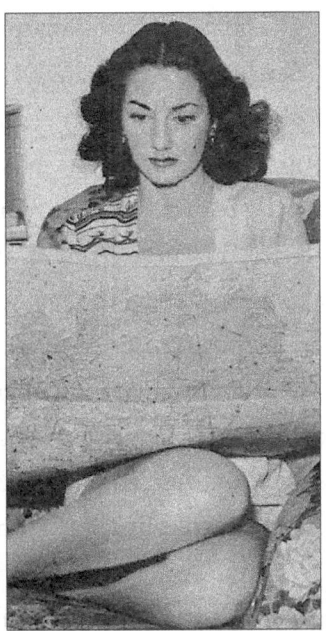

Trying to locate her husband, Kirk Alyn, who is serving in the Merchant Marines.

At the piano with younger sister, Mary, admiring her father's art work.

PIX magazine was a popular magazine in the 1940's. The February 3rd issue of 1945 included a two-page photo spread with the title "Hollywedlock." Eight celebrity couples were featured. Shown in various scenes of domestic bliss were Susan Hayward and Jess Barker, Dorothy Morris and Marvin Moffie, Mr. and Mrs. Lee Bowman, Van Heflin and Frances Neal, Kathryn Grayson and John Shelton, Pamela Blake and Michael Stokey, Johnny "Body and Soul" Green and MGM "Glamazon" Bunny Waters.

The *Philadelphia Enquirer* was among the hundreds of newspapers that carried Louella Parsons' gossip column. On February 7, 1945, Parsons' announced that the cast of *The Harvey Girls* had given Virginia a baby shower. As usual, Parsons' had scooped everyone else on the story.

The photograph of Kirk Alyn and Virginia shows him holding up one of his shirts while his smiling wife irons another. The caption reads, "Chore. Like an ordinary housewife, 'deadpan' vocalist Virginia O'Brien, does the ironing herself and husband Kirk Alwyn [sic] in their Beverly Hills apartment. Kirk Alwyn divides his time between screen acting and work at aircraft factory. Virginia's latest film is *Meet the People*." This photograph was taken at the young couple's apartment, which was located across the street from the backlot of 20th Century Fox.

The photograph in *PIX* magazine was clearly taken sometime before its publication. Had the couple been photographed just prior to the magazines release, readers would have seen a noticeably heavier Virginia. On March 20, 1945, newspapers across the country announced that Virginia was given only a little more than a week to finish her part in her latest movie. This turned out to be for a good reason, and her fans breathed a sigh of relief when they read:

> Although her baby isn't expected until June, Virginia O'Brien has received an ultimatum from the doctor to wind up her role in *The Harvey Girls* within 10 days. She must

stay home and take it easy. Can't even drive her car. But she is lucky for one thing. Her husband, Kirk Alyn, is stationed with the Merchant Marines in Catalina and can get home most weekends.

A happy moment on the set of *The Harvey Girls* with Judy Garland.

Even after she had left the set of *The Harvey Girls*, the publicity machine at MGM continued to promote her role, and the movie. On April 6, 1945, newspapers like the *Ames Daily Tribune* carried this vital information:

> "Virginia O'Brien has added a quarter of an inch of muscle to her right forearm after wielding a hammer and tongs for her role as a lady blacksmith in Metro-Goldwyn-Mayer's *The Harvey Girls*.

While this sounds like typical Hollywood fluff, it may actually be true. In watching Virginia perform the work of a blacksmith, it is obvious that she is doing the work herself. Not only does she fire and strike the horseshoe, she works the bellows. Her pounding of the hot shoe on the anvil, like every bit of "business" in the blacksmith number, is done in rhythm. The rehearsal required to get all of this perfect would have easily built muscle.

Newspapers across the country announced the birth of the first child of Virginia and Kirk Alyn, born on June 20, 1945. United Press ran the news on June 22nd: "Dead-pan singer Virginia O'Brien has a new daughter, six-pound, three-ounce Theresa ... at St. John Hospital in Hollywood." Kirk Alyn is described as a "Coast Guard Seaman," and a "Coast Guardsman." All sources reported him as being stationed at the aforementioned Catalina Island.

In an interview with the author, Terri O'Brien stated that the location of St. John's was actually Santa Monica. Due to her fear of hospitals, after the successful birth of Terri, Virginia insisted that all her children be born at St. John's. In 1953, because of her fear of flying, the family took the train from New York to Los Angeles. This was done so that her son John could be born at St. John's.

While Virginia recuperated at home, MGM was at work on a short film. Initially, the film was titled *Morgan's Folly*. This was later changed to the title under which it was released, *The Great Morgan*. Frank Morgan played himself. Morgan is tired of acting and wants to become a producer. In order to show him the difficulties in producing, the fictitious MGM production head, K.F., gives Morgan permission to make his first film as producer.

The actor moves from his dressing room to a large office. On the door hangs a sign reading "Frank Morgan, Producer." Launching his first production proves to be harder than he thought. Morgan runs into problems when he can't remember his story ideas. His memory fails him again when forgets his reason for contacting costume designer Irene and art director Cedric Gibbons. He does not know that Douglas Shearer is the head of Metro's sound department.

Eventually, Morgan's historic melodrama. *The Burning Secret*, goes into production. While other films are completed on time, *The Burning Secret* is still filming after sixty days. When K.F. asks to see the finished product, Morgan himself insists on editing the film. In a rush, Morgan drops the cans containing the film. He has trouble putting them back in order.

Still confident of his abilities, Morgan announces that his producers fee is $10,000. In the screening room, Morgan discovers that he had edited his film and another short film, *Musical Masterpieces*, together. After watching a few moments of *The Burning Secret*, one of John Nesbitt's Passing Parade shorts, *Our Old Car*, fills the screen.

Morgan offers to fix *The Burning Secret*, but K.F. was entertained by the musical footage of the King Sister, Carlos Ramirez, Eleanor Powell, Tommy Dorsey, and Virginia O'Brien. In the closing moments of *The Great Morgan*, MGM's own Leo the Lion takes Frank Morgan's place in the screening room. Leo speaks the closing line, "If only I could act."

The Great Morgan is a 57-minute "compilation film." All of the musical numbers come from different MGM films. This is how Virginia appeared in the short without reporting to the studio. "Jive," performed by Virginia and Tommy Dorsey, was cut from *Ship Ahoy*. The number can be seen on Youtube.

It is clear that Virginia, Dorsey, and his orchestra are on the *Ship Ahoy* set. The same set where Eleanor Powell performs her "Matador" tap routine. If not for its inclusion in *The Great Morgan*, the Dorsey-O'Brien "(I Fell in Love with) The Leader of the Band" would have languished in MGM's vaults.

Virginia and Tommy Dorsey perform "(I Fell in Love with) The Leader of the Band." Cut from *Ship Ahoy*, the number wasn't seen by the public until the release of *The Great Morgan*.

The May 31, 1945 broadcast of the radio show *Encore* was a "best of" episode. Announcer Ken Carpenter told listeners it would feature the "best" liked segments from past shows. Brought back for an encore were Bette Davis, Fred Allen, Jimmy Durante, Gypsy Rose Lee, and the Loumel Trio. Benny Goodman opened the show with the high-flying tune "Airmail Special." This was followed by the story of Oliver Twist, which Edger Bergan told to Charlie McCarthy. Virginia offered her number from *Thousands Cheer*, "In a Little Spanish Town."

MGM ran blurbs at the end of August 1945 about a remake of *Three Wise Fools*. This project would have reunited Virginia and Frank Morgan. The third fool was to have been played by Lionel Barrymore. Sadly, those notices were premature. The film was made in 1946 with Lionel Barrymore, Margaret O'Brien, and Lewis Stone. If the role of

Rena Fairchild was the role Virginia was considered for, that part was played by Cyd Charisse.

By September of 1945, Kirk Alyn had served for 18 months in the Merchant Marines. Now he would return to Republic Studios to resume his film career. He was slated to appear in the series known as *The Ranger*.

Readers of the *Los Angeles Times* got their first glimpse of Theresa Alyn on October 6, 1945. The headline accompanying the photo of mother and daughter was "Screen Baby Steals Scene, First Picture." The two-paragraphs below the photo read:

> "Mugging" like a seasoned screen scene-stealer, Theresa Alyn, daughter of actress Virginia O'Brien and husband Kirk Alyn, had her picture taken yesterday for the first time.
>
> Theresa arrived three months ago, temporarily halting her mother's film career, but Miss O'Brien plans to appear before the camera again soon."

Before her return to film work, Virginia made a guest appearance on Campbell Soup's new radio show, *Request Performance*. Her visit to the show on October 21, 1945 found her acting in a skit that spoofed one of the most infamous radio broadcasts of all-time.

Ten days before Halloween, the man who had traumatized the east coast with his broadcast of *The War of the Worlds*, Orson Welles, was the host of the show that gave listeners "... *Whatever you ask for, you get, so get ready for a few surprises!*" This broadcast's surprise was Welles' comedic take on his own infamous *Men from Mars* heard seven years earlier.

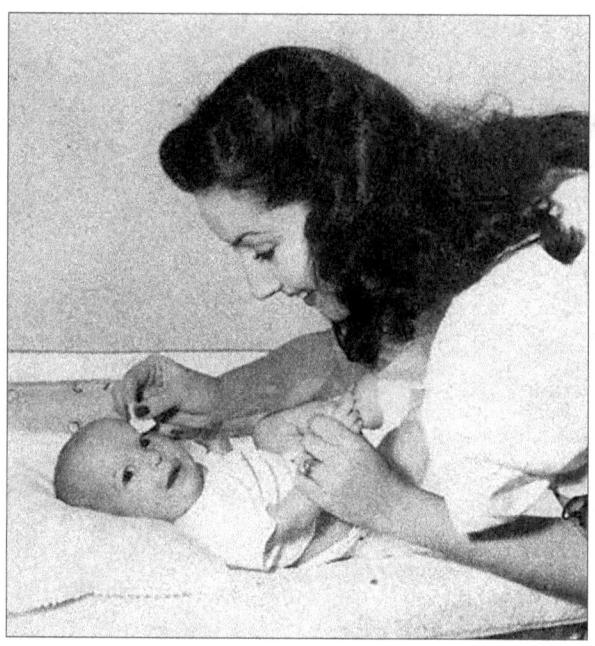

Virginia and her daughter, Theresa.

In this new version, titled *The Three Rover Boys Down East*, or *Rescue on the River*, the destination was the moon. Making that journey as the Rover Boys were Welles, Eddie Bracken, and Johnny Mercer. Virginia, as the sweetheart of one of the boys, was rescued from the river.

The following day, Virginia made a successful appearance at Hollywood's famed Cocoanut Grove. As reported on the 22nd of the month, she sang there for Admiral William F. Halsey. She must have been thrilled by the fuss Hollywood icon Cary Grant made. Grant told reporters, "Gosh, if I could pry her away from Metro and book her in England, she'd be a riot." A few years later, that very thing happened.

The Cocoanut Grove appearance was quickly followed by a radio show on WHMA that was advertised as "… a nation-wide star-studded victory bond program." Co-sponsored by the Motion Picture Industry and the War Activities Committee, the other stars that evening were Alan

Ladd, Rosalind Russell, Frank Morgan, Dick Powell, Janet Blair, and Jack Carson. Listings for the show do not mention the song Virginia presented.

Virginia and Eddie Bracken prepare
for the broadcast of *Command Performance*.
Author's collection.

The familiar title "She Can Smile Too" was seen in a publication known as the *Jax Air News* on November 8, 1945. The glamorous photograph is captioned: "Although she earned her film laurels for a unique style of poker-faced singing, Virginia O'Brien's smile is as warm as toast. She has been barnstorming the foxhole circuit since Pearl Harbor, but her next spot is in M-G-M's *The Harvey Girls*. While she is not smiling in this photo, at least her work entertaining the troops is acknowledged."

This photograph of Kirk Alyn and Virginia appeared in various newspapers on December 23, 1946. The caption read: Virginia O'Brien tries her famous dead-pan at breakfast. The kitchen curtains are of bright green print percale. Author's Note: Terri O'Brien remembered these curtains in their home at 12155 Morrison Street.

1946 saw the delayed release of *Ziegfeld Follies* and *The Harvey Girls*. One new film, *The Show-Off*, had her in a role so minor that she complained to the powers-that-be for the first time. In the other, *Till the Clouds Roll By*, she gave one of her most memorable musical performances.

"Around the Lot with Judy Garland" was a photospread created to promote *The Harvey Girls*, showing Judy Garland on the film's various sets. The star poses in various costumes and casual wear with the cast and crew. She and Virginia stand side by side wearing the simple black dress and white apron worn by Fred Harvey's waitresses. The photographs appeared in the January 1946 edition of *Screenland* magazine. Virginia wore more contemporary fashions for her next photo session.

Shortly before the opening of *The Harvey Girls*, in the January 2, 1946 issue of *Motion Picture Daily*, Virginia received a short review. "Virginia O'Brien is in the stellar assemblage doing specialties as she alone seems endowed." This particular specialty, her musical moment as the lady blacksmith, was probably the most memorable number in the film without the presence of Judy Garland.

Virginia was not in The *Harvey Girls* period costumes for the fashion photographs that were published ten days before the film's opening. Melbourne's *Argus* newspaper brought Hollywood fashion to Australia at the beginning of 1946. The January 8th edition featured photographs of Joan Leslie and Virginia. Leslie, a Warner Brothers star was photographed in a Dutch bonnet with a matching purse. There were two photos of Virginia.

She modeled the new "cut-like-a-sack" beige jersey dress. Snoods, which covered a woman's hair, were the latest in headwear. Virginia's polka-dotted snood matched the wide belt. In the second photo, she was pictured in elegant evening attire. Her black crepe dress was accentuated by a lipstick red belt of suede. Her shoes matched the belt, and a "winged" soon looked like a giant hair ribbon.

Premiering on January 8th, *The Harvey Girls* was among the top 60 money producers of 1946, earning $4,112,000 in the United States. The film's most popular song, which Virginia sang with Judy Garland and the cast, was "On the Atchison, Topeka, and the Santa Fe." The song won an Academy Award for its creators, Johnny Mercer and Harry Warren.

The Decca album of three 78rpm records consisted of six songs from *The Harvey Girls*: "On the Atchison, Topeka and the Santa Fe," "Wait and See," "Swing Your Partner Round and Round," "It's a Great Big World," and "The Wild, Wild West." Virginia joined Judy Garland and Betty Russell, who sang for Cyd Charisse, on "It's a Great Big World." "The Wild, Wild West" is her solo. Virginia's photograph, along with those of Judy Garland and Kenny Baker, is on the cover of the album, and a booklet that accompanied the album. Baker, Garland, and O'Brien all have short pieces about them in the booklet. Virginia's reads:

Virginia is Alma from Ohio in *The Harvey Girls*. Author's collection.

An Italian film poster for *The Harvey Girls*. Photo courtesy of Terri O'Brien.

"Virginia O'Brien was frightened into a career …

"With a wealth of expression in her voice, but absolutely none on her face, she employs what Hollywood calls the 'dead pan' with professional skill now, but at first she was a natural. She was terrified in the course of an audition.

"Miss O'Brien stood stiffly, almost motionless, but she sang. It was remarkable. The instructor for whom she was giving the involuntary demonstration saw the novelty of that frozen face. From that time on, her training consisted more of control of the facial muscles than voice cultivation."

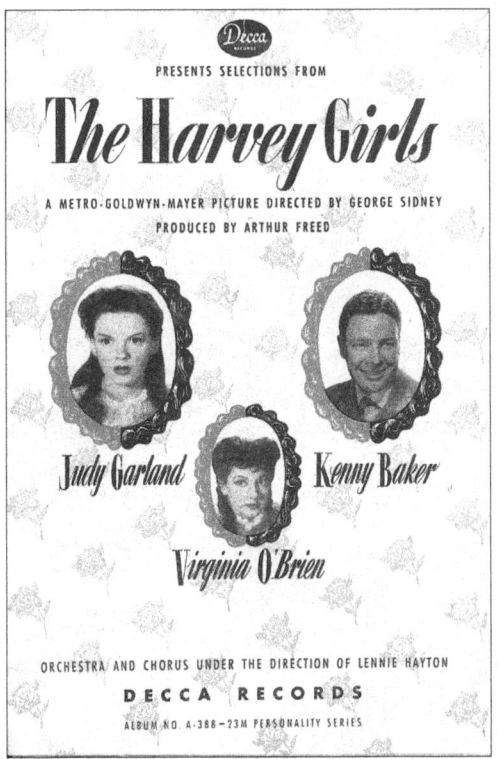

The booklet that came with the Decca album of songs from *The Harvey Girls*. Author's collection.

Within weeks of the opening of what was arguably Virginia's most significant film to date, her participation in another Red Skelton vehicle was announced on January 30, 1946. She and Marjorie Main were "... set for top comedy roles in MGM's forthcoming *The Show-Off*...." Her part was not a "top" role, and *The Show-Off* would prove to be her biggest disappointment at her home studio.

Until the release of *The Show-Off*, there was more publicity for *The Harvey Girls* and *Till the Clouds Roll By* in the beginning months of 1946. The February issue of *Screenland* magazine featured two photographs of her side-by-side. The caption reads: "Virginia O'Brien's voice as well as her brunette beauty attract attention in the star-studded *Till the Clouds By*, with Tony Martin, right."

A promotional photo for *Till the Clouds Roll By* (1946). The caption read: Relaxation ... Between scenes of Metro-Goldwyn-Mayer's new musical, "Till the Clouds Roll By," Tony Martin and Virginia O'Brien do a little kibitzing. The singers, wearing costumes of the 1890's, are featured in the spectacular "Show Boat" and finale scenes of the lavish Technicolor production.

Virginia and another of MGM's brunette beauties, Kathryn Grayson, also appeared in a 1946 issue of *Screenland*. It was another opportunity to promote their new film. Both were in costume, posing bustle to bustle on the set. "Kathryn and Virginia O'Brien learn the way of a maid with a bustle … Age before beauty? But what happens when both are beautiful." And what happens when both enjoy the sport of fishing?

Hollywood reporter Bob Thomas wrote of a contest between Virginia and her friend Kathryn Grayson. This was reported in papers carrying Thomas' column on February 11, 1946. It all started with a remark Kathryn made on the set of the "… river scene for the *Showboat* sequence in *Till the Clouds Roll By*."

> Said Kathryn: "When I was a kid in Winston-Salem, I was the best fisherwoman in the neighborhood."
>
> Said Virginia: "I once landed the biggest halibut ever caught off the Santa Monica pier."
>
> So now the gals and their respective husbands are going on a fishing cruise to determine which is the better angler. The loser will have to do the cooking.

The news on March 3rd was a bit more serious. Kirk and Virginia were involved in the first of two auto mishaps. While Virginia was "badly shaken," Kirk suffered a head wound that required five stitches.

St. Patrick's Day 1946 found Virginia in San Francisco. She had traveled there with her boss, L.B. Mayer. The all-knowing Hedda Hopper reported that Virginia would sing, and Mayer would give his annual speech. San Francisco papers featured a photograph of the two on March 14, 1946. In part, the caption read: "'Hibernia Temple' Mythical unit of the Shriners holds annual luncheon…. Among film and radio notables participating are … Louis B. Mayer, M.G.M. executive; Actress Virginia O'Brien."

Virginia joins Louis B. Mayer in San Francisco to celebrate St. Patrick's Day.

The second story appeared in newspapers, including the *Joplin Globe*, on April 14th. "Husband and wife were both treated for frostbite after heavy snowfall in mountains near Los Angeles, for several hours." Thankfully, these incidents were the only trouble the couple appeared to have in 1946.

With the long awaited opening of *Ziegfeld Follies* approaching, photos of astride Snow White, her "horse," with her towering plumed headdress, began to appear with great frequency. The caption accompanying this photograph dated May 2, 1946 read, "Virginia O'Brien sings the most amusing ditty in *Ziegfeld Follies of 1946* ... which Miss O'Brien warbles while galloping across the screen on a white 'prop' horse."

What was not mentioned was the fact that Virginia's song was added to the film after preview audiences had seen it. The majority of those first audiences did not like the opening sequences. Least of all, Lucille Ball's whipping of showgirls clad in black jaguar costumes.

Virginia's number was inserted after Lucy's ended, lifting the mood and garnering laughs.

Very few knew that Virginia had just learned of her pregnancy. It was only after receiving her doctor's approval that she mounted to ride sidesaddle and sing "Bring on those Wonderful Men." It was Virginia who revealed this in interviews decades later. The timing places the filming of her performance at the beginning of October 1945. After she completed this new sequence for *Ziegfeld Follies*, she began work on *The Harvey Girls*.

Astride Snow White and in costume for "Bring on those Wonderful Men" in *Ziegfeld Follies*.

As early as May 9, 1946, there were rumors that Buster Keaton would play Virginia's father in *Merton of the Movies*. Hedda Hopper included this news in her column that day. She added that MGM was looking for an 8-year-old boy with a "... sphinx face" to play Virginia's little brother. Hopper would later fabricate a story about the casting of that part.

"Kay Kyser agrees with Virginia O'Brien that her husband, Kirk Alyn, furniture manufacturer, should quit smoking sawdust," read the caption of a photograph in the *Cincinnati Enquirer*. Whether or not Kirk Alyn actually smoked saw dust was notknown. The photograph does show the mustachioed actor with a pipe in his mouth, while bandleader Kyser and Virginia grimace. The photograph appeared on May 12, 1946. Here we have another example of Hollywood's press machine weaving another unlikely tale. Terri O'Brien, in an interview with the author, says her father did not put sawdust in his pipe.

Bandleader Kay Kyser and Virginia react to Kirk Alyn's odd choice of smoking material.

John L. Scott of the *Los Angeles Times* reported in the paper's June 9, 1946 edition, that while Virginia was ready to act, she would do so while "keeping her good sense of humor from showing!"

The chance to act would come via her role in *Merton of the Movies*. This is how nearly all the publicity for the film was geared. MGM wanted to give the impression that Virginia had never really acted before. In other words, they were selling her now not as a comedic singer, but as an actress. Perhaps they were hoping that this might make audiences accept the fact that she wouldn't be singing in her next film.

The article retraced her stage-fright induced success in *Meet the People* five years ago. Virginia told Scott, "Really I was only in *People* here for three months, but they taught others my tricks". Those "tricks" would remain in place in that "Virginia has a hankering to grin, even laugh out loud." This she would not do until the studio gave her "the green light." In the meantime, her smiles were saved for "Kirk Alyn, just out of the Coast Guard, their one-year-old daughter, and friends."

Scott wrapped up his article with this about baby Theresa:

> "Oddly enough, when studio cameramen took first shots of her baby girl, the child revealed a perfect "dead pan," but Virginia can show other color photos proving that her infant has a big, beautiful smile. And mother will no doubt see that when daughter grows up she'll not get frightened during her first audition."

Lina Romay was a singer with Xavier Cugat's band. A photograph in the June 16, 1946 edition of the *Detroit Free Press* shows her with Kirk Alyn and Virginia. "Caught Kirk Alyn, Virginia O'Brien, and Lina Romay chatter-threesoming. "Deadpan warbler' Virginia is Mrs. A.," read the brief caption. Kirk still has his pipe, and his moustache.

Under the byline "A Special Correspondent," it was reported the Virginia O'Brien had become a member of "Hollywood's newest and most exclusive club...." Lana Turner was its president. Betty Grable was a member. Fellow members, who also happened to be under contract at MGM, included Judy Garland, Ann Sothern, and Gloria DeHaven. This report appeared in the *New Castle Sun* in New South

Wales on June 22, 1946. The secret group was the "Safety Pin-up League." The criteria for membership was a baby daughter, and the use of safety pins on said infant.

Hedda Hopper still kept track of news large and small in Hollywood. Her column mentioned that Kirk and Virginia were planning a trip to South America. What made this minor news item print-worthy on July 8 of 1946, was Virginia's preparation for this vacation. She was returning to high school that summer to take courses in Spanish and Portuguese. Whether she completed those courses, and took the south of the border journey is unknown. Appearances she made in the latter part of July indicate that the vacation may not have been possible.

Jerome Kern, who had passed away in November of 1945, was to be saluted at the world-famous Hollywood Bowl between July 18th and 20th 1946. Kern had made an enormous impact on the Broadway musical, most significantly with *Showboat*. His contributions to Hollywood musicals were acknowledged by his eight Academy Award nominations. He won the Oscar twice for "The Way You Look Tonight" and "The Last Time I Saw Paris."

"Kern Night" at the Hollywood Bowl featured all of the major stars of MGM's Jerome Kern biography *Till the Clouds Roll By*. Cast members Robert Walker, Frank Sinatra, Judy Garland, Lena Horne, and Virginia were on hand that night. Only Tony Martin was unable to attend. The singer was having his appendix removed at Cedars of Lebanon.

Gadfly Hedda Hopper reported on a swank affair at the Hillcrest Country Club in her "Looking at Hollywood" column (*Los Angeles Times* July 24, 1946). The 25th anniversary party with entertainment "… that would have bankrupted theater had the backers had to pay for it." With Jack Benny as emcee, the show began at 10pm and ended at 2am. Virginia was on the bill with Danny Kaye, Danny Thomas, Gene Kelly, Van Johnson, George Burns, Mickey Rooney, and Frank Sinatra. Employees who had been there since the 1921 opening received gold watches.

Tony Martin, Virginia, and MGM chorines pose for a photograph from *Till the Clouds Roll By* (1946). Virginia gave a memorable performance of "Life Upon the Wicked Stage." Photo courtesy Terri O'Brien.

From the Show Boat segment of *Till the Clouds Roll By*, left to right, Lena Horne, Virginia, William Halligan, and Tony Martin (1946). Photo courtesy Terri O'Brien.

Edwin Schallert of the *Los Angeles Times* column dated August 10, 1946, was headlined: "Alyn Starting Career in 'Trap' at Monogram." "Kirk Alyn, husband of Virginia O'Brien, seems all set for a movie career," Schallert wrote. His role in *The Trap*, the leading "juvenile part," was offered to Alyn by producer James S. Burkett. The producer was impressed by Kirk's performance as John the Baptist in *A Voice in the Wilderness*, one of the series from Cathedral Films about biblical subjects. *The Trap*, a "Charlie Chan whodunit," was seen as Kirk Alyn's break-in role.

The *Showman's Trade Review* seemed to be the only publication that recognized how wasted Virginia's talent was in *The Show-Off*. That publication's August 17, 1946 issue remarked "Two splendid performers like Virginia O'Brien and Eddie 'Rochester' Anderson are among the supporting members of the cast, but why is one of the mysteries of the pictures making, for they get very little to do." Virginia and "Rochester" remained friends for decades to come.

Agreements of Consent were standard practice between the studios and stars. On August 20, 1946, Virginia signed a slightly different consent form. Usually, these forms gave the studio the use of image for publicity purposes. This particular consent form gave the Motion Picture Relief Fund permission to use Virginia's "… name, autograph, photographic likeness and/or artist's sketch of my likeness…." This authorization gave the Motion Picture Relief Fund permission to sell her image "… throughout the world."

The state of California was having its first state fair since the end of WWII. In her August 28, 1946 column, Hedda Hopper announced the fair and the film stars who would be attending on opening night. The Hollywood attendees included William Bendix, Eddie Bracken, William Demarest, Marilyn Maxwell, Lina Romay, and Virginia.

The whole family was in on the act when the *Daily Examiner* of New South Wales covered the Debut of a Glamour Girl on September 14, 1946. The glamour girl was "The very young lady … Theresa Alyn, daughter of M-G-M actress Virginia O'Brien and husband Kirk Alyn." The family photo introduced the couple's first child, and reminded Australian fans that Virginia was in "… one sequence of the M-G-M Technicolor revue, *Ziegfeld Follies*."

During the summer and autumn months of 1946, Virginia was working on her eighth, and final, film with Red Skelton. Frank Morris' column "Here, there and Hollywood" appearing in the *Winnipeg Free Press* on September 25th, covered this scene as filming came to an end one evening:

> "It was getting close to six o'clock and the end of another studio day, so we only had time for a quick visit to the set of *Merton of the Movies*, where Red Skelton and Virginia O'Brien,

who plays opposite him, were resting between scenes. Virginia, who cultivates a dead-pan manner on the screen, is a vivacious, beautiful girl when the cameras are not rolling.

While the visiting Canadian was quick to spot the difference between the Virginia of real life versus the Virginia of reel life, something else caught his eye. This was the hug that Red Skelton received from a blonde who happened to pass by. While their embrace looked as if "… they hadn't seen each other for 10 years." Onto the ways of movie folk, Morris surmised, "Most likely their last meeting had only been the week before. But that's Hollywood for you."

Virginia and Red Skelton having fun on the set of *Merton of the Movies*. Author's collection.

Two days later, on September 27th, members of the Conference of Studio Unions (CSU) and the International Alliance of Theatrical Stage Employees, an A.F.L. group, went on strike. There were picket lines at Warner Brothers and Metro-Goldwyn-Mayer. At Warner Brothers, 850 employees were taken across the lines in 17 buses. MGM stars reporting for work, and crossing the line on foot, were Greer Garson, Red Skelton, and Virginia. While the strike was resolved, Virginia must have caught a chill. That too, made the local papers.

Hedda Hopper wrote about Virginia's dancing newsboy on October 10, 1946. She had seen the paperboy "... doing an acrobatic dance on her front lawn." Knowing the studio still hadn't cast an actor to play her little brother in *Merton of the Movies*, she picked up the phone. That's how Virginia's paperboy got into the movies, or so the story goes. There are no scenes with Virginia's character, Phyllis Montague, and her little brother. Even the scenes with Phyllis' father were cut.

While there are no songs in *Merton of the Movies*, it seems that at some point in the production three songs were slated to be in the film. Whether they were actually recorded and filmed is unknown. It is possible they were recorded for the soundtrack but never filmed. If that is the case, the recordings may be somewhere in the MGM film archives now owned by Turner Classic Movies.

According to the November 17, 1946 issue of the *Lansing State Journal* Virginia was to sing three songs that made the "hit parade" in 1915. The article stated, "The songs are: 'Oh, By Jingo!' 'I'm Sorry I Made You Cry,' and 'All Aboard for Dixieland.' To carry out the authenticity of the film, which takes place in 1915 Hollywood, M-G-M decided to use hits of that period instead of new compositions." Virginia's fans can only hope that one of TCM's film historians finds the complete *Merton of the Movies* soundtrack with these songs.

Virginia recovered quickly from the head cold mentioned in Harold Heffernan's column (November 25, 1946). Although it is doubtful she followed the advice of Red Skelton, who suggested, "Just let it develop into pneumonia—the doctors know how to cure that." Whatever the cure, she was on-stage at the Biltmore Bowl just two days later.

> "The movie town last week put on its best manners and gave the Associated Press Managing Editors Association what old-timers reckoned was the biggest party in Hollywood's history.
>
> – Bob Thomas "Hollywood Column," December 2, 1946.

The "… biggest party" in the history of Hollywood took place at the Biltmore Bowl. MGM's grand lady, Greer Garson, welcomed the editors before Jack Benny took to the stage. The succession of stars included Jane Powell, Edgar Bergen and Charlie McCarthy, Roy Rogers, and Van Johnson. Thomas lauded Jimmy Durante for "breaking up Da Jernt."

Singers performing that evening were Dick Haymes, "… the best baritone in Hollywood," and Virginia, who "… deadpanned her songs." Judy Garland, introduced by Ronald Reagan, sang "I Got the Sun in the Morning" from Irving Berlin's *Annie Get Your Gun*. Judy Garland was cast in the film version of *Annie Get Your Gun*. She was too ill to complete the film, and was subsequently fired by MGM.

Garland's shocking departure left the role of sharpshooter Annie Oakley open to other musical actresses at Metro. A blurb in nationwide papers on October 28th announced, "Now it's Virginia O'Brien who's trying for the coveted role of Annie Oakley in the screen version of *Annie Get Your Gun*."

Virginia probably didn't mention her confidence issue to Mayer. She did make him aware of another reason she couldn't accept the assignment: "I told him I had a great fear of horses. It should have been in my [studio] bio." Virginia was gracious in her comments to Van Neste about the star who eventually played the legendary Oakley, saying "… she was great!" In truth, the loud, brash, homely woman who starred in the film makes it painful to watch. No Virginia O'Brien.

In the meantime, Virginia was still working on *Merton of the*

Movies. The fun she and Red Skelton had while filming was shared with the readers of Sheila Graham's "Hollywood Today" column on October 31, 1946:

> "Red Skelton is doing one of his silent sequences in *Merton of the Movies*, and there's plenty of ad-libbing between Red and Virginia O'Brien while Red is doing Sherlock Holmes and putting on different disguises."

Red's scrubwoman is greeted by Virginia with, "You'll have to do better than that—I'd know you anywhere." When Skelton goes behind the scenery to change into his next disguise, a cow wanders onto the set. "Oh, that's a wonderful disguise," Virginia opines. The cast and crew laugh. The laughter continues when Red chases the cow armed with a fork and knife. Grahams wraps up with, "And these actors and actresses actually get paid for this sort of thing!"

A lobby card from *Merton of the Movies*. Virginia's eighth and final film with Red Skelton. Author's collection.

Truth was a newspaper published in Brisbane, Queensland. On December 8, 1946, Red Skelton was quoted in the paper's "Talking of Talkies" column. "Pressed by Virginia O'Brien for definition of comedian on the set of *Morton [sic] of the Movies*...." Skelton's reply was, "A comedian is a fellow with a good memory, who hopes no one else in the room has one too!" Some four decades later, Virginia would say that her friend Red wore her out. Nevertheless, his kinetic presence coupled with her low-key underplaying created a memorable comedic team.

"Virginia O'Brien tired of sitting around doing very little, is going on an extended personal appearance tour," wrote columnist Sheilha Graham. This tidbit appeared in Graham's column on January 13, 1947. No details of the tour are given in this first news item of the new year.

On February 27, 1947, Virginia was among 600 alumni of North Hollywood High School gathered for a special event. While it was the 10-year reunion of Virginia's class, it was also open to other graduating classes. This was the first home-coming alumni day since the outbreak of World War II. Other film stars in attendance included Noah Berry Jr., and a one-time student body president named Alan Ladd.

The National Orange Show was, in its time, a Southern California event as well known as the Rose Bowl Parade. On March 16th and 17th of 1947, Virginia was the star of the show. On those dates, she performed a 2pm matinee and an 8pm evening show. The article in the March 16, 1947 edition of the *San Bernardino County Sun* was extensive. Virginia was referred to as "... a tall, graceful brunette who parlayed a deadpan expression into a brilliant success on the stage, radio and in the cinema...."

This article did not mention *Meet the People* as the scene of her first experience with her frozen façade. For the first, and only time, it was reported her face "froze" during her first singing lesson. This prompted her decision "... to capitalize on this novel vocal style." It was her mastery of this approach that led to her "... immediate hit in the Hollywood stage revue *Meet the People.*" That success led to her signing a long-term contract with Metro-Goldwyn-Mayer, and her involvement with the Broadway musical *Keep Off the Grass.*

Her latest film, *Till the Clouds Roll By*, was mentioned. She was called a "… film colony rarities, a native daughter of Los Angeles." The article gave her height as "… five-feet-six-and-one-half inches…." When she was not before the camera or a live audience, she "… has very expressive and mobile eyes and features…." The article concludes with an enticement for those who would be attending the Orange Show: "She will offer her famed frozen-faced vocal stylings supported by an excellent vaudeville revue, complete with 16 Orange Show girls."

"Virginia O'Brien's tonal charm is unmistakable," wrote music critic Robert H. Allen in his "Hot Off the Wax" column. He was praising her new Decca recordings of "Say That We're Sweethearts Again" and the humorous "I'm Going Back to Whur I Come From." This column was seen in various newspapers on May 11, 1947. Virginia's name appeared next in association with a major concert given for veterans of World War II.

On Wednesday July 2, 1947, the Hollywood Bowl presented the 3rd annual Music for the Wounded Concert. The *Los Angeles Times* ran an article titled "Gayety Will Mark Show for Wounded" on June 25, 1947, featuring photographs of Red Skelton, Danny Kaye, Frances Langford, and Virginia. Others on the bill included Gene Autry, Jimmy Durante, Jack Haley, and Frank Sinatra. Producer Al Armer was building a special runway, "in order that members of the audience may see the stars more closely…." The 175-piece orchestra was conducted by Alfred Wallenstein.

The film industry magazine *Harrison's Reports* was the first to comment favorably on Virginia's work in her final MGM feature. The magazine proclaimed the third version of *Merton of the Movies* "Good!"

The comments about Virginia read in part, "Virginia O'Brien, as the young actress who falls in love with Skelton and helps him reach success, handles the requirements of her role with ease."

Virginia's eighth film with Red Skelton was her last under her contract with MGM. *Merton of the Movies* came from a popular book of the same title. Written by Harry Leon Wilson in 1919, it was published and adapted for the Broadway stage by George S. Kaufman and Connelly. The production ran for 392 performances in 1922.

Two years later, in 1924, the story was adapted again, this time for the screen. The silent film was directed by James Cruze. It starred Glenn Hunter and Viola Dana. This version is now considered to be a lost film.

Eight years passed before it became 1932's *Make Me a Star*. Now it was a pre-Code romantic comedy directed by William Beaudine and starring Joan Blondell as "Flips" Montague. Viola Davis preceded Blondell in the role. In 1947, the part was played by Virginia. Red Skelton played Merton, with Robert Alton at the helm. A glamorous photograph of Virginia taken to promote *Merton of the Movies* was captioned as follows by MGM:

> "NO MORE "FROZEN FACE" ... Vivacious Virginia O'Brien recently declared she will no longer adhere to the "deadpan" type of screen role for which she has been famous. She says her roles from now on will highlight the straight dramatic quality which characterizes her portrayal opposite Red Skelton in Metro-Goldwyn-Mayer's *Merton of the Movies.*

No more frozen face. Virginia as Phyllis Montague in *Merton of the Movies*.

Virginia's portrayal of Phyllis Montague, the silent-screen stunt woman who helps Skelton's Merton Gill find success in Hollywood, won her some of the best reviews of her career. The October 1947 issue of *Screenland* magazine wrote of her "kissing lesson" scene with Skelton: "… there's a gal who finally comes into her own as a terrific comedienne." On November 2, 1947, the film critic for Connecticut's *The Bridgeport Telegram* enthused, "… now Miss O'Brien emerges from Hollywood a full-fledged leading lady … she now plays a sprightly, vivacious part that matches her off-screen personality."

Unfortunately, these strong reviews, and the public's response to Virginia since the beginning of her MGM years came too late. *Merton of the Movies* was the last film she made at her home studio. In her 1999 interview with Dan Van Neste for *Classic Images* magazine, Virginia remembered how she learned she was being let go. "When it all came to an end, it was quite sudden. I remember I was having my hair done at the beauty parlor when I read in the papers that my contract had not been renewed. No one told me."

Just before she was released from her contract, Louis B. Mayer offered her a role that could have saved her career. Before his offer came along, she would return to radio for her last appearance on *Command Performance*. This broadcast was heard on September 2, 1947. The "... lovely and vivacious Mistress of Ceremonies," was Penny Singleton, the actress best remembered for the 28 *Blondie* movies she made between 1938 and 1950. Considering the situation at MGM, Virginia's choice of songs seems ironic. She sang "Everybody Has a Laughing Place." While she no longer had a studio to report to every day, she still had her family.

Ventriloquist Bob Wiss was a student at the University of Illinois in 1947. Wiss entered and won an amateur talent contest on local radio station, WGN. As the winner of "Stars of Tomorrow," the second-year student beat 90 contestants. His prize, a $500 bond, was presented to him by "... movie actress Virginia O'Brien," reported *The Daily Illini* on September 16, 1947. Wiss was an NROTC student and a Phi Kappa member.

On October 28, 1947, the following appeared in Dorothy Kilgallen's widely read "The Voice of Broadway" column: "Now it's Virginia O'Brien who's trying for the coveted role of Annie Oakley in the screen version of *Annie Get Your Gun*...." Considering the fact that L.B. Mayer offered the role of sharpshooter Oakley to Virginia, she probably wouldn't have had to try too hard to get it. After some consideration, she declined.

At the time, Virginia said she turned it down out of fear of her ability to carry a movie on her own. This is understandable, as it was something she had never done. *Annie Get Your Gun* would have been her first "name above the title" movie. It wasn't until 1999, in her interview with Dan Van Neste, that Virginia reveled another reason behind this decision. She told Van Neste:

> "L.B. Mayer did call me to his office to replace Judy Garland in the film *Annie Get Your Gun*, but I just didn't feel I could do it. I've always had a certain lack of self-confidence about shouldering a whole show. I told him I had a great fear of horses. It should have been in my [studio] bio."

While Virginia said that the actress who finally played the role was "great," the truth is she is far from it. The overly loud, brassy individual makes the movie virtually impossible to watch. Her Annie Oakley is strident, and annoying.

Virginia would have made a lovable Oakley. The woman who played her can't be loved by the audience, let alone her love interest, Frank Butler (Howard Keel). MGM would have been wiser to recruit the lady who created the role on Broadway, Virginia's one-time hero, Ethel Merman.

While Virginia was no longer employed by MGM, the first news of 1948 gave reason to celebrate. The announcement was seen by the readers of the Hollywood column written by Jack Lait Jr. on January 19, 1948.

> "Trade Chatter: Virginia O'Brien almost lost her deadpan when she found out her hubby, Kirk Alyn, is gonna be Superman in the Columbia movie serial."

With that happy news, the Alyn-O'Brien family started a new chapter.

Daddy's little girl. Virginia and daughter, Terri, visit Kirk Alyn on the set of one of his films in matching mother and daughter outfits. Circa 1948. Photo courtesy of Terri O'Brien.

Chapter Eight

Deadpan Solo

Chapter Eight, Part One: Exit Superman

Early in May of 1948, Virginia and Kirk Alyn boarded the Queen Mary. The couple's destination was the United Kingdom. Virginia had been hired to perform at the London Casino. Although they weren't released until July 1948, Kirk had recently completed sixteen episodes of Columbia Pictures *Superman* series. The arrival of the screens first Superman was a big deal in the UK, but what about Virginia's deadpan routine?

Happily, Virginia was a smash. British audiences welcomed her warmly. At the London Casino, she played to full houses. Rounding out the variety show were local favorites including the popular impressionist, Leslie Strange. American dance team Harrison and Fisher were on the bill, as were Freddy Carpenter's Casino Girls.

The casino's producer, Bernard Delfont, gave an opening night party, which was covered in *The Stage* section of the local newspaper on May 6, 1948.

"Virginia O'Brien At Bernard Delfont's party, given for her at the Casino.

> Virginia O'Brien stressed the international appeal of her type of dead pan humour. She said that, not relying overmuch on dialogue, it can more easily appeal to audiences

of any nationality and environment. She found that when, as in the case of a foreign audience, it is necessary to ensure that all allusions and jokes in dialogue are understood clearly, facial expressions and pantomime assist in breaking the ice. Miss O'Brien considers variety as the spice of life, and American friends who have already appeared here tell her that it is at its best in England now."

The May 12, 1948 issue of *Variety* reviewed her show at the London Casino. The reviewer noted that unless the headliner was a "universal favorite" their appearance in the UK was "pointless." The fact that Virginia was known only to film audiences was seen as a disadvantage. "This is not belittling her talent," the critic wrote. The audiences' appreciative response was obvious and the review highlighted her successes. "Her skits of "Ramona," "Salome," and "Virginia" were nicely received." Other numbers that went over well included songs she had not performed on screen: "Go to Sleep My Baby," "Feudin' and Fightin'," and "When You Wore a Tulip and I Wore a Big Red Rose."

Virginia and Kirk stayed on after her closing at the nightspot. On May 20th, she was called upon to substitute for her friend, Allan Jones. As the British press put it, Allan was "unable through indisposition to appear." Virginia carried on, and it was reported that the crowded house gave a hearty reception to Virginia O'Brien.

Also on May 20th, a photograph of "Actress Virginia O'Brien, with actor-husband Kirk Alyn at a Beverly Hills dinner" appeared in *Radio Call* magazine. Taken before their departure for London, it shows a typically wide-eyed Virginia dressed to the nines—hat, gloves, and what appears to be a fox fur. Alyn looks every inch the leading man in his suit and tie.

Virginia, Kirk Alyn, and Gene Kelly in Australia's *Radio Call* magazine.

The same page in the Adelaide, Australia publication featured to photos of Virginia's *Du Barry Was a Lady* co-star, Gene Kelly. The dancer was pictured as D'Artagnon in MGM's 1948 version of *The Three Musketeers*. The other photo showed Kelly in casual wear as he dances at a cafe with actress-wife, Betsy Blair, a golden red-head.

Musical Merry-Go-Round was a series of short films that were shown in movie theatres before the main feature. Later, they were also seen on television. The fourth film in the series has host Martin Block acting as a disc jockey on a radio show. Virginia is his in-studio guest. Together, they discuss the career of Les Brown and His Band of Renown, and play some of Brown's records.

Block is on-the-air playing Brown's recording of "Leap Frog," when Virginia stops by for an informal visit. She is not introduced to Martin Block's listening audience, nor are her remarks broadcast. The eleven-minute film was released on July 17, 1948. First up is a flashback showing Brown during his college days at Duke University. His group, The Blue Devils, was one of the first college bands to record. That early record was of the tune "Swap Fire."

This is followed by another flashback of Brown and his band playing his biggest hit, "Sentimental Journey." This sequence is set on a train. The blonde who sings the number is uncredited, and her rendition does not measure up to Doris Day's original interpretation. At the song's end, we return to Block and O'Brien in the studio. During his introduction of the next song, Block makes an awkward transition that leads to Virginia's moment in the song.

After complimenting her smile, Block asks why we never see it on-screen. O'Brien predictably replies that she got into the deadpan on the stage, and that it was now second nature. "We can almost see it on your records, like this one… " is Block's introduction to her recording of "Carry Me Back to Old Virginny".

While her record is playing on the turntable on Block's desk, we see her singing it in a dream sequence. The segment begins when she tells Block how nervous she was on her first day at Metro-Goldwyn-Mayer. She explains to him the song kept running through her mind the night before. "I had the strangest dream," she recalls. "I guess you might call it a nightmare."

The set on which this newly filmed rendition of the song was filmed is decidedly surreal. The night sky with stars' backdrop, white 1920's camera with a crank that turns on its own, empty director's chair with glasses, and megaphone suspended in mid-air is reminiscent of a Salvador Dalí creation. Perhaps the strangest thing of all in Virginia's dream sequence is that her song has nothing to do with Les Brown.

In 1948, Virginia recorded with arranger-conductor Victor Young. The joint session produced two songs on *Decca's Personality* series. The record was reviewed favorably in the July 31, 1948 issue of *The Cash Box* magazine. "More novelty wax, with thrush Virginia O'Brien, of movie fame on deck for the vocal offering," the uncredited review began. "Both sides, styled with a western kick, show the gal in stock phrases that satisfy."

Ciro's nightclub in Hollywood was the host of a fundraiser on the night of November 17, 1949. The United Hostesses were donating all of the evenings proceeds to the Blue Baby Fund. The fund helped the children of WWII veterans. The *Los Angeles Times* reported that "such luminaries as Victor Borge, Betty Garrett, and Virginia O'Brien were donating their talent."

A news item from the UK appeared in the *Barrier Daily Truth* of New South Wales on December 16, 1948. This was the report that Virginia had appeared on the BBC's *In Town Tonight* radio program during her engagement at the London Casino. Readers learned that Virginia had "stumbled on to" the asset of her frozen-faced delivery. Prior to that she had planned to go into law, following in the footsteps of her father. Singing was merely a hobby until the audition for *Meet the People*. Virginia "engagingly" told listeners another variation of her discovery:

> "I got ready to launch into a hot number, but as soon as I opened my mouth to sing,
>
> I became terrified and just froze. I stood there like a rock and sang with a frozen face. My teacher was so struck with the novelty of it that he made me study control of the facial muscles so as to cultivate the style—and when I tried out for the stage revue *Meet the People* in 1939, I'm told my sphinx-like face caused quite a sensation."

Released in 1948, the A side of Decca #24304 was "Dude Ranch Serenade." Summed up in the review as, "Makes for loads of laughs throughout, with Virginia in a well-deserved vocal spotlight." The B side tune was "Wrong Train," a song in which, Virginia tells of the squabbles she gets into when she takes the wrong train. The reviewer from *Cash Box* found the product, cute as a bug, and encouraged producers to look at Virginia as a potential coin culler for the music ops.

1949 would be the year Virginia made her television debut. On March 1st of 1949, Virginia appeared on the popular television show the *Texaco Star Theater*. The show's star, Milton Berle, had recently returned after recovering from nervous exhaustion. The other guests that evening including the acrobats known as The Gauchos, comedian Billy Gilbert, Pat Rooney Sr., and Robert Alda. Two years after this broadcast, Alda and Pat Rooney Sr. appeared together in the Broadway musical *Guys & Dolls*.

Robert Alda is best known today as the father of actor Alan Alda. He sang that night, and then joined Berle in a sketch about the foreign legion. Berle and Billy Gilbert did a comedy routine. Virginia sang

"Go to Sleep My Baby," and also played a role in a parody of movie making in Hollywood. A song and dance performed by Berle and Rooney closed the show. Virginia and Robert Alda would work together again at the end of 1949.

"One day last September, Peter Lorre shook the hand of a wounded veteran, bed-ridden in a San Francisco's hospital," began an AP article in the March 21, 1949 issue of Indiana's *Rushville Republican*. With this visit, Lorre initiated a tour of veteran's hospitals undertaken by fifty film stars. The purpose of the tour was to have the stars sit and talk with veterans who were too ill to leave their beds. Virginia, having overcome her fear of hospitals, was on the tour along with Eddie Cantor, Dinah Shore, and Dick Haymes. Clifton Webb served as singer Dorothy Kirsten's master of ceremonies.

In April of 1949, Virginia would become the first in a series of "big name" performers working at the Sundown Club in Phoenix. Her one-week engagement was announced in the *Arizona Republic* on April 13, 1949. She would be performing there on her 30th birthday (April 18th).

Students at Moberly Junior College were entertained by a number of Hollywood celebrities at their annual MJC banquet for juniors and seniors.

During the summer months of 1949, Virginia went on a brief tour unlike any she had been on before. Along with her husband, she took part in the Movie Star World Series. Between June 19th and July 20th, up to forty stars played baseball to raise funds for the City of Hope Hospital in Duarte, California. The opposing teams were named for the drama and comedy masks. Victor Mature was the captain of the Tragedians. Bob Hope led the Comedians.

The goal was to raise $7,500,000 to build a new 700 bed unit at the "… non-sectarian institution [that] treats a variety of diseases—tuberculosis, cancer, heart disease…." The *Philadelphia Inquirer* dated June 26, 1949, ran an article that summed up the proceedings:

"Forty of Hollywood's top stars will play a night softball game at Shibe Park on July 13. Such stars as Zachary Scott, James Craig, Jack Carson, Bill Demarest, Keenan Wynn, and Eddie Bracken will be in the game. Glamour girls like Virginia Mayo, Gloria DeHaven, Jane Russell, Virginia O'Brien will function as "batboys" in costumes especially designed by Edith Head, Hollywood designer."

While these were amateur games, the *Philadelphia Inquirer* also pointed out the dangers. At the opening game, a future US President was injured "... Ronald Reagan suffered multiple fractures of the right hip sliding into first base. Reagan went into a traction cast for at least six weeks." Evidently, Kirk "Superman" Alyn, as the press referred to him, made it through tour without any injuries. Kirk's friend Bill "Hopalong Cassidy" Boyd umpired a game at Cleveland Park. Virginia was also joined by a friend, "... glamorous Kathryn Grayson" who was a fellow "batboy."

Kirk Alyn, Virginia O'Brien, William Boyd, Albert Dekker, and Grace Bradley Boyd choose sides before the 1949 Movie Stars World Series charity game at Wrigley Field.

Terri O'Brien traveled with her parents by train for the Movie Star World Series games. Her fondest memory is when Hopalong put his huge white cowboy hat on her head. This happened during their visit to New York City. Cowboys were her heroes. She loved playing cowboy, and remembers using the "lasso" she made in the living room of the O'Brien's Los Angeles home.

"Movie Stars Set For Wacky Game In Cleveland Park" was the headline of a brief article in the July 7, 1949 issue of the *News Journal*. The paper promised a game that "won't be like any athletic contest seen before in these parts...." The male stars at this stop in the tour included James Craig, Sonny Tufts, and Peter Lawford. Here the ladies were referred as "bat girls." O'Brien and Grayson were there along with Celeste Holm. Umpire Cassidy showed up with "his two trusty six shooters and rarin' for action." A young starlet named Marilyn Monroe went unnoticed in the press for the series.

"Movie Star Day" was held on July 11th in Akron, Ohio. This was a break from baseball as the stars accompanied sixty-two members of the Pittsburgh Models Club to Ascot Park. This was part of the eight races in the Pittsburgh Models Day Purse. Attending the luncheon at the Ascot Park club house with Virginia were Bill Boyd, Phillip Reed, Donald O'Connor, and Laura Elliot. The event was duly reported in the *Pittsburgh Press* on July 10, 1949.

When the stars played in Boston, they were hosted for a weekend by Ben Wolf and Harry Siegal. This weekend at the seashore was reported in the July 30, 1949 issue of the *Showman's Trade Review*. There were 30 stars in the group, who on July 18th went to the Paddock Club at Suffolk Downs. Hopalong Cassidy tossed hundreds of his lucky coins to fans. Aside from Virginia, other stars included ice skater, Belita, and Virginia Mayo. When the Movie Star World Series ended, Virginia returned to Los Angeles and a new theatrical experience.

The famous Turnabout Theatre produced shows in Hollywood

from 1941 to 1956. Performances there were regularly sold out, as the shows were popular with the general public. Top Hollywood stars were also among the loyal supporters. The shows consisted of a marionette performance in the first half. A stage revue, featuring actors, was presented after the intermission. Famous talents were featured in the revue, actress Elsa Lanchester being the most popular. The folk singer Odetta was another audience favorite.

The Turnabout sprang from a group called the Yale Puppeteers. Some of the puppets had appeared in the 1933 film *I Am Suzanne*. The name of the theatre came from audiences standing, and then "turning about," to see the second half of the show. This required a theatre with a stage at either end. That theatre was located at 716 North La Cienega Boulevard. Another distinction were the seats. Adjacent seats were humorously labeled Hot 'n Bothered, Salt 'n Pepper, etc.

"Virginia O'Brien Cleverly Entertains at Turnabout" was the title of a *Los Angeles Times* article in the August 2, 1949 issue. . Virginia was appearing in) Foreman Brown's revue *On Second Thoughts*. The writer, credited only as G.K., likens her to the lovely Colleen the Irish poets rave about. G.K. continues his own rave review:

> "Virginia is a brilliantly clever chanteuse, as well as beautiful to look at. Not sentimental Irish ditties, oh, no. She has a unique gift: she can put over in her "art-less way" a hard, burlesque number with demure ladylike delicacy."

Turnabout audiences were treated to "Say That We're Sweethearts Again" from the film version of *Meet the People*. Next, G.K. writes of a "spy number" in which Virginia is hanging close on the line. "Spying is an awful mess," she pans after dreaming that she is the femme fatale spy, Mata Hari. In reality, she is doing laundry for "Molotov and the other Russian boys."

**Photograph used to publicize Virginia's
1949 appearance at the Turnabout Theatre.**

Another song tells of her boyfriend, and how friendly he is to her girlfriend. He is a little too friendly. After she breaks up with him, he marries the other woman. The tag line to this common tell is, "Now that they have settled down, he often drops around to see how friendly he can get with me." The critic found the revue lives up to its star or beyond.

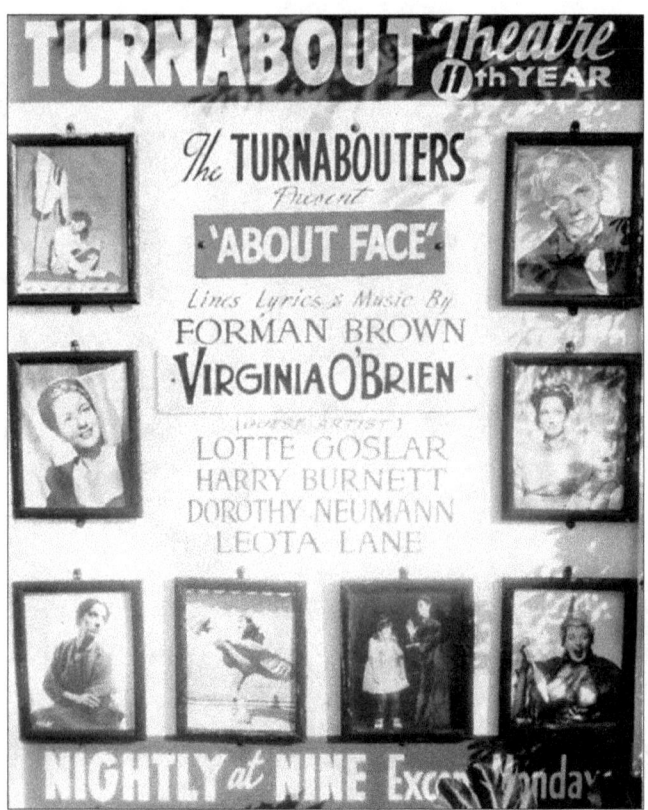

Window display at the Turnabout Theatre
featured Virginia's photograph.

An ad in *Radio Daily* magazine dated August 1949 for the Minifilms corporation, featured the wild-eyed, mustachioed comedian Jerry Colonna. The ad promoted a TV production titled *Big Time* starring Colonna. "Hollywood's first top-flight all-star television variety show," was filmed in the KLAC-TV "Cinemascope" technique. The date of the broadcast is not included. Directing was Le Roy Prinz, who was a musical production director at Warner Brothers. Colonna's guests were Robert Alda and Virginia.

Vaudeville was thriving in 1919, the year of Virginia's birth. Thirty years later, it was considered to be dead, and Los Angeles was given credit as the town that killed it via the movies. On September 1, 1949, it was revived at The Orpheum Theater in Los Angeles. Former vaudeville headliners were in the audience for the opening night. Among them were Lionel Belmore, Vera Lewis, Kingsley Benedict, Virginia Pearson, and Sheldon Lewis. The Orpheum Theater had announced a new policy of four vaudeville performances daily. Virginia was the headliner of the premiere show. All of this was reported in the *Oakland Tribune* on September 2, 1949. The music was provided by Rene Williams and the Orpheum Orchestra. Among the other acts joining Virginia were the DeHavilland Trio, Joey Rardin, and the Wiere Brothers.

Also in September of 1949 was the rebroadcast of Virginia's appearance on the BBC radio program *In Town Tonight*. To promote it, a lengthier version of the article from the December 16, 1948 *Barrier Daily Truth* was published in the September, 21 1949 issue of the *Daily Examiner* of New South Wales. This included a new closing paragraph about the Hollywood mogul who saw Virginia in *Meet the People*:

> "Everyone knew Louis B. Mayer, head of M-G-M was in the audience and worked like mad to impress him. With the exception of Virginia O'Brien, who did not much want a stage or film career, hence did not set out to impress. As luck would have it, she outshone her colleagues in Mr. Mayer's eyes and was plunged willy-nilly into Hollywood, which has made her one of its most popular musical-comedienne film stars."

A benefit show and dance was to be held at the clubhouse at Santa Anita Park. The fundraiser was sponsored by actress Janet Leigh to raise money for the Le Roy's Boys Home in La Verne, California. The *Los Angeles Times* reported that on Saturday October 15, 1949, Leigh would perform in an "entertainment production" along with Joy Hodges, Pamela Britton, Virginia O'Brien, and Robert Mitchum.

Christmas always found Virginia performing. On Friday December 9, 1949, she was on the roster with several stars for the Children's Christmas Party. The party, which was hosted by "Sherman Oaks business people," included a Ferris wheel, auto rides, free candy, and a theatre show. In the theatre show, Virginia was joined by Robert Alda, Don "Red" Barry, Tom Drake, Ellen Drew, Jack Oakie, and Stan Laurel of Laurel and Hardy.

Comic Ed Wynn had a career that started in vaudeville. He had been popular in the theatre, films, and radio. Now, like other comedians of his time, he was on television. *The Ed Wynn Show* broadcast on December 22, 1949, had two other great comics as guests, Buster Keaton and Billy Gilbert.

In the audience that night, observing the show from their balcony seats, were Virginia's friends Lucille Ball and Desi Arnaz. Two weeks later, Lucy and Desi were Wynn's guest. It's possible that Arnaz was studying how Wynn's show was filmed. Later he would apply that knowledge to the production of *I Love Lucy*.

After her appearance on *The Ed Wynn Show*, Virginia took some time off. She had good reason for doing so, as she was expecting her second child. Christmas came early in the Alyn household. On December 5, 1950, Virginia became a mother for the second time. She and Kirk had another daughter, and Terri was a big sister. The baby girl was christened Elizabeth.

Incredible as it may seem, Virginia returned to work before the end of December. *The Saturday Night Revue* was hosted by comedian Jack Carter. On the Christmas Eve broadcast of 1950, Carter welcomed the great character actor Charles Coburn and Virginia as his guests. The song, or songs, Virginia performed that night are unknown.

In March, Virginia returned to television for what would be her first teleplay. She starred in "Love Comes Stealing" by Olive Kelsay on the *Hollywood Theater*. Her role was that of a spoiled rich girl. Her love interest is an architect who has a strong dislike for rich girls. The show was broadcast on March 26 and 30, 1950.

In April of 1950, the possibility of Virginia returning to the silver screen was announced. Newspapers printed a brief blurb where she talked about the character she was being tested for: "A batty character if ever there was one. But it's a change of pace for me and I'd love to do it." That film was *Harvey*. Jimmy Stewart was starring in the lead role of Elwood P. Dowd, the charming gentleman whose best friend is a six-foot tall invisible white rabbit named Harvey. *Harvey* had been a huge success on Broadway, breathing new life into the career of Barbara Stanwyck's one-time husband, Frank Fay.

Only three years had passed since Virginia's last film, but three years was all it took to have a newspaper photograph captioned, "Remember her? She's funny Virginia O'Brien, deadpan songstress, seen with her husband, Kirk Alyn." The photograph appeared in newspapers, including *The Cincinnati Enquirer*, on July 9, 1950. One can only imagine how Virginia must have felt. If she was hurt, she never let on. By this point in her life, she had certainly survived the highs and lows of show business.

From the end of 1950 to August of 1953, Virginia and Kirk lived in New York. One reason for the move was Virginia's semi-regular appearances on *The Ken Murray Show*. Murray's Saturday show was broadcast on CBS. Virginia joined the show on five documented episodes. If there were additional visits, those broadcast dates are unknown. Before starting her visits to Ken Murray's show, Virginia and Jackie Copper were guest panelists on the March 8, 1952 broadcast of *Celebrity Time*. The topic that evening was great paintings and sculptures.

Erskine Johnson, who wrote the syndicated "In Hollywood" column, mentioned Virginia's plans for the future on April 30, 1951. "Behind the Screen: Virginia O'Brien, the dead-pan thrush," he began, "… has turned over the nursery to a governess, changed agents and is ready to resume her movie career." Said resumption wouldn't take place for another four years.

The Santa Monica Ballroom was the location of "L.A.'s Top TV Show." On Saturday nights, musician and orchestra leader Spade Cooley's show was televised at 8:30 and 9:30pm on KTLA channel 5. The ballroom had a seating capacity of one thousand. Cooley's guests on May 5, 1951 were Virginia and Rudy Vallee.

Her first installment of *The Ken Murray Show* was seen on March 8, 1952. Robert Sterling, a name from Virginia's days at MGM, was a guest. Virginia must have had fun with her "musical visit to a Mexican bullring." Joining her for that number were trumpeter Rafael Mendez and flamenco dancer Trini Reyes. Ole!

On March 22, 1952, Ken Murray and Virginia welcomed guests silent screen heartthrob Ramon Navarro, actress Coleen Gray, ice-skater-movie-star Sonja Heinie, and current heartthrob Tony Curtis. The following Saturday, March 29th, Virginia returned to join John Barrymore Jr., Maria Riva (Marlene Dietrich's daughter), and cartoonist Al Capp. Joining them was the composer of "The Tennessee Waltz," Pee Wee King.

On April 1, 1952, there was a change of pace. Murry still acted as the host, but the event was the *Parade of Stars Auto Show*. This was the first broadcast of an annual show. The sponsor was Auto-Lite. The program was live from the Waldorf-Astoria Hotel on WCBS at 9:30pm. The website tv.com calls the show a "... glitch-ridden telecast." In addition to Ken Murry and Virginia, viewers were treated to model Laurie Anders on horseback, and whistler Minda Lang. One wonders whether the high spot was the whistling, or Ken Murray's chat with Auto-Lite president Royce G. Martin. **more**Virginia's last appearance with Ken Murray was on April 26, 1952. For that show, she was joined by her co-star from *The Harvey Girls*, Angela Lansbury. Murray also welcomed actor Bob Cummings and Hawthorne's Bears.

While she was living in New York, Virginia's mother passed away on April 16th, 1952. Edna's brief obituary was published in the *Fresno Bee*. A lengthier version appeared on April 18, 1952 in the *Los Angeles Times* as follows:

> "Funeral services for Mrs. Edna Lee O'Brien, 65, mother of actress Virginia O'Brien, will be conducted tomorrow at noon in the Little Church of the Flowers, Forest Lawn Mortuary arranging, with internment in Forest Lawn Memorial Park. Mrs. O'Brien died Wednesday. She lived at 12036 Laurel Terrace, North Hollywood. Besides her daughter she leaves husband, Thomas F.; two other daughters, Mary, film actress, and Mrs. Fran Sande*; a sister Mrs. Rubey Bacon, and two grandchildren."

The fact that her mother's service was held on her thirty-third birthday must have saddened Virginia greatly. She was unable to attend the funeral. Four months later, the family returned to the West Coast.

> [* Author's note: Virginia's sister Fran was married to character actor Walter Sande (pronounced San-dee). *Halliwell's Who's Who in the Movies* includes the following on Sande: "(1906–1972) American character actor, usually a background heavy." Some of his credits are *To Have and Have Not* 1944, *Dark City* 1950, *Bad Day at Black Rock* 1955 and *The Gallant Hours* 1960. He also appeared on the television version of *Tugboat Annie* in 1956.]

November 1952 found Virginia making appearances on the stage and television. On November 4th, Virginia and "… and actor-husband, Kirk Alyn, filmland Superman" were seen on *Everywhere I Go* hosted by Dan Seymour. Her appearance at the Triton club and restaurant on New York City's Main Street East was more substantial. Billed as "The beautiful movie star famous as the "dead pan" singer. Scintillating comedienne," she played two shows nightly from November 10th through November 17th, 1952.

Before she left New York City, columnist Earl Wilson overheard Virginia saying, "In small towns most girls over 21 are spoken for. On Broadway, most of 'em are spoken about." Wilson printed this quote from Virginia as his "Wish I'd Said That" item. Newspapers carried it on February 22, 1953.

The famous Steel Pier in Atlantic City hosted many entertainers, including Virginia. Author's collection.

Atlantic City's Steel Pier was famous for the wide variety of entertainers it hosted. The *Altoona Tribune* dated July 14, 1953, boosted the upcoming engagements of Louis Prima and his orchestra, as well the Ray Anthony and his bandsmen. From July 19 to July 25, the gala stage show starred Virginia. She was sharing the bill with "comedy favorite" Jackie Miles.

During one of many interviews with Terri O'Brien, she told the author of her fond memories of the Steel Pier. Standing in the wings, she watched her mother perform every night. During the day, her favorite activity was watching the pier's legendary High Diving Horses.

On August 25, 1953, Virginia's longtime supporter Louella Parsons reported the following: "Virginia O'Brien, who, with her husband, Kirk Alyn and the two children, had been living in New York for two years, telephoned to say they are back home. Virginia expects her third child very soon. Very soon was September 14, 1953. Two days later local papers announced, "Virginia O'Brien and Kirk Alyn are very happy over the arrival of a baby boy. They already have two little daughters." Theresa and Elizabeth's baby brother was named John. He was born at Virginia's hospital of choice, St. John's in Santa Monica.

Virginia next appeared as "A special added attraction … Direct from Hollywood" on the April 16, 1953 television show *The Stars of Broadway Open House*. The headliner was "Popular Comedy Star of Television," Jan Murray. This program was broadcast from the Skouras Academy of Music, located on 14th Street in New York City. Nearly a year went by before she made another television appearance.

On March 15, 1954, Virginia visited *The Betty White Show*. Only the broadcast date is known. Television websites give no information as to the song, if any, Virginia performed. Most likely, this live broadcast consisted of a chat with the congenial hostess. Surviving footage of White's show can be seen on YouTube. It is possible that Virginia's appearance is yet to be unearthed.

"Irish Nightingale" read the caption beneath a photograph of Virginia in the March 15, 1955 edition of the *Bakersfield Californian*. On the 16th, she would "serenade the Trade Club for a St. Patrick's Day show at the Bakersfield fairgrounds."

Virginia and Kirk Alyn attend the opening of The Cruel Months at the North Hollywood Playhouse in November of 1954. Left to right: Lee Roberts, Mrs. Lyle Talbot, Lyle Talbot, Virginia, Kirk, Bill Fawcett, Mrs. Bill Fawcett, Joanne Rio and Dick Patton. Miss Rio was said to be Liberace's fiancée. That romance was probably shorter than the run of The Cruel Months which closed in three days. Photo courtesy of Terri O'Brien.

The first mention of Virginia's return to movies was published in Harold V. Cohen's "The Drama Desk" column in the March 19, 1955 issue of various newspapers. Cohen reported, "Virginia O'Brien ... who has been away from the screen for several years, has been set for a role with Donald O'Connor in *Francis in the Navy* for Universal-International."

In another blurb, her role was described as that of a WAVE who would escort O'Connor through a naval hospital "psycho ward." The role was not as important, or as serious as it sounds. The picture would not be released for five months. In the meantime, there was a difficult issue to contend with in her private life.

In a town known for divorces, the twelve-year marriage of Kirk Alyn and Virginia O'Brien had lasted much longer than most. On June 25, 1955, the news of their divorce was reported nationwide. Most papers, like the *Long Beach Independent*, with its question, "Where's That Stony Face?" took a light approach. The photo of Virginia in that paper was captioned "She Can, Too, Smile."

Smiling for photographers after winning her divorce from Kirk Alyn. Courtesy of Terri. O'Brien.

After her divorce, brighter news came on August 24, 1955 with the release of *Francis in the Navy*. Beginning in 1950 with *Francis* (also known as *Francis the Talking Mule*), and ending in 1956, there were seven films in the popular series. The sixth entry, *Francis in the Navy*, almost didn't get made. Star Donald O'Connor had enough of playing the character Peter Stirling.

At the request of his daughter, O'Connor returned for his final movie with the talking mule. One interesting bit of trivia about *Francis in the Navy*, is that it was Clint Eastwood's first credited screen role (he played "Jonesy").

Virginia puckers up for Donald O'Connor in *Francis in the Navy* (1955).

This was Virginia's first screen appearance since 1947's *Merton of the Movies*. As Nurse Kittredge, Virginia was one of three nurses in a row who kissed Donald O'Connor. Virginia's is the longest, and funniest, of the three. However, she did not get the opportunity to do what she did best … sing. She would get to do that at her next live engagement.

Chapter Eight, Part Two: Benefits, Nightclubs, and Television

Virginia's Trapshoot Specialty? If she didn't actually shoot, she was there. The event took place at Harold's Trapshooting Country Club in "The Biggest Little City on Earth," Reno, Nevada. One hundred marksmen participated, and producer George Moro presented a specialty number titled "Pull, Pull," featuring the Riverside Starlets.

This opening night performance took place on Thanksgiving evening in 1955. On Saturday the 26th of November, the proceedings where covered in the *Reno Gazette-Journal*. Accompanying the article was a photo of Virginia, her hair noticeably shorter than during her MGM years. She is surrounded by four young men, The 4 Stags, the dancing act. The audience responded enthusiastically:

> "They applauded the ['Pull, Pull'] number. and then gave Virginia O'Brien, Professor Backwards, and Les Marcellis little short of ovations as they completed their acts."

The article went on to mention that the audience knew "veteran trouper" Virginia from her films and television appearances. Special mention was made of her "Wabash Blues" number. The numbers she made famous caught the fancy of the holiday minded audience. The 4 Stags were cheered for working smoothly with the star. Another review, published on November 27 in the *Nevada State Journal*, concluded with, "... she sparkles particularly on some of her old favorites, like 'A Bird in a Gilded Cage.'" With this successful engagement, 1955 came to an end.

In February 1956, Virginia returned to a familiar scene. She was performing at another annual police ball. Music was provided by bandleader and radio star, Skinnay Ennis. The evening reunited Virginia with The Stags (formerly The 4 Stags), who appeared with her at the Riverside Casino in November of 1955. The event was a benefit for the San Bernardino Police Department.

Among the popular sounds of 1956 was the music of Alvino Rey. A native of Oakland California, Rey was referred to as the "of the pedal steel guitar." Evidently, it was a sound that Virginia liked. She was actually seen smiling on his April 1956 opening night at a club called The Shalimar on Ventura Boulevard, reported Dave W. Himlin in his "Valley Ramblings" column, the blurb appearing in the *Van Nuys Valley News* on April 19, 1956.

The following day, April 20th, Virginia was among several stars who bid farewell to the Turnabout Theater. The theater where she made a successful appearance in August of 1949. After 15 years and 4,535 performances, the theater was closing. Journalist Aline Mosby wrote on that day "... the Turnabout owners came to the belated conclusion that Los Angeles isn't a good theater town. So the company is moving—lock, stock and even its quaint streetcar seats—to the traditionally more cultural San Francisco." Other Turnabout alum joining Virginia that day were Elsa Lancaster, Gilda Gray, Queenie Leonard, and the Duncan Sisters.

In May of 1956, Virginia's photograph appeared in numerous US newspapers. The bold headline read "L.A. From N.Y. In 59 Hours." The caption better describes exactly what was going on: "Actress Virginia O'Brien looks surprised and Tom Clark looks happy as he sits in his Renault in Los Angeles after a drive of 59 hours, 12 minutes from New York with his wife." Virginia, standing outside the driver's window, was planting a kiss on the record-breaking driver. Clark and his wife returned to New York in a safer 120 hours.

"Virginia O'Brien to Headline New Show in Chi Chi's Starlite Room," read the headline below Virginia's photo in the May 29, 1956 issue of the *Desert Sun*. Chi Chi was a popular nightspot in Palm Springs, and the club became a home base for Virginia, where she continued to perform into the 1970's. The article referred to Virginia as the "outstanding singing comedienne of stage, screen, and television."

The MGM films listed here were *Ship Ahoy*, *The Harvey Girls*, and *Till the Clouds Roll By*. Virginia was the headliner at the Chi Chi. Appearing with her to round out the evening's entertainment were "sure audience pleaser" comedian Buddy Lewis, and one Jacqueline Hurley, who had "America's most unusual acrobatic act."

A 1956 publicity photo for nightclub appearances showed off Virginia's new hairstyle. Author's collection.

In July of 1956, Virginia returned to the stage at one of Los Angeles' fabled nightclubs on the Sunset Strip. From July 7th through July 12th, she performed at Ciro's. She shared the stage with the Bobby Ramos' Rhumba Band and the Mischa Novy Orchestra. In 1956, a seven-course dinner at Ciro's started at $3.45. There was no cover charge for the show.

Phoenix welcomed Virginia for the first time in six years. She last performed there at the Sundown Club in 1949. Now she was opening an eight-day engagement at KoKo. Phoenix newspapers reported on August 22, 1956: "… Many will remember her in such films as *Panama Hattie, Du Barry Was a Lady, Ziegfeld Follies*, and *The Harvey Girls.*" Sharing the bill for the run was a trio of singers who called themselves "Day, Dawn and Dusk."

From Phoenix, Virginia traveled to Walla Walla for the New Southeastern Washington Fair. Her appearance there took place on August 30th. On this "Family Night" at the fair, she was the first entertainer in the "Television Personalities of 1956" series. As a "sensational television star," she was accompanied by the Claude Gordon Band.

In September of 1956, Virginia was reunited with her co-star from *Ringside Maisie* and *Panama Hattie*, Ann Sothern. Sothern had joined the ranks of film stars who made a successful transition to television. Her show *Private Secretary* ran from 1953 to 1957. Ann played Susie McNamara, the private secretary of Peter Sands, played by Don Porter.

The episode that brought Virginia and Ann together again was appropriately titled "The Reunion." Virginia is Tootie Stevens Walters, one of three classmates who get together with Susie. The other high school friends are played by June Vincent as Lucille Applegate Carter, and Gloria McGhee as Mary Lou Daley. Together they convince Susie that she is a social failure. In turn, Susie tries to straighten out their lives. Of course, everything is happily resolved.

Virginia's successful engagement at Chi Chi's in May was repeated when she returned to the club in September. Again, a beautiful photograph of her accompanied an article in the *Desert Sun*. The September 22, 1956 article was titled, "Two Headliners Returning to the Chi Chi Sunday." The other act on the bill was the Salmas Brothers. The brothers had launched their act at the Palm Springs club in 1955. On opening night, they were called back for five encores. Details about Virginia included the following: "She has appeared on leading TV shows, including *Ed Sullivan, Steve Allen, Perry Como, Milton Berle* and *Bandstand Revue*."

Her guest spot on Ann Sothern's show was followed by one of her more unusual television credits. *Northwest Home* was broadcast from Oregon. *TV Guides* dated October 9, 1956 summarized that days show as "A fashion show featuring shoes to fit any occasion." The host is identified only as Barbara. "Nightclub entertainer Virginia O'Brien," was Barbara's featured guest.

Virginia's next appearance would be at Ciro's on the Sunset Strip. She would perform there for a special luncheon with the theme of "Fashions on a Holiday." The event was presented on Saturday November 17th by the California Federation of Women's Clubs Junior Membership. The *Van Nuys News* dated November 15, 1956, included an article title "Ciro's Fete for Juniors to Show Holiday Styles," which informed readers that actor Michael O'Shea would be the commentator. Virginia would be backed by George Poole and his combo.

In 1944, Virginia had joined voices with Frances Langford and Ginny Simms on the Christmastime broadcast of *Command Performance*. On November 28, 1956, *The Desert Sun* featured photographs of the three singers at the Starlight Room of the Chi Chi club in Palm Springs. Frances and Virginia were there for Ginny Simms opening night. Langford was photographed with Bob Hope. The photo of Virginia had comedian Morey Amsterdam at her side. This was the event of the season, preceded by a cocktail party for 200 guests at Simms' home in Mesquite.

Christmas continued to be the time when Virginia would appear at events, especially those that involved children. In 1956, the Santa's Toy Clinic opened with a "Parade of Stars" on Ventura Boulevard in Encino, California. Other stars joining Virginia in the parade included Adele Jergens, Lori Nelson, Lt. Rip Master (of the *Rin Tin Tin* television series), and Johnny Carson. Virginia cut the ribbon that officially opened the clinic.

In the December 12, 1956 edition of the *Valley News Sun* Jewell Johnston praised Virginia's dedication: "Not only did Miss O'Brien sing and dance, but she helped entertain the children at the tables while they were eating, seeing that each had plenty of food and seconds if they were needed." This was not the only volunteer work that Virginia participated in during the Christmas season of 1956.

Once again, the *Valley News Sun* reported Virginia's generosity in the December 23rd issue. Santa Claus appears in a photograph along with a huge group of children seated at tables. This event was the "... annual Sepulveda Optimist Club-sponsored Yule party for handicapped and otherwise underprivileged children." The dinner was donated by the hosting Rafters Restaurant. This evening brought 1956 to a close.

Television viewers caught Virginia's appearance in color on *Club Sixty* on March 1, 1957. This would be her first television show broadcast in color. *Club Sixty* was hosted by Paul Gray, a humorist guaranteed to "... satisfy the most critical observer." Singers appearing on *Club Sixty* were backed by Joe Gallicchio and the NBC orchestra. By March 4 of 1957, she was appearing at the Town & Country nightclub in St. Louis. The club was located in the Congress Hotel. Billed as "That Famous Deadpan Comedienne," Virginia had a successful engagement that ended on March 10th.

The Embassy Room at the Ambassador Hotel in Los Angeles hosted a luncheon on April 9, 1957. The event was a meeting of the Junior Auxiliary of the Los Angeles Jewish Home for the Aged.

Joining Virginia to entertain that afternoon were Joan Blondell and Louise Beavers. There was a special connection her for Virginia, as the auxiliary president was the sister of L.B. Mayer, Ida Mayer Cummings.

Virginia participated in many fundraisers for the City of Hope Medical Center over the years. One such benefit was the Masquerade Ball of 1957. The ball was hosted by the City of Hope Panorama Chapter on November 9, 1957. The *Van Nuys* newspaper reported on November 7th that the "Highlight of the evening will be the appearances of several movie and television stars, among whom will be Virginia O'Brien."

In 1958, Virginia married for the second time. Her new husband was Vern Evans. Their marriage was mentioned in a brief blurb that appeared in newspapers nationwide during the last week of January 1958. One such paper was *The Monroe News Star*. "Virginia O'Brien, who made her fame as a frozenpuss singer, unfroze long enough to say yes to Verne Evans, an airplane firm official. They'll waltz down the aisle on June 9."

The first report that the couple was expecting a baby was announced in a surprising way on April 11, 1958. Mike Connolly's syndicated Hollywood column reported on an engagement Virginia had to fulfill during her pregnancy.

Connolly wrote, "It's a hard, hard world when a fairly well-known star like Virginia O'Brien has to travel 1500 miles from Hollywood to play a saloon stand (the Cave Club in Vancouver, B.C.) when she's seven months pregnant. The management disapproved of her appearance, so all hands agreed to cancel half of Virginia's two-week date at the spot (besides, it was Lent and business was lousy!)."

On June 25th of 1958, Virginia gave birth to her fourth child. The couple had a girl named Gale. The baby was named after actress Gale Storm. In 1982, when Gale was 24 years old, she would proudly pose next to her mother for a photograph. The photo was published in the eighth book of Richard Lamperski's *Whatever became of...?* series.

Virginia took some time off after Gale's birth. As it turned out, she would need her strength when her father suffered his second heart attack.

"Tom F. O'Brien, 77, known as the nemesis of the pickpocket during his tenure as a Los Angeles Police Department captain…," the November 27, 1958 *Los Angeles Times* article began. He was stricken at his home at 12036 Laurel Terrace. His famous daughter was mentioned, as was his passing of the State Bar in 1930. He recovered at Sherman Oaks Hospital. Life continued for the O'Brien family, and "Honest Tom" got to spend some time with his new granddaughter, albeit brief.

Virginia was among a group of entertainers including the singing groups The Albins, and The Petites who, backed by the Bill Regis Orchestra, appeared at the "… long-awaited opening of the Red Hill Tennis Club." The debut of the club was celebrated with two nights of dinner, dancing, and performances. The gala was reported in the *Tustin News* on June 4, 1959.

The years since her release from MGM had not been easy. Like any "trouper," she took what she could find. Comedian George Jessel became something of a champion for Virginia in 1959-60. On May 3rd, she guested on his television show along with Mona Freeman, Lia de Leo, and Walter Lantz. On September 15, 1959, she shared the bill with George Jessel and Dean Jones at Billy Gray's Band Box. This was a one-night-only performance. She would see Jessel again in four months. Another visit to Jessel's TV show came on November 21, 1959. The other guests on that occasion were columnist Cobina Wright and actress Elaine Edwards.

At the end of 1959, Virginia again took part in a program for the Los Angeles Jewish Home for the Aged. This would be the "Festival of Lights" at the Beverly Hilton. Others who participated in the program for the aides who worked at the home included singer Mike Mason, Reed Hadley, and Tamara Toumanova.

On January 9, 1960, Virginia returned as a guest on *The George Jessel Show*. Jessel's other guests included singer Jack Smith, Lady Lawford, and actress Maria Palmer. Comedian Jessel was a fixture in showbiz circles. The comedian started his career in vaudeville. This broadcast was not reviewed, and Virginia's song selection is not known. Also on January 9, 1960, the following appeared in the entertainment columns of newspapers nationwide. "Remember Virginia O'Brien, MGM's wartime pretty-stoneface? Her daughter Terry's one of the "Pretty Kittens" at the Fremont Hotel, Las Vegas." The truth is, she was the leader of the Pretty Kittens. Virginia's eldest daughter, Terry (who now goes by Terri), was beginning to make a name for herself.

Thomas F. O'Brien passed away on January 16th. The *Los Angeles Times* ran the 77-year-old deputy district attorney and police captain's obituary on January 20, 1959. There was a military service at his Calvary Cemetery graveside. He was survived by four daughters, a son, a brother, 14 grandchildren, and 18 great-grandchildren.

Comedian Doodles Weaver is known today as the uncle of actress Sigourney Weaver. Between 1936 and 1981, Weaver appeared in more than 140 films and television shows. One of his Broadway credits was *Meet the People*, the same revue that launched Virginia's career in Los Angeles. The live version of *The Doodles Weaver Show* played at Larry Potter's Supper Club in 1959. The *Los Angeles Times* reported on February 21, 1959 that Weaver was inaugurating a new entertainment policy. The show featured Weaver's orchestra. As emcee, he would be welcoming the Ink Spots, the Lancers, Mel Torme, Jacqueline Fontaine, and Virginia.

For her next professional engagement, Virginia was the featured performer in a show titled, *Showgirls of 1960*. She joined the cast in February of 1960 while they were performing at the Statler Hilton's Terrace Room. This was announced in the *Los Angeles Times* on February 13th, which stated that Virginia was added to "… freshen things up." She would continue to do that when the show moved to a new venue.

At the San Francisco nightclub, Bimbo's, billed as a "Spectacular Extravaganza," it boasted a company of 40. The *San Mateo Times* June 28, 1960 edition called Barry Ashton's show "... the top spectacular ever produced in San Francisco." Virginia's specialty was "The Sleepwalker." It was a job. The show was sold-out nightly, with shows at 8pm, 10:30pm, and 1am. Another dry spell came after it closed.

Democrat Virginia O'Brien was front and center when Democratic National Chairman John M. Bailey attended the FDR Dinner in Beverly Hills. Los Angeles area newspapers reported that Mr. Bailey "laid an egg" at the fundraiser. He made the mistake of following Virginia's act, rather than being the last speaker of the March 1961 event.

"Vive Hollywood" had performances at the Starlight-Hilton's Terrace Room in January of 1963. In his "Night Life" column for the *Los Angeles Times*, Walter Guenther first mentioned the show on January 6th. He reported that the "... variety spoof on filmland" was set to open on Thursday, January 10th. Virginia was the star. She was "... supported by singers Bill Mullikin and Jodi McDowell." Another blurb about the show appeared in local papers on January 20, 1963.

In July of 1963, the City of Hope, also known as Duarte Hospital, celebrated its 50th birthday. Los Angeles television channel KTLA was there on July 9 to broadcast the celebration. Actor Eddie Albert hosted the program, and Virginia was a special guest. The other performers included singers Jennie Smith and Johnny Prophet, and actress Coleen Gray made an appearance.

Hedda Hopper was still writing her column in the 1960's. On October 24, 1963, she wrote of a new audience discovering Virginia for the first time:

> "The film sensation of Stockholm is the old Marx Brothers film *The Big Store*. On opening night after Virginia O'Brien's

"Rock-A-Bye Baby" number, the audience cheered and demanded that the operator run that part of the film again. He did. Most of the teenagers in the audience had never heard of Virginia—they were electrified."

Hedda was one a roll. Her column dated November 5, 1963 carried this note: "I'm laughing now. Virginia O'Brien, Jack Oakie and Patsy Kelly join up for a pilot about ESP. Virginia may do some records to try out her silly deadpan sound on teenagers." It appears that neither idea came to fruition.

Another full year went by before Virginia appeared at the *11th Annual Deb Star Ball*. Broadcast from the Hollywood Palladium on December 22, 1963, the hour-long show was hosted by Gordon and Shelia MacRae. Hans Conried interviewed attendees. Virginia was the guest singer. The debutantes, age 16 to 22, included Raquel Welch. The young ladies were escorted by Bill Bixby, Hugh O'Brian, and Walter Pidgeon.

In 1964, very little was published about Virginia. One minor television appearance came on a show called *Day in Court*, the daytime show only making the TV listings in Los Angeles area papers on June 28, 1964. It was 6 months before her next major nightclub engagement.

"Sans Souci" was the title of a song that Peggy Lee wrote. The phrase is French for "no worries" or "carefree." Virginia had no worries when she appeared at the Lafayette's Sans Souci in Los Angeles. She opened in December of 1964, and closed in January of 1965.

Tedd Thomey's "In Person" column, which appeared in the *Long Beach Independenti*, reviewed the show in the January 15, 1965 issue. "Lucky Accident Creates a Career" was the headline. Thomey wrote of her show at the Lafayette Hotel:

"At the Lafayette's showroom, Virginia is backed by the fast-swinging de Fuentes Brothers on guitar, drums, and piano. She does only a few deadpan comedy numbers during each show, preferring to demonstrate her lusty voice on such songs as "San Francisco" and "Hello, Dolly," which she belts out very beautifully.

Thomey ended with some notes on Virginia's height, "5 feet, 7½," and weight, "140 pounds," and that she jokes with the audience about "the size of her derrière." She blames eating too much during the holidays on the later. He also mentions her marriage to a "space lab engineer," and the ages of her children, "6 to 19."

Based on her fear of horses, it's probably unlikely that Virginia rode in the equestrian ride sponsored by the Agoura Corral. On June 13, 1965, a ride went from the Paramount Movie Ranch to Lake Encanto Park in Cornell, California. That evening, Virginia and singer-actor Randy Boone performed. Boone had recurring roles on three popular TV westerns: Wagon Train, The Virginian, and Cimarron Strip.

Virginia's only known appearance on *The Ed Sullivan Show* took place on November 11, 1965. To say that the entertainers Sullivan gathered that night were eclectic would be an understatement. It would be a reunion with her former MGM co-star, Bert Lahr. Ed's other guests were The Dave Clark 5, Woody Allen, and the Berry Sisters. Chester Morris and Maureen O'Sullivan presented a scene from *The Subject Was Roses*. Backed by "her own rock and roll band," Virginia performed "Ramona."

1966 brought an interesting variety of public appearances at benefits, and political dinners.

April saw Virginia at a fundraiser for the American Cancer Society. The April 24th Les Girls fashion luncheon received press on April 11th and 21st, 1966. Held at the Cocoanut Grove, the event was hosted by Jerry Lewis and Connie Stevens. In addition to Virginia, Dean Jones and Vicki Carr performed that afternoon.

The Van Nuys newspaper, *Valley News*, covered a benefit for the

Junior Ballet Theatre Foundation on May 31, 1966. A photo of Virginia shows her modeling a dinner gown for the event, which took place at the Beverly Hills Crystal Room on June 10th. Under the heading Honorary Chairman, a short paragraph read "Virginia O'Brien, national entertainment personality and honorary event chairman, looks forward to greeting Hon. Gerard Peres, new French consul general in Los Angeles, and Jan Clayton, among others at her celebrity table." Clayton is best remembered for playing the role of Ellen Miller on televisions *Lassie* from 1954 to 1957.

The Film Welfare League was known for its annual Luau Party. Los Angeles papers carried the news that the luau was to be held at the Ambassador Hotel's Club Room on Friday August 28th. Virginia participated as a celebrity hostess and performed later that evening.

California Governor Edmund G. Brown was attending the "Salute to Long Beach." Virginia was one of the entertainers performing at the dinner dance. The *Long Beach Independent* wrote up the event on October 14, 1966. Members of the 39th District danced to the music of the Benny Lorin Orchestra. The Perris Hill setting was familiar, as Virginia had entertained troops there during WWII. Unfortunately, when she was singing "Ramona" for the governor and 5,000 guests, the lights went out.

Hopefully, the lights stayed on for the Crystal Ball hosted by Santa Barbara's County Medical Society. Taking place on November 18, 1966 at the Newport Beach Balboa Bay Club, the party benefited the fund to educate young people going into the nursing profession. Virginia provided the entertainment along with Joe E. Ross and magician Rudy Miller. The crowd was anticipating an appearance by actor Raymond Massey.

The caption in The *Los Angeles Times* read, "Councilman John Patrick Cassidy discusses the art of roping with vocalist Virginia O'Brien." Yes, roping. Virginia was entertaining at the December 10, 1966 "Cookout with Cassidy" barbecue. *Yee-haw!*

Vern Evans and Virginia O'Brien were married for eight years. They dated for 1 year after getting together in 1957, and married in 1958. Eight years later, in 1966, they divorced. The marriage of Vern and Virginia ended quietly. There was no mention of it in California newspapers. It also appears that no court documents were filed. Shortly after that divorce, Virginia married real estate developer Harry B. White in 1969. Her third, and final marriage, was the longest lasting.

Chapter Nine

Saluting MGM

Virginia wrapped up the 1960's with a return to the stage in March of 1969. The Masquers Club was presenting the stage version of *Merton of the Movies*, and Virginia would be playing the casting director. Ray Loynd of the *Los Angeles Times* mentioned her in his March 28th review of the show, stating simply that she had been Red Skelton's co-star in the 1947 film.

On January 28, 1970, the *Los Angeles Times* reported that the Stop Arthritis Telethon would be televised for almost 20 hours on Saturday February 1st. The hosts were Gene Raymond and Jane Wyman. Producer Jack Rourke had secured appearances by Bobby Troupe, Nellie Lutcher, Ann B. Davis, Edgar Buchanan, Virginia, and Nichelle Nichols of *Star Trek*.

In 1971, Virginia was interviewed at length by film historian and author, Richard Lamparski. His interviews with stars from the Golden Age of Hollywood led to the publication of the series of books titled *Whatever Became of ... ?* Virginia would be profiled in the eighth edition, published in 1982.

This interview was broadcast on Lamparski's radio show. He opened with the standard question about how her career began. Virginia spoke of that opening night thirty-one years ago, and said that she had never expected to have a professional career in show business. Yes, she had taken dance lessons with the goal of dancing like Eleanor Powell. Then she revealed for the first time that her parents stopped the lessons because they were concerned that she was too frail and not eating. The dancing lessons were replaced by singing lessons at the studio of Al Siegel —not directly with Al, but with one of his instructors. She explained that Siegel only worked with those students who he felt were "… really going somewhere."

Everything changed when producer Danny Dare visited Siegel's studio. He was impressed by Virginia and asked if she wanted to join the company of *Meet the People*. Since she had never planned on "… doing anything" with her singing, she declined. Unwilling to take no for answer, Dare called her parents. Finally, after considering the offer, she accepted.

After several weeks of rehearsal, she found herself in front of an audience for the first time. She told Lamparski she thought she was moving her arms and doing fine. Then they started laughing. She finished the song and fled the stage in tears. Danny Dare explained why the audience laughed, and told her to keep doing what she was doing. After that, doing the deadpan night after night was easy, because she was always terrified. Recalling how her knees knocked, she said if she had cymbals strapped to them she would have been a one-man band.

When asked if she ever wanted to do anything else at MGM, Virginia spoke to being "typed" in Hollywood. Once she was typed, her arranger would get a call from the "top office" when they needed her to liven up a picture. Her song would be dropped into the film, and "… suddenly, there I was." She also told Lamparski that she never really complained to the studio about expanding her roles.

Lamparski told her when he lectured, he was frequently asked about her. Even if they didn't know her name, they enquired about the beautiful singer with the immobile face. Virginia felt that she was remembered because once she started singing, the camera stayed on her. There were no "cutaway" shots during her songs. "Unless you were blindfolded," she laughed, "you had to look at me."

When asked about her lack of interest in show business, she said that was simply because her family was "… always around it." She gave the impression that she was blasé about the whole thing. It was not a surprise to see Bing Crosby, James Cagney, or Pat O'Brien on Uncle Lloyds yacht. She also said that she didn't think what she did was a "talent."

To a question about her first husband, she replied, "Oh, you mean Soupy-Doupy?" Remembering their trip to London, she said she was surprised to see "Superman's Wife Arrives" in the papers. Kirk Alyn had only recently finished his work on the Superman series, and it still generated excitement in the UK. There seemed to be a hint of jealousy when she explained to Lamparski that MGM had arranged this trip; this was her tour.

To bring his listeners up-to-date, Lamparski asked, "Where have you been?" "Working," came the honest reply. She spoke of wanting a "different sound" behind her, and working with a Latin group in Alaska. She wanted to move there, but her husband preferred Mexico. While Harry said it was too cold, she disagreed "… it was only 15 below the last time I left."

Next came the inevitable question, "What was it like to work with Judy Garland?" Virginia said she was a sweet girl, and the greatest talent she had ever worked with. She also said that by the time they got to *The Harvey Girls*, Garland, who she had worked with before, was "changing." She couldn't put her finger on it at the time, but now, in retrospect, and with knowledge about Judy's situation, she understood why.

Speaking of Garland's unending appeal, she talked about a recent show she had given for the prisoners at Terminal Island. Afterwards, the warden came up to her to say that only days before he had seen Virginia's photo on the cover of a Judy Garland album. "Thanks to her," Virginia said, "I'm on so many record covers, and in so many books ... no one will ever replace her."

When Lamparski asked in an untoward manner if Garland was "disturbed" during the filming of *The Harvey Girls*, Virginia made a graceful pivot and took the conversation in another direction. She said that Judy was late, and that her habitual tardiness caused the delays that resulted in Virginia's "disappearance" from the film halfway through. Eventually, taking her gowns out, and having a double replace her for a dance number was no longer effective. She also mentioned the complications of filming her number in *Ziegfeld Follies* just before work began on *The Harvey Girls*.

Virginia segued from her pregnancy and her inability to finish *The Harvey Girls* as planned, to the end result, "... my wonderful daughter, Terri." She spoke proudly of Terri's group the Cover Girls, and their success in Reno and Las Vegas. She said she wished she had joined Terri for her three-and-a-half month tour of Vietnam. This led to a question about another family member, her husband. "Did Harry know about Virginia O'Brien before he married you?" Lamparski queried. "*Oh, yes!*" came the laughing reply. "He saw all of my movies while he was in the service."

Richard Lamparski next asked about her new act, and any changes she desired. Virginia said she would like a "Western" sound behind her. She would like to dance a bit. Then she spoke of the difficulty of creating something new, and the unforeseen obstacles that could halt a production. She had recently been rehearsing a new show at The Masquers in Hollywood, where she was a "Masquerette." She had seven "kids" in the show, and was adding more ballads. This project came to a sad end when producer-director Gene Altmate suddenly died of a heart attack. After that, legal entanglements prevented them from taking the show on the road.

The interviewer then asked his subject about her income during the MGM years. Virginia spoke of making $5,000 a week when she went out on tour, but stated honestly that she hadn't made "bundles" of money. Veering away from the topic of money, she spoke of her father, "Honest Tom," and his friendship with Louis B. Mayer. She said she was seen as "Tom O'Brien's daughter" at MGM and, as a result, none of the actors were allowed to take her out. On the one bowling date she went on with John Raitt, she remembered her sister, Mary, tagging along. She didn't seriously date until Red and Edna Skelton introduced her to Kirk Alyn.

Lamparski wondered if anyone had ever tried to make her break character. She said that since she went into "… a kind of a trance," making her break into a smile didn't work. Her biggest smile, after singing "In a Little Spanish Town," was a phony grin. Only Red Skelton could get her laughing spontaneously.

The interview wrapped with her speaking again of her children. She said her youngest, Gale, was going to be "Peggy Fleming the second." Virginia was pleased that she was still recognized everywhere she went, and said she would "… never have a facelift." In his closing comments, Richard Lamparski mentioned some upcoming appearances, one on the *Mike Douglas Show*, and another on Steve Allen's current talk show.

Steve Allen welcomed Virginia to his television show on June 9, 1971. His co-host was Joanne Carson. Whether or not Virginia warbled a tune is unknown, since the show was not reviewed. The other guests were long-time Academy Award President Jack Valenti, and Desi Arnaz. One can only wonder if Desi and Virginia shared memories of a certain redhead.

Perhaps the first indication of a nostalgia craze, leading to reborn careers and the release of *That's Entertainment*, was the revue *The Big Show of 1928*. Even though she was only nine in 1928, Virginia signed on for what would prove to be a very successful show. "And Ensuing

Years" may have been added to the title to explain the presence of the cast members who, like Virginia, were too young to have been working in 1928.

The new revue was truly an all-star production. Virginia was in good company with Cab Calloway, Louis Jordan and his orchestra, The Ink Spots, and burlesque legend, Sally Rand. Together, these stars of yesteryear thrilled their sentimental audiences. Only fifty-two, Virginia was a baby among old-timers whose careers stretched back to vaudeville.

Reviews were good all-around. *The Big Show of 1928* debuted at the Huntington Hartford Theatre in Hollywood, where it ran for two weeks. In a review from the December 29, 1971 edition of the *Los Angeles Times*, Virginia was singled out for being A Good Sport:

> "Also on hand is Virginia O'Brien, whom I never saw in movies but who is certainly a very good sport about not being in them anymore. Her deadpan comedy is so subtle that I had a hard time finding it, but her self-respect is bracing in an evening so lacking in it."

The Merv Griffin Show that aired on January 10, 1972 was dedicated to *The Big Show of 1928*. The congenial host, and one-time big-band singer, welcomed cast members Rudy Vallee, Sally Rand, Louis Jordan, and Virginia. Griffin introduces Virginia with the obligatory story of how she froze on the opening night of *Meet the People*, and how that led to her "… deadpan trademark."

Virginia sings "In a Little Spanish Town" backed by Griffin's band. The tempo is a bit slower than it had been when she first performed it in *Thousands Cheer*, her voice pleasantly deepening over the years. She segues into "Rock-a-Bye Baby" from *The Big Store*, displaying her comic timing, and winning laughs. As the audience applauds, she joins Griffin and the other guests.

Saluting MGM

Merv mentions *Meet the People* again, recalling cast members Bill Orr and Nanette Fabray. He asks if Louella Parsons was involved with the revue. "No," Virginia replies. "But I did go on the road with her after I left *Meet the People*," referring to her tour with Louella and *Her Hollywood Stars of 1941*. Griffin asks if the deadpan routine was just a gimmick, and Virginia says she had a genuine case of stage fright, and adds, "… they were staring at me, so I just stared back at them."

To Griffin's question about the last thing she did in movies, O'Brien laughingly replies, "I don't like how you phrased that." She tells him it was "… a mule picture," then clarifies that it was *Francis in the Navy* with Donald O'Connor. "What were those days at MGM like?" Griffin asks. Virginia says she felt like the studio was a city, her home, where everyone was treated like royalty.

The host then shows Virginia some photographs from the MGM years. One shows a young Frank Sinatra leaning against a speaker on the soundstage while Virginia records "I Fell in Love with the Leader of the Band" from *Ship Ahoy*. She tells Griffin, "He was telling me how to phrase. Maybe if I'd listened to him, they wouldn't have cut it from the picture."

Out of the blue, Merv says he felt her wide-eyed, no expression visage "strange." Without missing a beat, Virginia replies, "Boy, I'm sure glad I came tonight!" When the laughter dies down, Griffin shows her the last photograph. It shows her in a coffin. He asks about the story behind this macabre image. Virginia explains that it's from a revue called *Hanky Panky*. She and Cass Dailey presented it at the Huntington Hartford Hotel before she joined *The Big Show of 1928*. Virginia's segment with Merv ends with her speaking proudly of her children. Palm Springs area newspapers carried the blurb on April 30, 1971, that "… dead pan comedian, breezes into the Chi Chi this weekend, tonight and Saturday evening for the *Hank Panky* show."

After the Merv Griffin broadcast, the cast of *The Big Show of 1928* would go through a series of changes. At first, the nostalgic variety show was headlined by Rudy Vallee. There was probably some friction when the star billing changed to, "Starring Sally Rand and Rudy Vallee." Rudy Vallee on-stage, and off-stage was two very different creatures. Vallee had become the type that fellow showfolk dislike—a stuffed shirt, a conservative man who didn't mix with the rest of the cast.

Vallee's feelings, regarding the camaraderie of his fellow players, came to a head during a bus ride to the next city on the schedule. The antics, jokes, and singing grew louder. Rudy Vallee made it known that he was not happy. Virginia, trying to cajole him into joining the fun, was rewarded when Vallee responded with a single, derogatory slur.

The use of this word revealed that Mr. Vallee was no gentleman. There was a moment of stunned silence, after which the gaiety continued. The tables were turned, and Vallee, getting a taste of his own "cold shoulder" treatment, left the show. Since he was the one of three cast members performing in 1928, the year was changed to 1936.

Hanky Panky, the show Virginia spoke of during her appearance with Merv Griffin, was set to re-open. An article appeared in the March 2, 1972 edition of the *Desert Sentinel* (Desert Hot Springs, Ca). Virginia would be returning to the newly titled *The Hanky Panky Revue Comedy Capers Revue.* Hunt to the reporter for the Desert Sentinel, "They've written a musical comedy version of *Dracula* with special sound effects that will be a delight to everyone. Several one-man shows are being lined up for John Barrymore Jr., Cass Daley, Virginia O'Brien, etc., for Thursday nights." Between this revamped revue and *The Big Show of 1936*, Virginia was staying active.

The cast of *The Big Show of 1936* continued to change. Ben Blue, who had appeared with Virginia in *Panama Hattie*, was a welcome addition. New cast members Jackie Coogan and Beatrice Kay were audience favorites. Two furry Hollywood icons, Rin Tin and King Kong, had their turn in the spotlight. "King Kong was a fake! He wasn't much bigger than Jackie Coogan, but on second thought, that's pretty big," wrote Philip F. Crosland, arts editor for Wilmington, Delaware's *The News Journal*.

Crosland's July 19, 1972 review followed a performance at Mitchell Hall in Newark, where the show was added as an "extra attraction" at the University of Delaware Summer Festival of the Arts. In bold print, above photos of Coogan, Cass Daley, Beatrice Kay, Vince Barnett, and Virginia, the headline read "Old Magic of '36 Stars Regales Campus." Of course, Virginia clearly impressed the arts editor:

> "Virginia O'Brien, whose wide-eyed unsmiling countenance brightened a number of motion picture musicals in the 1940s, looked much as she did in those days as she sang 'Say That We're Sweethearts Again,' 'Tea for Two,' and 'I Want To Be Happy.' She proved a real show-stopper in her floor-length red gown."

More than thirty years had passed since Virginia's stage debut in *Meet the People*, and "show-stopper" was still the showbiz term most used to describe her impact. Virginia and the rest of the company kept the tour going throughout 1972 in Toronto (1/15), Cleveland (2/7–2/12), Phoenix (3/6–3/11), St. Louis (7/6–7/11), Wilmington (6/26–6/27), New Jersey (7/17–7/22), and San Francisco (8/8–8/13). The theatres they played were huge. At St. Louis' Municipal Opera, Virginia dead-panned through two songs from *No, No Nanette*. Six thousand people applauded her renditions of "I Want to be Happy" and "Tea for Two."

No, No Nanette was credited with bringing about the nostalgia craze that seemed to be sweeping the nation. The hit Broadway musical brought Rudy Keeler, the tap dancer Virginia watched on Uncle Lloyd's sets, back to the stage. The wonderful 1930's comedienne, Patsy Kelly, was also in the show. Everything old is new again, wasn't just a phrase. Stars, songs, films, cars, and clothes from the 20's and

30's were now sought-after prizes. Hence, the birth of revues like those Virginia would appear in for many years to come.

> "Virginia O'Brien looks great. She is 48 now, looks it, admits to it, and parries it against the feebler thrusts of everyone in the roadshow *Big Show of 1936*. She is the youngster of the group, a strange assortment of entertainers for the over-50 crowd, ranging from Sally Rand hidden in a lavender spotlight to Allan Jones warbling tunes from Man of La Mancha." – Casey Charness, *Film Fan Monthly* September 1972

The Casey Charness article, simply title "Virginia O'Brien," was the first to look at her as a star of an era we would never see again. Running four pages, it covered the well-known story of the stage fright that launched a career. All of the stars she worked with, and every one of her MGM films, is mentioned here.

Mr. Charness makes some interesting observations: "… this Los Angeles comedienne whose voice was to singing as Katharine Hepburn's to acting: flat, straight and distinctive." Virginia expresses her feelings about the label of "deadpan singer." "I never felt restricted in my specialties," she told Charness, "In fact, I was the first person executives would think of when it was time to lighten the weight of a critical sneak preview."

Also addressed is her height, and the fact she didn't smoke. Both cost her film roles. The 5' 7½" was too tall to co-star with Gene Kelly in *The Three Musketeers*. She lost another role in an unnamed film directed by Henry Koster. "He said, 'Now Virginia, go over to that table and pick up a cigarette' … I thought, he must be kidding." Her refusal to smoke meant the loss of cigarette commercials too.

On the issue of career versus family, she said, "MGM wanted you to have babies between movies, but I wanted babies between babies." She felt that television had a hand in the demise of her career, because its growing popularity forced studios, including her own, to slash their rosters. Despite her feelings, she was excited about an offer to appear on Henry Fonda's television show.

Another opportunity went by the wayside when she was offered a great part in the Los Angeles production of one of Broadways biggest hits. "Angela Lansbury wanted me to do the Vera Charles part in *Mame*... But they transported the New York cast intact...."

In spite of her usually optimistic attitude, the article ends on a sad note: "I go out to MGM," she told Charness, "... it's like a ghost town, a real ghost town. Very depressing." Two years after the publication, movie-goers would see that ghost town in the 1974 film *That's Entertainment*. A film embraced by nostalgic fans, and one that would shine the spotlight on Virginia and her MGM family.

Virginia stayed with *The Big Show of 1936* into 1972, playing at a long list of venues that included the Felt Forum at Madison Square Garden, Pittsburgh's Heinz Hall, and Philadelphia's Academy of Music. At the St. Louis Municipal Opera's open-air amphitheater, Virginia sang for an audience of 6,000.

In his review of a one-night-only performance in Asbury, New Jersey, critic William Wolf commented on the strong laughs Virginia received for "... holding fast to her deadpan expression. When the production finally returned to the west coast, *The Big Show of 1936* was the inaugural production at the re-opening of San Francisco's Orpheum Theatre. That engagement was a sell-out from August 8th through August 13th (1972). After the San Francisco closing, Virginia returned to Los Angeles.

"Jam-packed with show-biz personalities, and even more jam-packed with nostalgia..." is how reporter Fran Erwin described the luncheon at the Hollywood Palladium on November 24, 1972. This gathering of the PPB and AFRTS members was saluting Bing Crosby.

In other words, the Pacific Pioneer Broadcasters and the American

Forces Radio and Television Service were giving the crooner the Carbon Mike Award. The "show-biz personalities" in attendance included Miss O'Brien, Edgar Bergen, Mel Blanc, Dorothy Lamour, Eddie "Rochester" Anderson, and The Andrews Sisters. The next time Virginia's name appeared in print it was linked to a bizarre prediction.

A brief mention of a musical version of *Dracula* seen in "Criswell Predicts," the column of Mae West's personal psychic, Cris Criswell (aka Charles Criswell King). His prediction on December 12, 1973 was "… Cass Daley, Vega Madux, and Virginia O'Brien will captivate you in the spoof *My Dear Dracula* on their national tour." Criswell missed the mark. No tour was announced, and the show was never heard of again. Not surprising, since he had also predicted that Mae West would be President of the United States.

Earl Wilson covered Dean Martin's show at the MGM Grand Hotel in Las Vegas. Wilson's December 18, 1973 "Off Broadway" column reported that Cary Grant introduced Martin, saying, "Well, Old Red Eye is back …." Former MGM stars at Wilson's table included Jane Powell, Howard Keel, and Shirley MacLaine. MGM's two O'Brien's, Margaret and Virginia, joined them.

Virginia was not mentioned in another newspaper article until ten months after the Dean Martin opening.

The Cinema Buffs organization promoted the preservation of classic films. In early October, the Cinema Buffs honored filmdom's top supporting players. Held at the site of the first Academy Awards, the Blossom Room at the Hollywood Roosevelt Hotel, the event was billed as "A Tribute to the Featured Player." Fran Erwin of Van Nuys, in the *Valley News*, reported on the Cinema Buffs event on October 18, 1974.

Featured player, Ben Cooper was the emcee. Mr. Cooper recalled, "Joel McCrea once told me that in all the movies he made, he insisted on being surrounded by good character actors …." McCrea understood the value of a featured player like Leon Ames, Hayden Rorke, Lurene Tuttle, Virginia Christine, Natalie Schaefer, and Virginia O'Brien. All of these "lesser known personalities" were honored that night. The honors would continue with the release of *That's Entertainment*.

That's Entertainment: 50 Years of MGM was broadcast on May 28, 1974. Hosted by George & Alana Hamilton, the program was produced for ABC's Wide World of Entertainment. The show consisted of footage from the May 17, 1974 premiere of *That's Entertainment*, and the opening night ball.

Joyce Harper of the *Philadelphia Enquirer* proclaimed the event "A Premiere to End Premieres" (May 24, 1974). Harper wrote of Gene Kelly winning the evenings biggest round of applause, Elizabeth Taylor's stunning "... deep blue chiffon Grecian-type gown by Edith Head," and Fred Astaire's singing of "Change Partners." Among those MGM alumni who looked "the entire staff of MGM's Grand Hotel," were Howard Keel, Marjorie Main, Ann Rutherford, and Virginia.

Marsh Hunt, Virginia, Ann Miller, unknown, and Jane Withers. Circa 1974.

The impact of this once-in-a-lifetime reunion of MGM greats was still making news a month later. On June 23, 1974, columnist Dick Kleiner called the occasion, "One of Hollywood's brightest nights ever.... The guest list was walking history." Klein ended his memories of the soirée thus: "I sat with the O'Brien girls—unrelated. Margaret has lost weight and looks great. Virginia was holding hands with her husband of five years, Harry White. When they got married they each had four children."

In September of 1974, articles began to appear about Virginia's return to movies. It had been twenty years since she made her last screen appearance. Like 1955's *Francis Joins the Navy*, the star of this new movie was also a mule. Francis could talk, and Walt Disney's *Gus* kicked field goals. While her role was very brief, she plays a newspaper reporter who interviews Ed Asner. She looked wonderful, and appeared to be having fun. Unbeknownst to her, this would be her last film.

It was no surprise to find Virginia attending a birthday party for her favorite MGM co-star and friend, Eleanor Powell. Virginia's castmate from *The Big Show of 1936*, Cass Daily, was there as well. The surprise party was hosted by Ray Sandlow, the owner of The Gary Theater in Los Angeles. Eleanor had visited the theater as a special guest when they screened her movies.

On November 30, 1974, the *Los Angeles Times* ran a photograph of Cass and Virginia posing with the birthday girl. Powell has the white military jacket she wore in the 1937 film *Rosalie*, a birthday present, wrapped around her shoulders. Another singer in attendance that evening was Cheryl Morris. In an interview with the author, Cheryl, who was the last singer to be hired by Harry James, reminisced about Eleanor Powell and Virginia O'Brien. Cheryl, who sang "Easy to Love" that evening by special request, shared this about Virginia:

> "Oh, how I loved that lady. How 'regular' and nice she was. That night she looked fabulous in her bright orange gown.

It was an evening I'll never forget. I think she was so much more than we ever were allowed to see on the screen.

"They kept her in a 'niche,' and though it was fun, she was such a gorgeous, charismatic woman, and had so much more to give. She was incredibly 'down to earth' and fun. I didn't know precious Virginia as much as I grew to know Ellie Powell. I wish I had stayed in touch with her after that night. I am grateful that we were close for that whole night."

An article from December 12, 1974, titled "6-Hour Yule Benefit Slated" announced that Virginia would headline the show *Christmas at the Harbour*. The annual event benefited the Oralingua School for the Hearing Impaired and Mentally Challenged Children at the Pacific State Hospital.

It was mentioned that Virginia had appeared on Broadway with Jackie Gleason, Jimmy Durante, Ray Bolger, and Jane Froman. It makes the incorrect claim that her contract with MGM was for ten years (it was for seven). Also mentioned are the films *The Harvey Girls*, *Panama Hattie*, *As Thousands Cheer*, and *Ziegfeld Follies*. MGM co-stars Frank Sinatra and Judy Garland are singled out. The benefit was planned down to the minute, and Virginia was to perform at 7:40pm. She would be including a medley of "Tea for Two" and "I Want to Be Happy."

In July of 1975, articles began to appear about Virginia's return to movies. It had been twenty years since she made her last screen appearance. Like 1955's *Francis Joins the Navy*, the star of this new movie was also a mule. This Francis talked, Walt Disney's Gus kicked field goals.

Hollywood journalist Vernon Scott wrote a glowing article about Virginia and her return to the screen. Carried by UPI, Scott's article was seen in newspapers nationwide on July 30, 1975. "Virginia O'Brien in 'Gus'—Deadpan full of life, she'll make another movie," was the title. The interview was conducted in the commissary at

Disney Studios. Direct quotes make up at least eighty-five percent of the three-column piece.

Scott begins with the typical summary of her days at MGM. "Her delivery brought down the house," he writes. *Du Barry Was a Lady, Panama Hattie,* and *Till the Clouds Roll By* are cited as three hits in which she did just that. He reminds readers that her last screen appearance was "a quarter century" ago in *Francis in the Navy*. After this, we are brought up to date with the mention of Virginia's four children, "… the youngest of whom is 16…."

Virginia spoke of her nightclub act, telling the journalist, "I sing a lot and dance a little… [But] I can't drop the deadpan numbers from my act. People yell for them." Her third husband is not named, but referenced as "… a retired real estate contractor and inventor who flies his own airplane." Scott states that Virginia does not have to work because the couple has "… property holdings in California and Nevada, one of which is a gold mine." Virginia continues to work for one simple reason, "I love show business… I guess I'm a ham."

As numerous writers did before him, Vernon Scott, via Virginia's quotes, retells the origin of her singing style. Of that fateful performance in *Meet the People,* Virginia shuttered as she spoke of the experience:

> "When the spotlight hit me I froze … my knees actually knocked together like castanets. My arms were frozen at my sides … the best I could do was move my shoulders. So I did. Everything was rigid except my mouth. The audience wasn't sure what they were seeing … they were quiet at first. Then people began to laugh. They roared. But I kept singing.

She recounts fleeing to the wings in tears at the end of her solo. "I was awful, but I was the hit of the show." On the second night of the production, no one had to tell her to repeat her opening night performance. Scott writes, "She was still terrified and just as big a hit."

Virginia told him she "... stayed scared for years. This ended when she realized that she could sing well. With what may have been a bit of regret, she also remarked, "But I never had a chance to prove it in those MGM musicals." On another note, she revealed that when various televisions acquired some seven-hundred MGM movies, that they would not take *Merton of the Movies*. She felt her last MGM movie was "... the worst picture ever made. It was so bad they made us do it a second time and it was still terrible."

At the conclusion of the interview, to prove that she was still in good voice, Virginia startled those also dining in the commissary. She broke into "... her best known song," giving "In a Little Spanish Town" the full treatment. At the end of her vocalizing, and his article, Scott wrote of the captive audience, "But they remembered her well and were pleased by the brief rendition."

Gus opened in the United States on July 7, 1976. The website Wikipedia acknowledges the film as Virginia's last, unlike the IMDb and TCM websites. It was also the last film of *Hogan's Heroes* star, Bob Crane.

A Pet is a Special Friend was a program created for second-grade children by The Women's Auxiliary to the Southern California Veterinary Medical Association. To support this organization and the Animal Welfare Project of Actors and Others for Animals, a fundraising dinner dance was held on April 26, 1977. That night the attendees were entertained by Virginia, as well as Anson Williams, Peter Marshall, Rose Marie, Dorothy Lamour, Art Lund, Charles Nelson Reilly, Burt Convey, Dick Haymes, and Betty Garrett.

The event was held at the Hollywood Palladium. Actors and Others president, Earl Holliman, told the press that the dinner would resemble a "40's bash." Milt Raskin, formerly of the Tommy Dorsey Orchestra, and his band provided the music. One of the prizes was an appearance on *Police Woman*, on which Holliman co-starred with Angie Dickenson.

In December of 1978, producer Alan Eichler booked big band great Helen Forrest into Studio One's Backlot Theater. During her successful two-week run, Forrest sang to many friends who came to see her. On December 12th, Dick Haymes and Virginia were in the audience. While he had worked with Helen Forrest, Anita O'Day, and Eartha Kitt, the younger producer was a bit hesitant when he introduced himself to Virginia. The two hit if off immediately, and when he expressed his interest in creating a show for her, she happily accepted.

Another great lady who performed at Studio One Backlot in 1979 was Maxene Andrews of the Andrews Sisters. In an interview with the author, Maxene's longtime partner, Lynda Wells, recalled a funny incident involving Maxene, Virginia, and Martha Raye. Having just given an incredible performance to a packed house on opening night, Maxene was singing "Apple Blossom Time," when she suddenly saw someone crawling toward the stage. When the mysterious figure emerged from the shadows and literally crawled onto the stage, it turned out to be Martha Raye.

Clearly feeling no pain, the inebriated Miss Raye took over and, much to the delight of the audience, proceeded to entertain the crowd for twenty minutes. Maxene Andrews wisely let her friend do this. Who was going to tell Martha Raye to stop? No one did, nor did they want to. At one point, Martha even took her false teeth out and placed them in Maxene's water glass. While Raye did her unexpected solo turn, Maxene took refuge at Virginia's ringside table on the same level as the stage. Nearby sat Rock Hudson, laughing helplessly at Raye's impromptu antics.

Attempting to regain control, Maxene came back on stage, followed so closely by Virginia that it seemed as though they were joined at the hip. Maxene looked over her shoulder at Virginia and said, "Oh great, we've got another one!" The audience howled when she asked Virginia, "Do you want to sing too?" Virginia launched into one of her trademark songs much to the terror of Andrews' young pianist, who faked it as best he could. The spontaneous performances of Raye and O'Brien were welcomed by Maxene, who had been nervous about performing that night without her sisters. Lynda Wells remembered Virginia fondly and said that Maxene Andrews "adored her."

Dining at the Masquers Club: Harry White
(Virginia's husband), Virginia, and Alan Eichler.
Photo courtesy of Alan Eichler.

These personal memories of Maxene Andrews opening at Studio One's Backlot Theater were also covered in the *Los Angeles Times*, dated September 27, 1979. Critic Dennis Hunt wrote of the sixty-one-year-old Andrews voice, "There is plenty of warmth and some strength in it … Her style is very casual and her material suits that style." Hunt's review closed with his observations of Martha Raye:

> "Raye, now 63, was a riot with her surprisingly raunchy ad-libs. One of her spontaneous bits brought down the house. In the middle of singing sweet "Little Girl Blue," already a shambles because of her non-stop joking, Raye pulled out her false teeth and gummed her way through the rest of the song."

Alan Eichler and Virginia became friends during the time it took to create a new show for her. Today, he is happy to share his memories of the still-beautiful, vivacious lady who would occasionally show up at his house unannounced. One challenge they faced was finding the right pianist for Virginia. Eichler quickly realized that her "deadpan" style actually employed jazz timing. Her accompanist would have to adapt to this, as well as her sense of comedic timing.

Another problem was the fact that Virginia had to relearn many of the songs she sang in her MGM days. Eichler's objective was to remove material that seemed ill-chosen for what would be consider her "come-back." Virginia joked that it wasn't a come-back, because she had never been away. Her producer concurred, remembering her as someone who "... always wanted to work," and "... a very together performer."

Musical Nostalgia was the title of a musical evening advertised in The *Los Angeles Times* on February 19, 1980. This "bit of 40's and 50's nostalgia" took place at the Hollywood Palladium. Under the direction of Lee Castle, the Jimmy Dorsey Orchestra played for Virginia, the Ink Spots, and Eddie Fisher. The "nostalgia" show played for five nights, from February 17th to the 23rd. Tickets were ten dollars.

Tom Cooper was the owner of the Vagabond movie theatre in Los Angeles. The Vagabond was a revival house, showing movies from the Golden Age of Hollywood. Cooper was successful in getting the stars of that era to appear at the Vagabond when he screened their films, and others. In August of 1980, Cooper's theatre hosted a 27-week film festival of 200 films. Ads in local papers appeared on August 20, 1980, inviting fans to "Join Gene Kelly." There were in-person tributes to Kelly's MGM friends: Kathryn Grayson, Margaret O'Brien, Eleanor Powell, Vincent Minnelli, Charles Walters, Betty Garrett, Marsha Hunt, and Virginia O'Brien.

"Virginia O'Brien To Appear At MGM Series At Vagabond," read an advertisement published on October 22, 1980. In part, it read "Virginia O'Brien, a featured player in many golden age MGM musicals, is scheduled to appear ... before the showing of *Du Barry Was a Lady*." Virginia's visit to the theatre was on October 27th.

The other film showing that day was *The Duchess of Idaho*, which featured the last on-screen performance by Virginia's friend, Eleanor Powell. (Virginia would return to the Vagabond in May of 1984, when she was honored with a two-film tribute.)

On November 9, 1980, another MGM star and her loyal followers were written up in the *Los Angeles Times*. "Jeanette MacDonald's Spirit Lives On" was the headline. Jeanette's fan club was launched in 1937, and forty-one years later it was still going strong.

Their annual meeting was described as a "... family reunion," with a banquet hosted by actor Gene Raymond. Regular attendees were Eleanor Powell, Alan Jones, Tom Drake, Leon Ames, and Virginia.

The world-famous Hollywood Brown Derby had the red carpet rolled out, and searchlights piercing the night sky on December 12, 1981. Three stars were honored that night as a part of the 60th Anniversary of the Motion Picture & TV Fund. Ernes Meer, who designed crystal chandeliers for "... the Vegas MGM Grand Hotel, the Academy Awards show, even Liberace has one in his car," donated $10,000.

Virginia mingled that night with Don Defore, the cast of Hill St. Blues, Prince Hohenlohe, and Baron von Buelow. The honorees were Milton Berle (70 years in showbiz), Danny Thomas (humanitarian), and Vivian Blaine (outstanding entertainer). Mr. Meer also provided

Monk Ekkehard wines from his vineyard... All the better to wash down the Maine Lobster and Russian caviar.

On August 24, 1984, Virginia and Alan Young appeared in the Long Beach Civic Light Opera's production of the classic Jerome Kern musical, *Show Boat*. Alan Young is best remembered as Wilbur Post from televisions long-running *Mister Ed*. Dave Ross of the Long *Beach Press Telegram* found the old warhorse, known among actors as "Slow Boat," to be stately, as grand as its story, awesome as its sets.

Alan Young played Cap'n Andy, captain of the Magnolia, the paddle-wheel boat of the show's title. Ads for the show announce Virginia as a "Special Guest Star," with a box around her name (an old billing trick to make a star's name more prominent).

Robert Koehler, a theatre critic with the *Los Angeles Times*, found Virginia's Parthy Ann only a shadow of the boat's bossy party pooper that she should be. He also felt that Young's Cap'n Andy was forcedly gay (in the original sense of the word). Alan Eichler recalls Virginia's portrayal of Parthy Ann differently: "She became better with time, and very quickly, she was perfect in the role."

Virginia got far better reviews as herself in her one-woman show, *Virginia O'Brien Salutes the Great Musicals of MGM*. This cabaret act was the final result of Alan Eichler's vision and determination to get the entertainer he admired in front of appreciative audiences again. It paid off. Over the next five years, she brought her act to Los Angeles venues like The Masquers Club, the Cinegrill at the Roosevelt Hotel, and a club on Santa Monica Boulevard called Gardenia.

For many of these performances, as well as others, her bass player was her daughter, Terri. As a professional musician, Terri did the job she was hired to do. It wasn't until her mother introduced the musicians that the audience knew who the lovely young bassist was Virginia's firstborn.

Kathryn Grayson visits Virginia the Gardenia after a 1984 performance. Photo courtesy of Alan Eichler.

Variety is practically the bible of the entertainment industry. On December 9, 1984, the venerable trade paper reviewed Virginia's act at the Vine St. Bar & Grill. *Variety* critic Kirk found Virginia to be, "as big a giggle as ever when the '40s MGM film-musical star unveiled her nitery act...."

> "O'Brien's 45-minute turn supplied a delightful sampler of songs from her pics, interspersed with witty asides about her co-stars and her career, and pointed up, if such reminders were necessary, the wealth of classic tunes supplied by that studios productions.
>
> If the 'act' itself still needs a little fine-tuning—O'Brien needed a few reminders from her pianist about song segues and the like in turn caught—the overall presentation is a charmer, thanks both to the songs and O'Brien's fun presence.

Her blank-stare delivery—accompanied by the slightest twitch of the shoulders or some mechanically exaggerated hand gestures—tickled the funny bone frequently, as did more or less 'straight' renditions of a medley of MGM favorites which included 'On the Atchison Topeka and The Santa Fe,' 'Donkey Serenade,' 'Can't Help Loving That Man of Mine,' and 'Till The Clouds Roll By.'"

Sillier fare—a strictly-for-fun 'Ramona' and 'She's Only A Bird In A Gilded Cage,' for example—was interspersed with solid pacing in terms of the overall effort."

The Vine St. Bar & Grill became Virginia's home in a way. She appeared there again in August of 1985 and 1986. Her success at Vine St. led to the publication of one of the longest articles dedicated strictly to her in decades. Jack Hawn's December 14, 1984 *Los Angeles Times* piece, "Virginia O'Brien Still Delivers Deadpan Gaze," was a long overdue tribute. Hawn's article began:

"She was, as film buffs might attest, a striking, dark-haired beauty with about as much expression as a wall clock and a voice that could bellow like a braying jackass."

The piece had the standard story of L.B. Mayer catching the frightened singer in *Meet the People*, and signing her to a contract. Jack Hawn wrote of the Vine St. gig, and the new album she had recorded at the Masquers Club. "I've never really retired," Virginia said. "Except for taking time off with the children, I've been busy, playing theaters and clubs on the East Coast mostly." Her Los Angeles roots, and important relatives, all stepped forward from the past, but Virginia's current work was the focus.

Virginia wore a "... multi-colored sequined-and-beaded gown," at Vine St. The show was a live performance of the album. Virginia was fine until "... she forgot the lead-in lines to a number." She told Hawn, "I was nervous." He found irony in the fact that it was that very nervousness that "... helped launch her career, now approaching half a century." The article concluded with an acknowledgement that there were many miles on that blank expression, yet it was successful for her, and "... notably Keely Smith and Cher." To which Virginia proudly replied, "But I originated it. They're much younger than me."

Virginia began 1985 on a good note. Columnist Liz Smith wrote about the friendship between Elizabeth Taylor and Liza Minnelli on February 5, 1985. "And now for a new duet—Liz and Liza!" Minnelli and Taylor were frequently seen at Michael Feinstein's piano bar lounge at the Le Mondrian Hotel on Sunset Boulevard.

Liz Smith continued with, "Liza sometimes gets up and sings for hours while Elizabeth sips her Perrier and applauds. The other night Liza sang with the once famous Virginia O'Brien of the 40's, who appeared in *The Harvey Girls* and *Till the Clouds Roll By* with Liza's mama, Judy." Liza Minnelli was just nine months younger than Virginia's daughter, Terri. Virginia had always been close to Liza. There singing reunion must have been a joy.

The Louis B. Mayer Theater was located at the Motion Picture and Television House. This was a retirement community for those involved in show business. The event in March of 1985 that brought out a huge crowd of celebrities was the 18th annual *Ding-A-Lings* show. George Christy of the Copley News Service covered the affair in his "Hollywood, Etc." column on March 20, 1985.

Among those attending were Jimmy Stewart, Robert Stack, and Lynn Redgrave. Roddy McDowell recalled breaking ground, with a spade, when he was a child for the future Mayer Theater. When Howard Keel asked McDowell about Claudette Colbert's age, the answer was "82," to which Keel replied, "What a great set of legs on her." Virginia's part of the show "... had the audience phrasing her rendition of "Life

Upon the Wicked Stage" and "On the Atchison, Topeka and the Santa Fe" ("The songs I sang with Judy Garland in *The Harvey Girls*").

Virginia would perform at many of these shows over the years, usually with her daughter, Terri, playing electric bass. Terri remembers performing in *Ding-A-Lings* shows on the following dates: February 1, 1987, February 4, 1990, June 11, 1992. Also, on June 12, 1988 they were in a show there called *All Our Yesterdays*.

Another annual *Ding-A-Lings* received a lengthy write-up in the February 23, 1986 edition of the *Los Angeles Times*. This production was a take-off on *The Love Boat*. Recovering from hip replacements, Fayard Nicholas of the legendary Nicholas Brothers used a cane during his tap routine. Ninety-five-year-old Nettie Oetell sang "Funny Face." Described as "perennially straight-faced," Virginia brought the house down with "Ramona."

While she didn't have a legion of gay fans like Judy Garland, Virginia O'Brien was a welcome celebrity in the gay community. She participated in gay pride events, and was one of the early stars to take part in the battle against AIDS.

She was among the celebrities her friend Alan Eichler praised in a letter to the *Los Angeles Times* on August 8, 1995. The veteran producer was responding to the August 11 article "Hollywood Powers Help AIDS Victims" by David Fox. Eichler wanted to make certain that the efforts of yesterday's stars were not forgotten. He wrote, "The fact that some of them may not be 'powerful' only makes the courage of their convictions more admirable."

Those mentioned in his letter included Vivian Blaine and Sammy Davis, Jr., both doing public service television spots. Rita Moreno headlined the APLA's show at the Hollywood Bowl, when others declined to appear. Mamie Van Doren rode in the APLA's 1984 parade. Jean Simmons, Patti Page, Sheree North, Terry Moor, Adele Jergens, Marie Windsor, Tippi Hedren, Betty Garrett, and Virginia all appeared in "the first major AIDS benefit in L.A.," the production of "Women Behind Bars." This show was presented by Gregory Harrison and Catalina Productions.

Like Mamie Van Doren, Virginia also rode in several gay parades. One photo shows her in a summer dress holding a matching parasol and smiling broadly. She is seated in a pink Volkswagen Bug convertible. Years later, when her daughter was asked by a friend about the reason behind Virginia's numerous gay fans, Terri replied, "Because she was always there for them."

Terri and Virginia at the Vine St. Bar & Grill in 1985.
Photo courtesy of Terri O'Brien.

In 1985, Virginia was front and center, appearing on the hour-long "Leigh Spears Show." Broadcast weekly on KFOX 93.5, the show was an important part of the gay rights movement. Host Leigh Spear was the son of the leader of the Jackie Gleason Orchestra, Sammy Spear.

In an interview for the *Santa Cruz Sentinel*, it was stated that, "Spear says the inability of his father to bring up the topic of his homosexuality led to a superficial relationship during his childhood."

Entertainment was the basis of his radio program, but he also wanted to discuss AIDS with callers. He also plans to have a segment on every show where lesbians could address their issues. Among the entertainers who visited with Spear during his 4pm broadcast were Charo, Kathryn Grayson, Jackie Gleason, and Virginia.

Singer Roberta Sherwood had hits with "Up a Lazy River" and "You're Nobody Till Somebody Loves You." On December 27, 1985, she was the recipient of the Film Welfare League's Lifetime Achievement Award. Virginia presented the award to Miss Sherwood at Hollywood's Le Bel Age Hotel.

August of 1986 saw Virginia's return to the Vine St. Bar & Grill. Her appearance there was filmed on August 3rd. Fans hope that this film will eventually be digitalized and released on DVD. Later in the month, on the 28th, Virginia appeared at an event to honor a star from the silent era.

She was among those who felt that Rudolf Valentino should be remembered. Virginia told the mourner at the annual pilgrimage that, "Rudy, as he was known to his friends and fans, was a phenomenon—a star of unparalleled appeal." Valentino's most loyal mourner, The Lady in Black, was there, as she had been for every anniversary of the film legend's death in 1926. In the coming years, Virginia would continue to appear, and entertain, at celebrations honoring Hollywood's history.

On November 5, 1986, the calendar section of the *San Bernardino Country Sun* advertised Virginia's appearance at the Chris Davis Supper Club in Rialto, California. She would be headlining the 8pm show, *The Fascinating Forties*. This was an annual show presented by the Chorus of Sweet Adelines. The show was promoted again in the same paper on November 7, 1986. This included an article about the

"Frozen Face" who was bringing her act to the private club. There was a current photo of Virginia and the obligatory list of her film credits.

Virginia in 1986.

In a warm letter to the author, Lyle Palaski recalled his memories of Virginia. That letter is included here with his permission:

> When video was all the rage in the 80's I became the buyer for the Video West stores in Los Angeles and I worked out of the West Hollywood store. I met Mark Mayes in 1985 and in 1986 or 1987 out of the blue he told me he wanted to take me downtown to see   something which turned out to be Virginia O'Brien's act.

I did not know who Virginia O'Brien was at the time, even though I was in my early 30's, but I quickly learned because her act used film clips from her movie roles. I was thoroughly entertained as was Mark who had known her from those MGM musical roles long before I did. It turns out that I did know her from a couple years earlier when a friend and I saw a double feature at the Vagabond Theatre on Wilshire of *Easter Parade* and the film Virginia was in, *Thousands Cheer*. Before *Thousands Cheer* they had also shown a short subject film that was all about Virginia! I was quite fascinated that night.

We enjoyed the show and, afterwards, Mark wanted to meet her and she generously came out into the room to meet and greet people so we got to talk to her. We had no camera with us, a photo would be a grand keepsake. I had on an MGM jacket that I had purchased on the MGM Lot when Mark and I had snuck on to the lot one day in an outing in Culver City. Mark told Virginia I worked for MGM video, which is only true if you say that I did because we bought and sold their product. She was interested to know if any of her films were on video and Mark said we could make a list and send it to her. I don't know what information we exchanged then ... if I took her phone number or address, but soon after I remember writing her with the information and she called me back.

Sadly, I don't have any letters from her. I wrote her a few times and then she'd call me back and talk for a while. In person and on the phone Virginia was very warm and giving. She told me some interesting things, such as being the honorary mayor of Wrightwood which I had to look up to see where it was. There was little of hers on VHS at the time, but she expressed interest in a couple things that were coming out, one of them being *Thousands Cheer* and I believe the other was *The Big Store*. I told her I'd let her know when they were coming out, but when they came out I just sent them to her as a gift.

One of our Video West customers was a man named Marc Courtland. He was a film historian of sorts and worked at the St. James Club, now called the Sunset Tower. I don't know how he was acquainted or came into contact with celebrities from the past, but he decided to ask the hotel if he could use one of the spare room spaces not being used where he'd invite a celebrity to come and view an entire film or short clips of scenes and the like which would be shown on video on one of the meeting rooms giant television screens.

In the 1980's that wasn't as gauche as it might sound now. These were Monday night events and free of charge and many were well attended. I remember meeting and talking to people like Betty Garrett, Anita Page, Gloria Stuart, Ann Miller, Patty Andrews and the like. One evening was with Virginia O'Brien and the film screened was *The Harvey Girls*. So, I got to briefly meet Virginia again that evening. There's a scene where Angela Lansbury first appears and walks toward the camera ... when that happened Virginia says out loud to much laughter, "Here comes 'Murder She Wrote.'"

I recall that these events happened for about three years, 1989-1991 or thereabouts. In the meantime, Marc Courtland had become afflicted with AIDS and was incurring a lot of medical expenses and was not faring well. The celebrities he'd been featuring decided to get together and hold one last Monday night event for him. It was to raise money to help with his medical expenses. It is my information that Cesar Romero and Virginia O'Brien were instrumental in the planning and execution of this event, helping to get people to attend and participate.

A couple years later MGM was planning *That's Entertainment Part III*, in part to celebrate their 70th anniversary. My friend Mark Mayes and I had pushed George Feltenstein, an executive producer for this film, someone who worked at MGM in the releasing department and we had become peripherally acquainted with, that Virginia O'Brien needed to be included in that film. Well, I remember seeing news footage of the premiere of this film and Virginia O'Brien was interviewed and the reporter asked, "Are you in it?" Virginia replied, "I don't know...I haven't seen it yet. I hope so." Well, to my chagrin, she wasn't. Later we asked George why not and whatever he said wasn't acceptable to me because I've forgotten it. It is sad that they couldn't have spared an extra two minutes in any of those three films to include one of her unique and vastly entertaining numbers.

In April of 1987, Virginia, along with one hundred and twenty others, attended the 50th reunion of the Class of '37. Finding the alumni was a difficult task, as the school records had been lost in a fire in 1982. There were other celebrates in her graduating class, some where there that night—Daniel Lee won an Oscar in 1971 for special visual effect in *Disney's Bedknobs and Broomsticks*.

Producer and writer Don Ingalls credits included *Fantasy Island,*

Gunsmoke, Have Gun Will Travel, Bonanza, and *Marcus Welby, M.D.* Actress Eva (McVeaugh) Gordan's first movie was *High Noon.* She too worked in television, appearing on *Simon & Simon, Cagney & Lacey,* and *T.J. Hooker.*

The April 23, 1987 edition covered the reunion, and reported that Virginia (O'Brien) White now lived in Wrightwood. Virginia, who said the reunion was a very special evening, revealed that she hadn't graduated with her classmates.

> "I dropped out of school three months before graduation. I returned to complete the work, but I received my diploma at my desk. In a way, this reunion is my graduation."

In 1987, the rock band Foreigner released the album *Inside Information.* The love song "I Don't Want to Live Without You" reached number five on the Hot 100. The music video of the song included clips from MGM films like *Royal Wedding* with Fred Astaire and *Father's Little Dividend* with Spencer Tracy. Near the beginning of the video viewers caught the opening moments of the "Show Boat" segment from *Till the Clouds Roll By.* Virginia is seen dropping her handkerchief, *which the gallant Tony Martin picks up and hands back to her. This is from the «Life Upon the Wicked Stage» number.*

Virginia visited with members of the Masquers Club again in September 1988. This was to attend a ball for "Gangsters and Their Molls" at the Hollywood's legendary Roosevelt Hotel. Many veteran stars who appeared in gangster films of the 1930s and film noir classics were in attendance: Marie Windsor, Ann Savage, June Lang, and Mae Clarke. Virginia was one of 350 guests at the sold-out event. The party goers danced to the music of the Art Deco Society Orchestra. The soirée was written up in the *Los Angeles Times* on September 14, 1988.

Masquers Club Variety Arts Ballroom Tribute to Virginia O'Brien.
Standing left to right Marsha Hunt, Jack Klugman, Virginia, and Cesar Romero.
Seated left to right, Betty Garrett and Marie Windsor.

Prior to his death in 1965, Stan Laurel gave his approval to a group that wished to honor his work with Oliver Hardy. His only condition was that it not be "a fan club" open to just anyone. Out of that, the Sons of the Desert, a society of Laurel and Hardy aficionados, was born. The name comes from the 1931 film *Sons of the Desert*. Bill Cassara was a devoted member and president of the Monterey "tent," as the individual groups within the Sons of the Desert were known.

The anniversary banquet, followed by the screening of a Laurel and Hardy film, was an annual event. Cassara invited a variety of movie stars to be the guest of honor at the banquet. In 1988 there were two guests of honor—Tommy "Butch" Bond and Virginia O'Brien. Bond is best remembered as the bully in twenty-seven of the *Our Gang* comedies. Unbeknownst to Bill Cassara, Tommy Bond had also worked with an actor Virginia knew quiet well.

Cassara invited friends and the guests of honor to his home the night before the anniversary banquet. Virginia arrived with Alan Eichler. She also carried the *Virginia O'Brien Salutes the Great MGM Musical* album. The album was played for everyone's entertainment. Cassara was not prepared for what happened next. "As soon as the first song started, Virginia joined in, belting out the opening number. We had Virginia O'Brien in stereo in my living room. I believe she sang along with every song on the first side. We were all delighted."

The banquet itself was held at Monterey's First Theatre. Built in 1846-47 by Jack Swan, it is the oldest theatre in the seaside town. Each year, Cassara created a brief montage of film clips to introduce the guest, or guests, of honor. Clips from Tommy Bond's career were screened first. Cassara was seated next to Virginia when the image of Kirk Alyn flashed on the screen. "No!" Virginia moaned loudly. When the shocked audience turned to see what was wrong, she explained "…that's my first husband." The scene that caused her amusing outcry was from one of the *Superman* films in the Columbia series. Standing next to Alyn was Tommy Bond as Clark Kent's protégé Jimmy Olsen.

Film clips from Virginia's career included her rendition of "Rock-A-Bye Baby" from *The Big Store*. Perceptive film historian Cassara remembered the conclusion of the "Sing While You Sell" production number when Virginia, the Marx Brothers, and others end up on the floor of the elevator. Knowing that Groucho says something to Virginia just as the elevator doors are closing, Cassara grabbed the opportunity. "What did Groucho say to you," he asked Virginia. She thought a moment before answering. "It was probably something dirty."

In his autobiography, *They Still Call Me Junior: Autobiography of a Child Star*, actor Frank Coghlan remembers seeing Virginia at the Jivin' Jack and Jills Reunion in 1988. Among the guests at the 1988 reunion were Leonard Maltin, Joan Leslie, Edward Dmytryk, Margaret O'Brien, and Billy Barty. The Jivin' Jack and Jills was a dance group that had appeared in nine feature films and one short between 1942 and 1945. The Andrews Sisters were in three of those movies. Several starred Donald O'Connor and Peggy Ryan, who were Universal's answer to MGM's Mickey Rooney and Judy Garland.

In March of 1988, Virginia brought her show to San Francisco's Plush Room. Her arrival was covered by the *San Francisco Chronicle*. Journalist Marian Zailian interviewed Virginia. Her March 20th article, "'40's Songbird Virginia O'Brien Soars Back," began:

"In the glittering string of musicals that the MGM studios made during the 1940s, everyone recalls that Judy Garland added her own particular shine to them, as did other leading ladies June Allyson, Lucille Ball, and Cyd Charisse.

But Virginia O'Brien? Who was she?"

Zailian answers her own question with a description of the tall, slim singer with the dark hair and hazel eyes whose deadpan delivery seemed to wink at her own beauty. Zailian writes that everyone agreed she was on her way to stardom, and yet she didn't become the star the studios tried to create.

Then comes the interesting, and accurate point, that after Virginia came, those who achieved stardom with a style that mirrored her own. In the 50s it was Keely Smith. In the 70s it was Cher. Why hadn't Virginia reached stardom, the journalist wondered. Virginia responded, "I chose not to take that trip."

In the Virginia O'Brien of the 1980s Marian Zailian saw a "pretty lady," who, at 67, still had her sense of humor, comic timing, and that "singular twinkle" in her eyes. She also found Virginia open to discussing the roads she did chose to travel. She spoke of her father, the LAPD captain, and her Uncle Lloyd, who directed at Warner Brothers with Mack Sennett.

"Uncle Lloyd used the house I was born in for comedies. He used the whole family in his films." She recalled her uncle directing her at two and a half to walk down a flight of stairs. Yet, she still maintained that she never thought of a career in acting.

> "What I was performing in was—in every sense of the word—'home movies.' What I wanted to do was dance on a theatre stage the way I'd seen Ruby Keeler dance in the film *42nd Street*, which Uncle Lloyd directed."

That she was, willing to expand my dreams. She decided she would become a combination of Ruby Keeler and Ethel Merman. An ideal that worked well during rehearsals. Her first performance for an audience was a different matter.

> "But opening night—wow! The song came out, but that's all that happened. I couldn't move. I couldn't lift my arms. I tried, but all I could do was raise my shoulders in a stiff little shrug. I was frozen with fear. I couldn't even smile. I finished my song and ran off in tears."

She kept on crying until the producer entered her dressing room. "Ginny," he said, "the audience loved you. Funniest act they've seen in years. Honey, you stopped the show." Virginia told Zailian, with a laugh, "I went out there as Ethel Merman, and came back a comedian." That comedian impressed audience member Louis B. Mayer. MGM beckoned.

O'Brien found the "grooming for stardom" to be slow. After a year, she had yet to step before the camera. She was allowed to join George Kauffman's revue *Keep Off the Grass*, and made her first trip to New York. The young singer was in awe of the Broadway talent she would be working with.

"What a cast! Ilka Chase, Ray Bolger, Jimmy Durante, and a young man nobody knew named Jackie Gleason. We all thought the show would run for years, but after four weeks in Boston, it lasted three weeks on Broadway."

MGM was ready to put her to work. Her first minor role called for no singing. "I didn't even talk," she recalled. She was called upon to do two things, scream and looked frightened. She found both "easy for me to do." This was in *Sky Murder*. While this was the first movie she made, her second film, *Hullabaloo*, was released first. A decision that allowed audiences to hear her sing in her screen debut.

"In those days, they always previewed a movie to get audience reaction. Originally, I sang 'Carry Me Back to Old Virginny,' straight first, then swung it. The audience reacted with thunderous applause. So, they put the film back in production and also gave me 'I Dream of Jeannie.' By this time, I had capitalized on my stage fright...." It was the press who hung the expression 'deadpan' on me."

She spoke of other MGM stars she worked with, including Red Skelton. "He would wear you out," she said. "He was onstage every minute. But he was the one who introduced me to my first husband, Kirk Alyn. He was the first Superman."

Then there was Judy, and *The Harvey Girls*. She was ready for the role that allowed her to be comic and romantic. Little did she know that Garland's late arrivals, and her own pregnancy, would change everything.

"Unfortunately, our star, Judy Garland had problems showing up...the shooting dragged on and on. As I got bigger and bigger, my role got smaller and smaller. Every scene became a challenge."

Her love scenes were cut, her lap was piled with pillows and she stood behind counters. When it became impossible to hide her increasing waistline, the solution was a blow. "Before the film was halfway through, my role disappeared completely."

Years later, Judy Garland's health would bring another opportunity her way. As she remembered, Louis B. Mayer "dumped" Garland. Virginia was offered her first starring role as Annie Oakley. In this interview for the *San Francisco Chronicle*, she stated that she turned it down because, "I was too busy playing wife and mother." In previous accounts, the reason was her awareness of the demands that came with "shouldering" a movie and her fear of horses that prevented her from filming *Annie Get Your Gun*.

At the close of the article readers were brought up to date on Virginia's life after MGM. She and Kirk Alyn had three children before their divorce, there was a second marriage and another baby (Gale). Her current life, with her husband of 18 years, was in Wrightwood, California. The couple lived in the ski resort because husband Harry White was a land developer with property in the surrounding San Bernardino mountains.

She had recently been offered a role in a TV sitcom, but turned it down. She was content with her life in Wrightwood, where she had been the honorary mayor. *The Plush Room* show was the result of a 1982 encounter with producer Alan Eichler. Seeing her in the audience at a show, he said, "You ought to be up there." Together, they created *Virginia O'Brien Salutes the Great MGM Musicals*.

The recording of Virginia's act at The Masquers Club.
Photo courtesy of Alan Eichler.

Unfortunately, this warm welcome to San Francisco was all but destroyed when *San Francisco Chronicle* theater critic Gerald Nachman gives Virginia's show a dismissive review in the newspapers in the March 24, 1988 edition. It was something he was known for, and perhaps even enjoyed.

Nachman's reviews were replete with errors. He would mention a song, and then write it was written by the Gershwins, when it was written by Irving Berlin. Songs were also incorrectly attributed to the musical, be they from film or stage. It took him two decades to give

Peggy Lee a good review, and even then, he misquoted her. His ineptitude was staggering.

The proud Mayor of Wrightwood, California.
Author's collection.

He added a year to Virginia's age and complained of her attempt to stretch 15 minutes of fame to 60. While he wrote that she was probably "quite a nice lady," he was complied to add, ""Once you get her away from the tambourine, antiquated shtick and sad little act...." His comments that the seasoned performer was out of her element, and that the show was a joyless hour, certainly effected ticket sales.

His only genuine praise was for the line "Just remember, I used to be your grandfather's pin-up girl." As for the songs, he enjoyed only "Where Did Robinson Crusoe Go with Friday on Saturday Night?" He closed with disdain for the audience sing-along closing of Cole Porter's "Friendship."

Where did Gerald Nachman go? Who cares.

Virginia, as always, went forward. Continuing to delight fans and appear at various charity events and salutes to Hollywood's Golden Age. While she no longer garnered the attention of the press, Virginia was active. She continued to perform into the early 1990s. Her act was nostalgic, but she didn't live in the past.

Chapter Nine, Part Two: More Stars Than There are in Heaven

"I'm trying to catch up to Mickey Rooney," said the star of *Love that Bob* as he stood next to his fifth wife at his 80th birthday bash. The *Los Angeles Times* dated June 11, 1990 had a photograph of Art Linkletter visiting with Bob and Janie Cummings. Also on hand to celebrate were Patty Andrews, Rosemary DeCamp, Jane Wyatt, Rose Marie, Red Buttons, and Virginia.

The big event in September 1990 was the American Cinema Awards, held at the Beverly Hilton Hotel with appearances by many of Virginia's friends and co-stars. In addition to Virginia, attendees included Ricardo Montalban, Ann Miller, Margaret O'Brien, Janis Paige, Jane Powell, Jane Russell, and Esther Williams. Frank Sinatra was honored that evening. The show was broadcast on September 12, 1992 by NBC.

September of 1990 also saw the release of the cast album of the London Palladium show, *Stairway to the Stars*. A review of the recording appeared in the September 20, 1990 issue of the Melbourne, Australia paper *The Age*. In his "Stage & Screen" column, Jim Murphy called the album an "agreeable surprise." Highlights were 75-year-old Georges Guetary, who, Murphy felt, "sounded exactly the way we heard him in ... *An American in Paris* around 40 years ago." Also praised was "that delightful deadpan girl Virginia O'Brien." After this review, there was little news from Virginia in 1991.

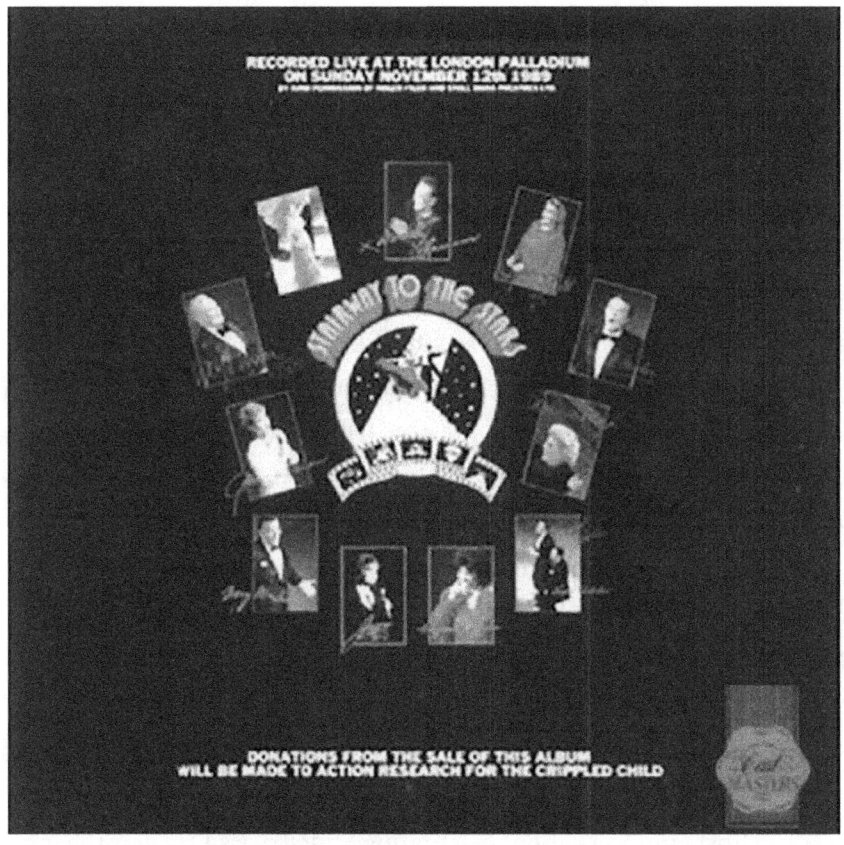

The CD of Stairway to the Stars.

One-time comedian Skip E. Lowe had a long-running show on public access television in Los Angeles. He interviewed many stars from the Golden Age of Hollywood on his program, *Skip E. Lowe Looks at Hollywood*. Lowe claimed to have found most of his guest by attending Hollywood cocktail parties. Virginia was among those guests in 1992. The airdate of his interview with her is unknown. However, the interview can be viewed on YouTube.

In their half-hour visit, Virginia shared many interesting memories with Lowe. She said because of her mother's fear of hospitals she was born at home. The family home was located in Chavez Ravine, which is now the site of Dodger Stadium. When asked about her father, she says that in those days the chief of police "ran the whole she-bang."

When questioned about her start, she remembers "singing up a storm" but being unable to move everything except her shoulders in *Meet the People*. She reveals that she made her screen-test and signed her contract two weeks after L.B. Mayer saw *Meet the People*. At first, she says her first film was *Hullabaloo*, but then quickly corrects herself and says *Hullabaloo* was the first film she sang in.

Virginia then recalls her screen debut in *Sky Murder* with Walter Pidgeon, and then notes the kind of trivia that only a dyed-in-the-wool film aficionado appreciates, the house used in *Sky Murder* is the same house used in *The Philadelphia Story*.

Her friendship with Groucho Marx and his daughter Miriam comes up when she and Lowe talk about *The Big Store* with the "crazy" Marx Brothers. She was a frequent guest at Groucho's home. Lowe then skips ahead to working with Judy Garland. Virginia calls Garland "a doll." Lowe, who was often befuddled, thinks Margaret O'Brien was in *The Harvey Girls*. Virginia corrects him.

The host enquirers about celebrating St. Patrick's Day. For the most recent St. Paddy's Day, Virginia had been the guest of Martha Raye. At the time Raye was in failing health and married to Mark Harris, who was thirty-three years her junior. Shifting to her personal life, Lowe mentions her current residence in Wrightwood and the duties of a small-town mayor. Virginia brightens while speaking of the towns annual chili cook-off, shows, and the bands that play on Mountaineers Day.

During the interview, Lowe shows his guest various career related items, including the cast album from the London show *Stairway to the Stars*. The album has a photo of the cast taking their bows. Virginia points out that she is standing next to Judy Garland's daughter, Lorna Luft.

Other central figures from her days at MGM, Virginia says the Red Skelton "wore you out." "Bosom buddies" is how she remembers her friendship with Eleanor Powell. Did Frank Sinatra ask her out? "Yes, once." But when she said he would have to come home to meet her parents, that was the end of that.

Unlike some Metro-Goldwyn-Mayer alumni, Virginia had fond memories of L.B. Mayer. "Was he tough?" She answers Lowe's query about the mogul: "Yes, but he was running an empire." She found him to be "down to earth." Recent activities with her contemporaries included taking a cruise from Hawaii to Los Angeles with Ann Miller and Virginia Mayo.

Lowe shows a film clip of Virginia singing "Fresh as a Daisy" from *Panama Hattie*. After viewing it, he comments on her tiny waist. "That was B.K. ... before kids," she quips. An upcoming show at the Motion Picture and Television Home, in which she'll appear as Ethel Merman while Fayard Nicholas plays Sammy Davis Jr., is mentioned. Virginia says she's been doing shows there for thirty-three years. Lowe then asks her if she believes in fate. Her straightforward answer is "I never thought about it."

The interview concludes with brief mentions of her recent work at local nightspots. At the tiny Gardenia nightclub, she had to walk around the block to make her entrance. She was proud of her five appearances at the Vine St. Bar and Grill. Virginia is upbeat and full of energy throughout the interview. At 73, she looks wonderful, and it's clear that she meant it when she said she would never have plastic surgery.

Tony Martin had known Virginia since they appeared together in *The Big Store* in 1941. They had also worked together in musicals, including *Till the Clouds Roll By*. Virginia had also worked with Tony's wife, Cyd Charisse, in *The Harvey Girls*. On October 28, 1992, Tony Martin received the prestigious Ella Award from the Society of Singers. Henry Mancini's wife, Ginny, was the founder of this society. Virginia was accompanied to Martin's award dinner by her husband, Harry White.

Virginia with longtime friends Tony Martin and Cyd Charisse.

Bridget Byrne, who covered the event for the *Los Angeles Time*, wrote, "The ballroom of the Beverly Hilton was crammed with a bevy of grand old troupers, the men in tuxedos, the women aglitter, as Martin's peers in his more than 50-years in radio, movies, television, and the record business gathered to sing his praises." The gathered bevy boasted MGM stars Debbie Reynolds, Esther Williams, Jimmy Stewart, Kathryn Grayson, Ann Miller, Virginia and, of course, Cyd Charisse.

Writing for the May 2, 1994 edition of *Variety*, revealed that *That's Entertainment III* almost didn't make it to the big screen. Originally it had been planned for television. The third film in the series devoted to the great moments from MGM films was seven years in the making. Archerd reported a "loft launching with rave reviews and an emotional preem ... and it makes its big splash Tuesday at New York's Museum of Modern Art." *That's Entertainment* was also a part of MGM's 70th anniversary. At the premiere, the on-screen hosts were present: Gene Kelly, Cyd Charisse, Ann Miller, and Esther Williams. Other MGM veterans included Virginia, Gloria DeHaven, Janis Paige, Ginger Rogers, Eva, and Zsa Zsa Gabor.

While she receives credit for appearing on the 1994 "making of" video *That's Entertainment III: Behind the Screen,* Virginia's appearance is all too brief. She is shown for a few seconds at the films premiere where Army Archerd welcomes her. She says she's happy to be there, but doesn't know if she's in the film itself. She isn't.

On May 29,. 1995, one of the final mentions of Virginia as an active performer was published in the *San Bernardino Sun.* "Boo, hiss the villain in musical comedy" was the unlikely headline. The Snowline Players was the amateur theatrical company in Wrightwood, California. Under the direction of Lora Steinman, the company was presenting the melodrama, "Ten Nights in a Barroom."

In part, the brief article read, "You can also cheer on veteran film actress Virginia O'Brien, a Wrightwood resident who makes a cameo appearance in the show. She will sing "I'm Only a Bird in a Gilded Cage." O'Brien was featured in *Hullabaloo, Lady Be Good, Du Barry Was a Lady, The Harvey Girls,* and *Ziegfeld Follies.*

Two Virginia's, Mayo and O'Brien, attended the Cinecon 32 convention, which ran from August 29 to September 2 of 1996. This annual gathering was the biggest and oldest convention saluting silent films and early "talkies." Director Stanley Kramer was also in attendance to see Tod Browning's 1921 film *No Woman Knows.* A program of Laurel and Hardy films celebrated the 70th anniversary of the sound process known as Vitaphone.

Terri O'Brien attends the March 12, 1997 tribute *Judy Garland: Over the Rainbow* with her mother. Photo courtesy Terri O'Brien.

The *San Bernardino County Sun* carried Harry B. White's obituary on December 24, 1996: "Harry B. White, 73, passed away 12/23/96. He was a Veteran of WWII where he served in the U.S. Army/Air Force. He is survived by his wife Virginia of 28 years. Father of John, Bob, Kathy & Suzette; stepfather of Terri, Liz, Gale & John." Harry, who had 16 grandchildren and 2 great-grandchildren, was interred at Forest Lawn Cemetery. Contributions to the American Cancer Society were requested in lieu of flowers.

Four stars were honored at a luncheon held at Studio City's Sportsmen's Lodge on Friday, April 4, 1997. Each received an award from the Southern California Motion Picture Council. The honorees were Dean Jones, Virginia O'Brien, Margaret O'Brien, and Francine York.

Virginia's friend, co-star, and the man who introduced her to Kirk Alyn, passed away on September 17, 1997. Red Skelton was eulogized by fellow comedian Milton Berle. Army Archerd covered the memorial service for the September 24, 1997 issue of *Variety*. The service was held at Forest Lawn Cemetery. Berle closed with a paraphrase of Skelton's familiar words said at the end of all his television shows: "... goodbye dear friend, and God bless." Skelton and Berle had known each other since the 1933 Chicago World's Fair. Virginia was there as were Bob Hope, Steve Allen, and Esther Williams.

Things were quiet for Virginia after Harry died. Between 1995 and her passing in 2001, Virginia's pace slowed as she was approaching her eighties. Although she continued to make public appearances, such as her involvement with the auctions of MGM memorabilia, co-produced by Turner Classic Movies and Bonhams, performing was no longer a necessity. Employees of TCM and Bonhams fondly remember her as a gracious lady who, upon return visits, greeted everyone by first name.

Now was the time to be honored for her fifty-five-year career. A career in which she worked in every medium: stage, film, radio, recording, and television. On such honor was when The Thalians, a group founded by Debbie Reynolds, recognized "The Legendary Ladies of the Silver Screen" in 1996. Other honorees included many of Virginia's friends from MGM: June Allyson, Marge Champion, Cyd Charisse, Nanette Fabray, Ann Miller, and Janis Paige.

Between 1996 and 1998 there was virtually no press about the one-time queen of the deadpan. Then, in January of 1999, the sweetest of tributes was paid to Virginia when Dan Van Neste published his article "Virginia O'Brien: Diva of Deadpan" in *Classic Images* magazine. An article that Mr. Van Neste graciously allowed to be reprinted throughout this book.

Soon after the publication of that article, Virginia moved into the Motion Picture and Television Country Home. While she claimed she had never retired, she was now only four years away from celebrating her eightieth birthday. That occasion came on April 18, 2000, the same year she marked her 60th anniversary in show business. It was here, at the senior facility where Virginia and her daughter had performed many times in the annual shows, that Virginia O'Brien peacefully passed away on January 25, 2001. Shortly after her death, a memorial service was held at the Motion Picture and Television Home. Virginia was buried at the Forest Lawn Memorial Park in Glendale, California.

While she is no longer here, her beauty and unique presence in the great MGM musicals remains. Since her passing, new generations continue to recognize the magic of films made during the era known as the Golden Age of Hollywood. New audiences discover and embrace favorite genres, directors, films, and stars. Discovering Virginia O'Brien will make people smile for many decades to come. Once she is seen, she is never forgotten.

Tributes:

2001: *Classic Images* March "Virginia O'Brien: Remembering a Wonderful Pal" *By Dan Van Neste*

2001: In the French magazine *la Revue de Cinema* dated March-April 2001, Luc Chaput included Virginia in his Salut l'artiste section. Virginia was still remembered by her fans in France, "Cette chanteuse et comedienne a connu un certain succes, specialment dans emotion de chansons aux cotes de Judy Garland (*The Harvey Girls*) ou de Red Skelton (*Du Barry Was a Lady*)"

2005: *Nostalgia Digest* Summer "Who Was That Lady?" by Walter Scannell

2014: *Nostalgia Digest Summer* "The Girl with the Frozen Face" by Garry Berman

New York Times Obituary: Virginia O'Brien; 1940's Film Star, 81, January 25, 2001

Virginia O'Brien, a familiar face and voice in film musicals and comedies of the 1940's, died on Jan. 16 in Woodland Hills, a Los Angeles suburb. She was 81.

Ms. O'Brien owed her film career to stage fright. When she made her stage debut in Los Angeles in 1940, she was too nervous to do anything but stand stock still and sing, virtually without expression.

Her performance wowed the members of the audience, who thought it was a comedy routine. One of those who joined in the laughter was Louis B. Mayer, head of Metro-Goldwyn-Mayer. Ms. O'Brien was soon on her way to a screen test and an MGM contract.

Her film credits over the next 10 years included '*Panama Hattie, Till the Clouds Roll By, Du Barry Was a Lady, Thousands Cheer, Lady Be Good*, and *The Harvey Girls*. She also appeared with Red Skelton in *Merton of the Movies*, and *The Show-Off*. Her last film role was in the 1976 film *Gus*.

She is survived by three daughters, Terri O'Brien, Liz Watkins, and Gale Evans, a son, John Feggo, seven grandchildren, and two great-grandchildren.

Virginia was happy and content in her final years.

Acknowledgements

Only the author's name appears on the book cover, but any biographer will tell you that they could not have done it alone. This book is a collaborative product. I want to acknowledge my collaborators. Some were close friends before my research began, others became new friends.

First and foremost, is Virginia's daughter, Terri O'Brien. It sounds cliché, but I simply could not have done it without her. She was always supportive, kind, and generous with her time and her collection of memorabilia from her mother's career. An added bonus was her sense of humor and our shared spiritual beliefs. And, yes, she is every bit as pretty as her mom.

Next, thank you to a man who I feel is one of our finest biographers, especially when the subject is a legendary musician. Thank you, dear James Gavin. James has "been there" for me every step of the way. What I call our mutual admiration society of two, began years before this effort. I can't think of anyone more in-sync with my passion for rare entertainers like Virginia, and the two singers he has painted full portraits of in his unequalled books, Lena Horne and Miss Peggy Lee.

I have had the help of three fellow BearManor Media authors. First, Dan Van Neste was an invaluable source of all things Virginia O'Brien. I can honestly say that if he hadn't written *Virginia O'Brien: Diva of Deadpan*, this book would have taken twice as long to complete. That article from *Classic Images* magazine was a god-send, my compass. As if that weren't enough, he gave me gratis permission to use "… every word." I did.

The next BearManor Media author who provided guidance is Scott O'Brien, whose biographies of Kay Francis and Sylvia Syms challenged me to be a better biographer. I know his devotion to the icons of the Golden Age of Hollywood inspire others writers as well. I look forward to a lasting friendship with him.

The third author from BearManor Media is Bill Cassara. My telephone interview with him was a delight. He provided the entire story of Virginia's visit to his home and of the Sons of the Desert anniversary banquet at which she was the guest of honor. Further, his book *Vernon Dent Stooge Heavy* led to the discovery of Virginia's working as a singer at the House of Murphy in 1938.

Alan Eichler, who created Virginia's salute to the Metro-Goldwyn-Mayer musicals, was tremendously helpful, and gracious in sharing his memories of working with Virginia. Without him, the section covering 1978 to 1988 would have been *very* sparse. I'm also grateful to him for recording Virginia's only album. All Virginia O'Brien fans owe him a round of applause for preserving her performance at The Masquers Club.

Thank you to Kevin John Charbeneau for the two fantastic photographs of Virginia performing at Fort Ord. Prior to this book, those photos were never published. The same is true of the memories of Virginia that Lyle Palaski shared. This is the first time they appear in print. Thank you, Lyle.

My thanks as well to the delightful Lynda Wells, who shared her memories of Maxene Andrews' hilarious encounter with Martha Raye and Virginia O'Brien. Another memorable story published here for the first time.

Ben Ohmart, founder of BearManor Media, has been one of the

Acknowledgements

easiest to work with people I've encountered in the world. His no-pressure attitude soothed me every time I went into panic mode. He answered every concern, and every email, *immediately*... no easy task from his home in Japan. His real gift to me was doing it all with a steady kindness.

Although he would say he didn't contribute anything to this book, the fact is, biographer and film historian John Fricke always contributes to my writing efforts. For that, and his encyclopedic knowledge of MGM's glorious musicals, I am most grateful. I also want to acknowledge everything he has done to honor the one-and-only Judy Garland. She could not have a better guardian.

Finally, the surprise contribution of Cheryl Morris. Had she not contacted me, I would have only had the date and location of Eleanor Powell's 1974 birthday party. While this was only one night in her life, and Cheryl's memories of it were packed with feeling. She offered, perhaps, the most vivid account of Virginia's humanity and presence.

The rest of you know who you are, but I want to shine the spotlight on you anyway. In alphabetical order Joan "The Goddess" Arthur, Dr. Jeff Burack, Joe & Diane Cohen, Jacqui Diaz, Mark Gebhardt & Rick Hocker, Arnie "The Incredible One" Goodpasture, The Hill's (Duke, Marsha and Jen), Ellie Hoffman & Barb Raboy, Ray Holt, Rae Ann Ianniello, Beth Lorber, Gene Marker & Edwin Chaves, Derrick Mapp, Matthew Martin, Bobbe Norris & Larry Dunlap, Penny Peck, Dr. Larry Tabor, and Mark Vieira.

Thank you to my amazing family: Marna & Ron Garriety, The Goppert's (Linda, Ted, Jenny & Jeff), Marti "Lady" Hicks, The Kellner's ("Big" Erik, Val, Christa & Heather), The Manibusens (Alisa, Jimmy & all of the J's), The Strom's (Erik, Debbie & Cole Bjorn), Sally Strom, Sara Wiener & Joanne Richter, Bella Wiener, and my incredible mother, Lana. Without her, I would run aground and sink.

Virginia O'Brien Portraits

Two portraits by MGM photographer Eric Carpenter.

Unless otherwise noted all photos in this book come from the collection of the author.

Index

Italicized page numbers have a photograph

Allyson, June 94, 123, 125, 127, 244, 257, 284
Alyn, Kirk (husband) 63, 86 – 88, 111, 128, 132, *134*, *138* – *139*, 140 – 145, *148*, *156* – 157, 160 – 161, 171 – *172*, 173 – *175*, *180*, 186 – 187, 189, 191, *192*, 193, 211, 213, 243, 246 – 247, 257, 288
Andrews, Maxene 46, 226 – 227, 266, 287
Annie Get Your Gun 164, 170 – 171, 247,
Asner, Ed 222
Astaire, Fred 221, 241

Bacon, Lloyd 2 – 3, 7 – 14, 211, 217, 244 – 245
Bacon, Rubey (aunt, nee Mary Rubey Cox) 2 – 3, 7, 9, 11, *12*, 14, 189
Ball, Lucille xii, 7, 46 – 48, 78, 89, 93, 107 – *108*, 119, 125, *126*, 128, 154, 186, 244, 278, 281 - 282
Benny, Jack 45, 56, 131, 159, 164, 279, 282
Big Show of 1928, The 213 – 215
Big Show of 1936, The 216 – 219, 222
Big Store, The 39 – 44, 48, 52, 73, 93, 204, 214, 239, 243, 252 – 253, 275, 283
Block, Martin 176 – 177
Bolger, Ray 26, 28, 45, 223, 246

Carson, Jack 131, 147, 180
Charisse, Cyd 145, 149, 244, *254*, 255, 257
Colbert, Claudette 36, *45*, 56, 76, 119, 233
Cooley, Spade 188

DaPron, Louis 18 – 19
DeHaven, Gloria 93, *94*, 123, 157, 180, 255

Dorsey, Jimmy 99, 228
Dorsey, Tommy 68, *71*, 72, 107, *108*, 113, 143, *144*, 225, 281-282
DuBarry Was a Lady vii, 104 – 115, 120 – 121, 176, 198, 224, 229, 255, 261 – 262, 275, 284, 288
Durante, Jimmy 26 – 28, 122, 144, 164, 167, 223, 249, 279 – 280, 282, 285

Evans, Vern (husband) 201, 208

Francis in the Navy 192 – 194, 215, 224, 275
Froman, Jane 26 – 28, 223

Garland, Judy 23, 78, 93, *133*, *141*, 148 – 150, 157 – 158, 164, 171, 211 – 212, 223, 234, 244, 246 – 247, 252 – 253, 256, 261, 267, 277, 279, 281, 283, 287 – 288
Grant, Cary 78, 146, 220, 276
Grayson, Kathryn 93, 100 – 101, 140, 153, 180 – 181, 229, *231*, 236, 254
Great Morgan, The 142 – 144, 275, 284
Gus 222 – 223, 225, 228, 262, 275

Harvey 187
Harvey Girls, The vii, 17, 26, 119, 133, *134*, 135, 140, *141*, 147 – 152, 155, 188, 197 – 198, 211 – 212, 223, 233 – 234, 239, 246, 252, 254 – 255, 261 – 262, 275, 281, 284, 288
Hattie, Panama 57, *58* – *61*, 76, 78, 80, 89, 91, 104, 107, 114, 198, 216, 223 – 224, 253, 262, 275, 281, 283

273

Hopper, Hedda 23, 29, 49, 112, 153, 155, 158
Hullabaloo 29 – 32, 35, 36, 37, 39, 53, 75, 122, 128, 246, 252, 255, 275, 281

Johnson, Van 123, 159, 164

Keaton, Buster 78, 82, 111 – 112, *113*, 114, 155, 186
Keeler, Ruby 7, 15, 18 – 19, 217, 245
Keep Off the Grass 23 – 28, 30 – 32, *33*, *34*, 35, 37, 56, 75, 167, 245
Kelly, Gene 66, 89, 93, 107, 108, *110*, 159, *175*, 176, 218, 221, 229, 255, 282

Lahr, Bert *64*, 65, 69 – *71*, 72, 78, 102, 105, 107, *126*, 129, 206, 276
Lady Be Good 35, 52, *53*, *54*, *55*, 56 -57, 75, 255, 262, 275, 281, 283, 289
Lansbury, Angela 188, 219, 239, 281
Laurel and Hardy 45, 186, 242, 255

Martin, Tony 40 – 41, *152*, 158, *159*, *160*, 241, 253, *254*,
Marx, Chico 41 – 42, *43*, 44
Marx, Groucho 39, 41 – 42, *43*, 44, 72 – 73, 92, 95 – 96, *97* – 98, 100, *101*, 243, 252, 277 – 278, 287 – 288
Marx, Harpo 41 – 42, *43*, 44
Mayer, Louis B. (aka L.B. Mayer) xii, 20, 25, 31, 125, *154*, 170 – 171, 185, 201, 213, 232 – 233, 245, 247, 252 – 253, 262
Meet the People (1940 revue) xi, 20 – 25, 30 – 31, 34, 37, 47, 49, 74, 104, 114, 157, 166 – 167, 178, 185, 203, 210, 214 – 215, 217, 224, 232, 252
Meet the People (1944 film) 106, 116, 120, 125, *126* – *127*, 128, 140, 182, 275, 281, 284
Merman, Ethel 19 – 20, 57, 78, 88, 106 – 107, 120, 171, 245, 253
Merton of the Movies vii, 17, 82, 155 – 156, 161 – 169, 194, 225, 262, 275
Miller, Ann 40, *221*, 239, 250, 253 – 254, 257
Minnelli, Liza 56 – 57, 233

Minnelli, Vincent 8, 229
Morgan, Frank 35, *36*, 122, 128, 142 – 144, 147, 278, 281
Mowbray, Alan 60
Murray, Ken 187 – 188, 276
Musical Merry-Go-Round 176, 275, 276

O'Brien, Edna (mother) 2 – 3, 5, 7, 11, 14, 79, *136*, 189
O'Brien, Mary (sister) 4, 6, 10, 14, 62, 67, 79, 112, *136*, *139*, 189, 213
O'Brien, Theresa "Terri" (daughter)
  Referenced 6, 18, 124, 142, *146*, 156, *172*, 181, 186, 190, 203, 212, 230, 233 – 234, *235*, 256, 262, 265. Photos courtesy of 6, 12, 13, 76, 118, 132, 133, 134, 148, 150, 159, 160, 172, 192, 193, 235, 256
O'Brien, Thomas (father) 2 – 5, 6, 7, 10, 12, 13, 23, 74, 89, 189, 203

Parsons, Louella 29 – 30, 35, 37, 39 – 40, 49, 66, 87, 140, 191, 215
Pidgeon, Walter 30 – 31, *38* – 39, 51, 205, 252
Porter, Cole 106 – 107, 110, 250
Powell, Dick 45, 56, 104, 125, *126*, 128, 147, 271, 281
Powell, Eleanor xii, 14, 35, 52 – 53, 64, 69 – 71, 72, 84, 93, 102, 143, 210, 222 – 223, 229, 253, 267
Powell, Jane 4, 164, 220, 250

Ragland, Rags 59, 78, 281
Ringside Maisie 47 – 48, 51 – 52, 75, 77, 198, 275
Romero, Cesar 240, *242*
Rooney, Mickey 23, 129, 159, 244, 250

Ship Ahoy 64 – 67, 69 – 71, 74, 76, 82, 84, 102, *103*, 111, 114, 143 – 144, 197, 215, 275, 281, 283 – 284
Shore, Dinah 128, *129*, *133*, 179, 279, 282 – 83
Showboat 153, 158
Show-Off, The 148, 152, 160, 262, 275
Sky Murder 37, *38* – 39, 75, 246, 252, 275

Sinatra, Frank *71*, 158 – 159, 167, 215, 223, 250, 253, 280 – 281
Skelton, Red vii, xii, 17, 44 – 45, 52, 55, 57, 59, 64, 69, 70 – *71*, 72, 82, 89, 93, 102, 107, *108*, 111, 118, 152, 161, *162*, 163, *165*, 167 – 168, 253, 257, 261 – 262, 276, 280, 282, 287 – 288
Sothern, Ann 47, 51 – 53, 59 – 60, *61*, 76 – 77, 89, 93, 157, 198 – 199, 281

Thousands Cheer vii, 75, 93, *94*, 95, 144, 214, 223, 238 – 239, 262, 275, 284
Till the Clouds Roll By vii, 148, *152*, 153, 158, *159* – 160, 167, 197, 224, 232 – 233, 241, 254, 275, 284

Two Girls and a Sailor 26, 120, 123 – 124, 275, 284

Van Neste, Dan 7, 11, 18 – 19, 28, 41, 59, 78, 126, 164, 169, 171, 258, 261, 265, 289

White, Betty 191, 276
White, Harry B. (husband) 208, 222, 227, 247, 254, 256
Winchell, Walter 26, 28
Wynn, Ed 52, 82, 186, 276

Ziegfeld Follies vii, 135, 148, 154, *155*, 161, 198, 212, 223, 255, 275, 284

Filmography

Hullabaloo (1940) - Virginia Ferris

Sky Murder (1940) - Lucille La Vonne

The Big Store (1941) - Kitty

Lady Be Good - (1941) - Lull

Ringside Maisie (1941) - Herself

Panama Hattie (1942) - Flo Foster

Ship Ahoy (1942) - Fran Evans

Thousands Cheer (1943) - Herself

Du Barry Was a Lady (1943) - Ginny

Two Girls and a Sailor (1944) - Herself

Meet the People (1944) - "Woodpecker" Peg

The Show-Off (1946) - Hortense

Till the Clouds Roll By (1946) - Ellie Mae

Ziegfeld Follies - Herself

The Harvey Girls (1946) - Alma

Merton of the Movies (1948) - Phyllis Montague

Musical Merry-Go-Round – Herself.

Francis in the Navy (1955) - Nurse Kittredge

Gus (1976) - Reporter

Archive footage: *The Great Morgan* (1946), *Walt Disney's Wonderful World of Color; Gus - Reporter* (1977) and *Classic Comedy Teams*; Marx Brothers segment (1986)

Television

All television appearances are as Herself:

Musical Merry-Go-Round (1948) Episode # 4 (also shown in movie theatres)

Texaco Star Theatre (1949) Episode 1.39

The Ed Wynn Show (1949) Episode 1.12

The Saturday Night Review with Jack Carter (1950) Episode 1.9

Parade of Stars Auto Show (1952) Live broadcast. No episode number.

The Ken Murray Show (1952)

The Betty White Show (1954)

The Geogie Jessel Show (1960)

ABC Late Night (1974) *That's Entertainment: 50 Years of MGM*

That's Entertainment III: Behind the Scenes (1994)

Radio

1942

Command Performance April 28, 1942: Program #11. AFRS origination. Host: Adolphe Menjou. Announcer: Paul Douglas. Guests: Virginia O'Brien, Red Skelton, Ozzie Nelson, Harriet Hilliard, Gloria Jean, Truman Bradley, Lucille Meredith, Billy Mills and His Orchestra, Jim Jordan, Marian Jordan, Joe Forte, Gail Patrick, Abe Reynolds, Tito Guizar. Virginia O'Brien starts the show with, "Deep in the Heart of Texas." Red Skelton appears as, "Junior, The Mean Widdle Kid," with Ozzie and Harriet as his mommy and daddy. Junior visits Daddy's office. A G. I. requests the sound of a slot machine playing off a nickel jackpot. Fibber McGee recounts his adventures during the last war, in "One-Man's Land."

Command Performance August 18, 1942: Program #27. AFRS origination. Host: Cary Grant. Announcer: Don Wilson. Guests: Virginia O'Brien, Joan Davis, Jose Iturbi, Bert Lahr, Ella Mae Morse, Freddy Slack and His Orchestra, Charles Previn conducts The Universal Studio Orchestra, Charles Previn (conductor). *The first tune dead-panned by Virginia O'Brien is, "Go to Sleep My Baby."* The program features the sound of a San Francisco fog horn.

Mail Call. August 20, 1942: Program #2. AFRS origination. Announcer: Truman Bradley. Guests: Red Skelton, Virginia O'Brien, Robert Young, Marsha Hunt. *The first tune is Virginia O'Brien rendition of, "Carry Me Back to Old Virginny."* Red is a drunken defense worker being quizzed by a spy. Robert Young and Marsha Hunt dramatize a scene from, "John Smith,

American" (although the main character is named "Joe"). A worker in a defense plant is kidnapped by two spies who demand to know about the bombsight he's working on.

Command Performance October 24, 1942: Program #38. AFRS origination. Hostess: Linda Darnell. Announcer: Don Wilson. Guests: Virginia O'Brien, Erskine Hawkins and His Orchestra, Red Skelton, Harriet Hilliard, Zero Mostel, Truman Bradley, Walter Scharf conducts The Republic Studios Orchestra. *Virginia O'Brien sings, "Boy, Did I Get Stinking at The Club Savoy".*

1943

Command Performance January 16: Program #48. AFRS origination. Hostess: Jeanette MacDonald. Announcer: Ken Carpenter. Guests: Virginia O'Brien, Dale Evans, The Mills Brothers, Eddie South and His Orchestra, Eddie Le Baron and His Orchestra. The opening song is, "Why Don't You Fall in Love with Me?" The sound of a baby crying is played for the G.I.'s.

Command Performance. March 20, 1943: Program #58. AFRS origination. Host: John Charles Thomas. Announcer: Ken Carpenter. Guests: Kenny Baker, Judy Garland, Virginia O'Brien, Woody Herman and His Orchestra. Judy Garland starts the show by singing, "Zing! Went The Strings of My Heart".

Blue Ribbon Town March 27, 1943: Host: Groucho Marx. Guest: Barbara Stanwyck.

Blue Ribbon Town April 3, 1943: Host: Groucho Marx. Guest: Hedda Hopper.

Blue Ribbon Town April 10, 1943: Host: Groucho Marx. Guest: Joan Bennett.

Blue Ribbon Town April 17, 1943: Host: Groucho Marx. Guest: Reginald Gardiner.

Blue Ribbon Town April 24, 1943: Host: Groucho Marx. Guest: William Bendix.

Blue Ribbon Town May 1, 1943: Host: Groucho Marx. Guest: Joan Blondell.

Blue Ribbon Town May 8, 1943: Host: Groucho Marx. Guest: Theda Bara.

Blue Ribbon Town May 15, 1943: Host: Groucho Marx. Guest: Veloz & Yolanda.

Command Performance May 15, 1943: Program #67. AFRS origination. Hostess: Joan Blondell. Announcer: Harry Von Zell. Guests: Dick Powell, Eddie Anderson, Judy Canova, The Sportsmen, Virginia O'Brien, Martha Tilton. *Virginia O'Brien opens the show with, "Boy, Did I Get Stinking at The Savoy."*

Command Performance August 14, 1943: Rosalind Russell, Judy Canova and Xavier Cugat. Rosalind Russell introduces Virginia saying the letters requesting her have "Piled higher than Mount Rainier. *Virginia responds to letters from enlisted men and sings "Say That We're Sweethearts Again."*

Blue Ribbon Town September 10, 1943: Host: Groucho Marx. Guest: Veronica Lake.

Blue Ribbon Town September 17, 1943: Host: Groucho Marx. Guest: Dorothy Lamour.

Army Forces Present September 25 Million Dollar Band (10:15pm): Virginia O'Brien.

Army Forces Present September 25 Who, What, When (10:30pm): Virginia O'Brien.

Blue Ribbon Town October 1, 1943: Host: Groucho Marx. Guest: Joe E. Brown.

Blue Ribbon Town October 15, 1943: Host: Groucho Marx. Guest: Orson Welles.

Blue Ribbon Town October 23, 1943: Host: Groucho Marx. Guest: Lucille Ball.

Blue Ribbon Town November 6, 1943: Host: Groucho Marx. Guest: Ida Lupino.

Blue Ribbon Town November 27, 1943: Host: Groucho Marx. Guest: Edward Everett Horton.

Command Performance November 27, 1943: Program #94. AFRS origination. Host: Herbert Marshall. Announcer: Harry Von Zell. Guests: Tommy Duncan, Bob Wills and The Texas Playboys, Anita Ellis, The 370th Army Air Forces Band, Tommy Cook, Conrad Binyon, Virginia O'Brien, Edgar Bergen, Frances Langford, Six Hits and A Miss, Skinnay Ennis. Bob Wills opens the show with, "New San Antonio Rose." Tommy Cook and Conrad Binyon portray two kids having an argument (in answer to a G. I. request). *Virginia O'Brien deadpans, "In A Little Spanish Town"*. Edgar Bergen tells Charlie McCarthy the story of, "Oliver Twist."

Blue Ribbon Town December 4, 1943: Host: Groucho Marx. Guest: Adolph Menjou.

1944

Command Performance January 15: Program #101. AFRS origination. Hostess: Frances Langford. Announcer: Ken Carpenter. Guests: Virginia O'Brien, Spike Jones and The City Slickers, Aileen Bauer, Red Ingle, Del Porter, Carl Grayson, Phyllis Brooks, The Revuers, Jimmy Wakely. The first opening number is, "Shoo Shoo, Baby," sung by Frances Langford.

Command Performance February 26: Program #108. AFRS origination. Hostess: Dorothy Lamour. Announcer: Ken Carpenter. Guests: Virginia O'Brien, Ruth Carroll, Jimmy Dodd, Ken Carpenter, David Rose, Vivienne Della Chiesa, Dick Haymes. Dorothy and Ken exchange snappy dialogue while playing a game of craps. David Rose conducts his own composition, "Holiday for Strings."

Command Performance April 22: Program #116. AFRS origination. Hostess: Gene Tierney. Announcer: Ken Niles. Guests: Roy Acuff and The Smoky Mountain Boys, Charlie Cantor, The Armed Forces Radio Service Orchestra, Virginia O'Brien, John Conte, Frank Morgan. Martha Tilton sings, "Besame Mucho." Charlie Cantor appears as "Clifton Finnegan" of "Duffy's Tavern". Frank Morgan tells about his farm.

Mail Call. May 24: Program #93. AFRS origination. Hostess: Paulette Goddard. Announcer: Don Wilson. Guests: Virginia O'Brien, The King Sisters, Edgar Bergen, W. C. Fields, Borah Minevich and His Harmonica Rascals, Meredith Willson conducts The Armed Forces Radio Service Orchestra. This broadcast is dedicated to the state of Kentucky. The opening number is, "Kentucky." Borah Minevich and His Harmonica Rascals play, "Brazil." Paulette Goddard listens to Mortimer Snerd's memories of his first date. Charlie McCarthy tries to apologize to W. C. Fields receives an apology from Charlie McCarthy for setting a skunk trap in Fields' garden.

Command Performance May 27: Program #121. AFRS origination. Hostess: Dinah Shore. Announcer: Ken Carpenter. Guests: Dick Haymes, Virginia O'Brien, The Louis Jordan Sextet, The Hoosier Hot Shots, Meredith Willson conducts The Armed Forces Radio Service Orchestra. The first tune is, "It Had to Be You."

Mail Call **July 5**: Program #99. AFRS origination. Host & Announcer: Don Wilson. A tribute to servicemen from the state of Colorado. The first tune is, "Time Waits For No One." Guests: Helen Forrest, Virginia O'Brien, Smith and Dale, Joe Smith & Charles Dale of "Smith and Dale".

Everything for the Boys **July 18**: Show #27. Hosted by Dick Haymes. Guests: Ella Mae and Virginia O'Brien. This broadcast featured a two-way conversation with GIs stationed in the UK.

Command Performance August 15: Program #132. AFRS origination. Hostess: Ginger Rogers. Announcer: Ken Carpenter. Guests: Jimmy Durante, George Murphy, Virginia O'Brien, The Golden Gate Quartet. *Virginia opens the show with, "Carry Me Back to Old Virginny".*

Command Performance November 1: Program #148. AFRS origination. Announcer: Ken Carpenter. Guests: Benny Goodman and His Orchestra, Edgar Bergen, Virginia O'Brien, The Loumel Morgan Trio, Bette Davis, Fred Allen, Gypsy Rose Lee, Jimmy Durante. On this "encore" broadcast all of the material come from previous programs. "Air Mail Special," is the opening number. Bergen and McCarthy do their Oliver Twist routine. Loumel Morgan sings, "Blues in The Night". Gypsy Rose Lee chats with Fred Allen.

Command Performance December 23: AFRS origination. Xavier Cugat and His Orchestra play, "Brazil." An extended Christmas special. The program was recorded October, 1944. Bob Hope (m. c.), Xavier Cugat, Jerry Colonna, Virginia O'Brien, Spike Jones and The City Slickers, Ginny Simms, Jimmy Durante, Henry Stimson (Secretary Of War), Dinah Shore, Jack Benny, Fred Allen, Kay Kyser, Frances Langford, Danny Kaye, W. C. Fields, Judy Garland, Spencer Tracy, Lee J. Cobb, Dorothy Lamour, Skip Homeier, Howard Duff, Ken Carpenter (announcer), Griff Barnett, Elliott Lewis, Harry Bartell, Verna Felton, George Marshall, The Ken Darby Chorus, James Forrestal (Secretary Of The Navy), Johnny Mercer, Don Wilson (announcer), Frank Nelson.

Mail Call **December 27**: Program #125. AFRS origination. The date above is the recording date. The program was released in January or February of 1945. Then first tune is, "Don't Fence Me In." Jimmy hires Monty as a tutor for his performance in, "Cyrano." Dinah Shore (m. c.), Ken Niles (announcer), Carlos Ramirez, Monty Woolley, Jimmy Durante, Virginia O'Brien, The Armed Forces Radio Service Orchestra.

1945

Encore **May 31:** Program specifics unknown.

Request Performance **October 21:** Program #3. CBS net, WBBM, Chicago air-check. Sponsored by: Campbell's Soup. The program is produced by the Masquer's Club of Hollywood. Johnny Mercer sings, "On The Atchison, Topeka and The Santa Fe." Eddie Bracken goes for a physical. Orson takes listeners on a "Rocket Trip To The Moon." He reminds listeners that he's going to the moon, not Mars. Residents of New Jersey are especially warned. Knox Manning is heard as the "reporter" broadcasting the launch of the rocket ship. Orson's description of being in outer space is remarkably similar to what astronauts would describe twenty years later. The cast does, "The Rover Boys Down East," or "Rescue On The River." Orson Welles (host), Johnny Mercer, Eddie Bracken, Ken Christy, Del Sharbutt (commercial spokesman), Knox Manning, Virginia O'Brien, Leith Stevens (composer, conductor), William N. Robson (director).

1947

Command Performance September 2: Penny Singleton and Jack Haley

Command Performance October 12: Linda Darnell, Edgar Bergen and Charlie McCarthy

Mail Call 1947: Program #217. AFRS origination. The first tune is, "Ride, Red Ride." The m. c. is referred to as, "Skipper Jay" (or "Skipper Jane"). The date is approximate. The Charioteers, Virginia O'Brien, Rafael Mendez, Ginny Simms, The Pied Pipers, Gertrude Niesen, Lou Holtz, Rita Hayworth.

1948

Symphonies Under The Stars. August 5, 1948: Program #33. AFRS Hollywood Bowl Series. The program originates from The Hollywood Bowl. Red Skelton as "Dr. Ricardo Skelzone" leads the orchestra. Danny Kaye is in top form. Irving Berlin sings "Alexander's Ragtime Band." Alfred Wallenstein (conductor), Pat McGeehan (m.c.), Red Skelton, David Forrester, Ed Gardner, Jack Haley, Frank Sinatra, Danny Kaye, Frances Langford, Gene Autry, Edgar Bergen, Frankie Laine, Virginia O'Brien, Jimmy Durante, Irving Berlin, The Jeff Alexander Choir, Matty Malneck and His Orchestra, Carl Cotner and His Orchestra, Mark Warnow and His Orchestra, Morris Stoloff and His Orchestra, Roy Bargy and His Orchestra, Axel Stordahl and His Orchestra, Carmen Dragon and His Orchestra, The Los Angeles Philharmonic.

Command Performance. June 28, 1949: Program #382. AFRS origination. *Virginia O'Brien sings, "Loreli".* The date above is the release date to the troops. Gene Tierney (m. c.), Jerry Colonna, Virginia O'Brien, Jack McCoy (announcer). Complete.

Virginia O'Brien on Radio - These are all the programs in the radioGOLDINdex database which credit this artist. These listings are accurate as of January 21, 2016. The programs are listed chronologically, partial dates appear first, unknown dates appear last. Copyright 2016, J. David Goldin.

Hullabaloo. **October 1, 1940. MGM syndication. Air trailer.** The date above is the scheduled release date of the film. Kay St. Germaine, Lennie Lynn, Virginia O'Brien, Charles Holland, Frank Morgan, George Stoll and His Orchestra.

Ship Ahoy. **1941. MGM syndication. Air trailer.** Eleanor Powell, Red Skelton, Virginia O'Brien, Tommy Dorsey and His Orchestra, Frank Sinatra, The Pied Pipers. Broadcast date unknown.

Lady Be Good. **August 5, 1941. MGM syndication. Air trailer.** Ann Sothern, Robert Young, John Carroll, Virginia O'Brien.

Panama Hattie. **1942. MGM syndication. Air trailer.** Ann Sothern, Red Skelton, Rags Ragland, Ben Blue, Virginia O'Brien, Lena Horne. Broadcast date unknown.

Meet The People. **1944.** Film sound track. Lucille Ball, Dick Powell, Spike Jones and The City Slickers, Bert Lahr, Vaughn Monroe and His Orchestra, Virginia O'Brien, The King Sisters. Broadcast date unknown.

The Harvey Girls. **1945. MGM syndication. Air trailer.** Angela Lansbury, Judy Garland, Kenny Baker, Virginia O'Brien. Broadcast date unknown.

Showtime. AFRS. "Carry Me Back To Old Virginny" Virginia O'Brien. Spike Jones and The City Slickers. Broadcast date unknown.

Treasury Song Parade. Program #382,383,384. Treasury Department syndication. Virginia O'Brien sings *"I Just Kissed Your Picture Goodnight," "I Can't Give You Anything But Love,"* and *"The Man On the Flying Trapeze"*: Virginia O'Brien, Lennie Hayton and His Orchestra. Broadcast date unknown.

Discography

"This is Spring" - COLUMBIA (USA): Discs 35632 1940-07-02; matrix: 26971; control: WCO26971; ~ 3 min

"Two in a Taxi" - COLUMBIA (USA): Discs - 35578 - 1940-07-02; matrix: 26973; control: WCO26973; ~ 3 min

"Clear Out of This World" - COLUMBIA (USA): Discs - 35578 - 1940-07-02; matrix: 26972; control: WCO26972; ~ 3 min

"I'm an Old Jitterbug" - COLUMBIA (USA): Discs - 35632 - 1940-07-02; matrix: 26970; control: WCO26970; ~ 3 min

"Say That We're Sweethearts Again" - DECCA (American) - 23868 - 1944-04-27; matrix: L3399; ~ 3 min

"A Bird in a Gilded Cage" - DECCA (American) - 24622 - 1944-04-27; matrix: L3400; ~ 3 min

"Dude Ranch Serenade" - DECCA (American) - 24304 - **1944-10-25**; matrix: L3657; control: (LA); ~ 3 min

"In A Little Spanish Town" - DECCA (American) - 24622 - **1944-10-25**; matrix: L3658; control: (LA); ~ 3 min

"Wrong Train" - DECCA (American) - 24304 - 1944-10-25; matrix: L3656; control: (LA); ~ 3 min

"The Wild, Wild West" - DECCA (American) - 23460 - 1945-09-07; matrix: L3959; control: (LA); ~ 3 min

"Life Upon a Wicked Stage" - MGM (1940s - 1950s) - 30002 - matrix: 46S3012; xref: (MGM-1); ~ 3 min

172 V Disc A Carmen Miranda – "Miranda Melody"

172 V Disc B Lucille Ball Virginia Obrien Red Skelton Gene Kelly Tommy Dorsey – "Friendship"

The Radio Years: Christmas 1944 - The Complete Broadcast of the Command Performance Christmas Show. Double CD. Radio Years RY 37/38 (1995). Mono ADD (Made in Italy)

CD I Tracks:

Introductory speech - Over There

2. Monologue - Bob Hope

3. Brazil - Xavier Cugat

4. Comic monologue - Jerry Colonna

5. "Let's Be Sweethearts Again" - Virginia O'Brien

6. "Holiday for Strings" - Spike Jones

7. Amor, Amor - Ginny Simms

8. Sketch: "O'mbriaco" Durante the patron of the arts - Jimmy Durante

9. Secretary of War Speech - Henry L. Stimson

10. "Babalù" - Xavier Cugat and Luis del Campo

11. "I'll Be Seeing You" - Dinah Shore

12. Sketch - Jack Benny and Fred Allen

CD II Tracks:

"Dance with the Dolly with the Hole in the Stocking" - Kay Kyser

"It Had to Be You" - Frances Langford

Sketch: The Sounds of Home - Kay Kyser

"Moonlight and Shadows" - Dorothy Lamour

Sketch - Kay Kyser, Dorothy Lamour and Bob Hope

Comic medley: The Movies - Danny Kaye

Comic monologue - W.C. Fields

"The Trolley Song" - Judy Garland

The Donkey - Christmas story - Tracie Spencer

Christmas Medley – Judy Garland, Dorothy Lamour, Ginny Simms, Dinah Shore, Frances Langford and Virginia O'Brien

"Hark the Herald Angels Sing"

"Oh Little Town of Bethlehem"

"Oh, Come All Ye Faithful"

"The First Noël"

"God Rest You Merry Gentlemen"

"Deck the Halls"

"It Came Upon the Midnight Clear"

"Silent Night"

The Motion Picture Soundtracks on CD:

The Big Store – Label: The Soundtrack Factory. Disconforme, 1999. SFCD33503. (Includes the soundtracks for *A Day at the Races* and *Go West*)

Lady Be Good – Label: Great Movie Themes. Saar Sri, 1998. CD 60029. (Includes the soundtracks for *Four Jills in a Jeep*)

Panama Hattie – Label: Great Movie Themes. Saar Sri, 1998. CD 60047. (Includes the soundtracks for *Blood and Sand* and *At War with the Army*)

Ship Ahoy – Label: Hollywood Soundstage. Howards International. CD 4006.

Du Barry Was a Lady – Turner Classic Movies/Rhino. Turner Entertainment Co., 2004. RHM2 7851. (Includes five songs from *Meet the People*. Virginia's "Say That We're Sweethearts Again" is not one of these five bonus tracks)

Two Girls and a Sailor – Label: Great Movie Themes. Saar Sri, 1998. CD 60023.

Till the Clouds Roll By – Label: Prism Leisure, 2005. PLATCD 1341.

Ziegfeld Follies – Label: MGM Records/Turner, 1994. CD 305124.

The Harvey Girls – Label: MCA Records, 1996. MCAD 11491. (Includes the soundtracks for *Girl Crazy* and *Meet Me in St. Louis*)

Additional CDs with songs from Virginia O'Brien films:

Cugat on Film – Label: Interstate Harlequin, 1999. CD 132. Virginia sings "Take It Easy" from *Two Girls and a Sailor*.

Alive and Kickin': Big Bang Sounds at M-G-M – Label: Turner Entertainment Co., 1997. R2 72721. Virginia sings three songs: "I Like to Recognize the Tune" with June Allyson and Vaughn Monroe from *Meet the People* "In a Little Spanish Town" from *Thousands Cheer*. "I Fell in Love with the Leader of the Band" an outtake from *Ship Ahoy*. Later used in *The Great Morgan*.

Virginia O'Brien Live on CD:

Stairway to the Stars – Label: First Night Records, 1985. OCR CD6021. Virginia sings "A Fine Romance" and "Life Upon the Wicked Stage". She joins the full company for the finale, "Hooray for Hollywood".

Virginia O'Brien Salutes the Great MGM Musicals - CD released on August 23, 2005 on the AEI label. Recorded live at The Masquers Club, Hollywood, CA. Produced by Alan Eichler.

In a Little Spanish Town

A Fine Romance

Life Upon the Wicked Stage

A Bird in a Gilded Cage

Say That We're Sweethearts Again

Oh! Lady Be Good

Fascinating Rhythm

The Wild, Wild West

Ramona

Till the Clouds Roll By

Filmography

The Donkey Serenade

Can't Help Lovin' Than Man

The Trolley Song

On the Atchison, Topeka and the Santa Fe

It's a Great Big World

Salome

Friendship

Rock-a-Bye Baby

<u>Bonus tracks:</u>

This Is Spring

Two in a Taxi

Clear Out of This World

I'm an Old Jitterbug

A Guest Star... Jimmy Durante

Bibliography

Books

Allen, Miriam Marx. *Love, Groucho Letters from Grouch Marx to His Daughter Miriam.* New York: Da Capo Press, 1992.

Andrews, Maxene and Gilbert, Bill. *Over Here, Over There: The Andrews Sisters and the USO Stars in World War II.* New York: Zebra Books, 1993.

Brideson, Cynthia and Sara. *Also Starring... Forty Biographical Essays on the Greatest Character Actors of Hollywood's Golden Era 1930 - 1965.* Albany: BearManor Media, 2015.

Cassara, Bill. *Vernon Dent: Stooge Heavy.* Albany: BearManor Media, 2015.

De La Hoz, Cindy. *Lucy at the Movies.* Philadelphia: Running Press, 2007.

Eames, John Douglas. *The MGM Story.* New York: Crown Publishers, 1977.

Fordin, Hugh. *MGM's Greatest Musicals: The Arthur Freed Unit.* Boston: Da Capo Press, 1996.

Fricke, John. *Judy Garland: A Portrait In Art & Anecdote.* New York: Bullfinch Press, 2003.

Fricke, John. *Judy: A Legendary Film Career.* Philadelphia: Running Press, 2010.

Gehring, Wes D. *Seeing Red: The Skelton in Hollywood's Closet.* Davenport: 2001.

Kniffel, Leonard. *Musicals on the Silver Screen: A Guide to the Must-See Movie Musicals.* Chicago: Huron Street Press, 2013.

Lamparski, Richard. *Whatever Became of...? Eighth Series.* New York: Crown Publisher, Inc., 1982.

Mayo, Virginia. *The Best Years of My Life.* Chesterfield: BeachHouse Book, 2001.

Nollen, Scott Allen. *Boris Karloff: A Gentleman's Life.* Baltimore: Midnight Marquee Press, 2005.

Parrish, James Robert and Bowers, Donald L. *The MGM Stock Company.* New York: Arlington House, 1973.

Richmond, Jennifer Ann. *Reels & Rivals: Sisters in Silent Films*. Albany: BearManor Media, 2016.

Vogel, Michelle. *Marjorie Main: The Life and Films of Hollywood's "Ma Kettle"*. Jefferson: McFarland, 2011.

Magazines

Movie Life September 1941 – Pin-up photograph

Screenland. October 1941 – Hollywood Makes Me Laugh.

PIX Magazine. February 3, 1942 – Photograph with Kirk Alyn.

Screenland. November 1942 – Inside the Stars' Homes: Thanksgiving with Virginia O'Brien.

Screenland. January 1943 – Photograph with Red Skelton (*Du Barry Was a Lady*).

Silver Screen. February 1943 – Photograph with Robert Stack.

Photoplay. March 1943 – "I Wish I Were…"

Radio Call. April 1943 – "Dead-Pan Star's New Picture"

Tune In. June 1943 – "Groucho Marx - Blue Ribbon Town Brings Back the Insanity and the Laughter". Photograph with Groucho Marx.

Movie Radio Guide. June 1943 – Blue Ribbon Town article. Photographs with Groucho Marx.

Movieland. August 1943 – Barbara Stanwyck cover.

Yank Magazine. February 18, 1944 – Virginia O'Brien Pin-Up.

Movie Show. November 1944 – Color portrait.

Primer Plano. December 1944 – Spanish movie magazine. Virginia O'Brien cover girl.

Silver Screen. February 1945 – "Thawing Out Frozen Face: The off-stage Virginia O'Brien."

Screen Stars. February 1945 – Gossip Corner.

Yildiz. May 1945 – [Turkish movie magazine] Photograph.

Screenland. January 1946 – "Around the Lot with Judy" (on *The Harvey Girls* set).

Film Bulletin January 7, 1946 – *The Harvey Girls* review.

Screenland. March 1946 – "Around the Lot with Judy" photo with Judy Garland.

Cine Roman [Italian movie magazine]. January 1, 1948.

Radio Call Vol. 11, No. 565 [Australia movie magazine]. May 20, 1948 – Photograph with Kirk Alyn.

Filmography

The Cash Box. July 31, 1948 – Record review of *Dude Ranch Serenade* and *Wrong Train.*

Film Fan Monthly. September 1972 – "Virginia O'Brien: by Casey Charness.

Variety. December 9, 1984 – Review: "Vine St. Bar & Grill Virginia O'Brien" by Kirk.

Hollywood Studio Magazine. 18 n5 1985 – "Lady Be Good" by Colin Briggs.

Classic Images n179. May 1990 "Ray's Way: Virginia O'Brien" by Ray Nielsen.

Classic Images n283. January 1999, Vol. 283 – "Virginia O'Brien: The Diva of Deadpan" by Dan Van Neste.

Variety n381. Jan 29/Feb 4 2001, – Obituary by Doug Galloway.

Classic Images n309. March 2001 – "Virginia O'Brien: Remembering a Wonderful Pal" by Dan Van Neste.

Classic Images n309. March 2001 – Obituary by Harris Lentz III.

Sequences: la Revue de Cinema n212. Mar/Apr 2001 – Obituary by Luc Chaput.

Psychotronic Video n34. 2001 – Film Article / Obituary by Tony Williams.

Nostalgia Digest. Summer 2005 – "Who Was That Lady?" by Walter Scannell.

Nostalgia Digest. Summer 2014 – "The Girl with the Frozen Face" by Garry Berman.

Virginia's former homes:

2638 Benedict Street, Los Angeles. Source: 1920 United States Census.

12036 Laurel Terrace, North Hollywood. Source: Los Angeles newspapers.

12155 Morrison Street in North Hollywood. Source: Los Angeles newspapers.

7500 Devista Drive, Los Angeles, California. Source: 1980's historical or correspondence records.

www.ingramcontent.com/pod-product-compliance
Lightning Source LLC
Chambersburg PA
CBHW060111170426
43198CB00010B/851